Marriages
and
Deaths
of
Montgomery County
Pennsylvania

1685-1800

Charlotte Meldrum

HERITAGE BOOKS
2007

HERITAGE BOOKS

AN IMPRINT OF HERITAGE BOOKS, INC.

Books, CDs, and more—Worldwide

For our listing of thousands of titles see our website
at
www.HeritageBooks.com

Published 2007 by
HERITAGE BOOKS, INC.
Publishing Division
65 East Main Street
Westminster, Maryland 21157-5026

International Standard Book Number: 978-1-58549-065-3

CONTENTS

iii

INTRODUCTION

Montgomery County was formed in 1784 from Philadelphia County. The area had already been largely settled by various ethnic groups. There were settlers in the southern part of the county as early as the 1680s. Many were Quakers, Welsh and English; there were a few Baptists; also members of the Anglican Church. The Germans began arriving in the county a few decades after the English and Welsh. Most were Lutherans and Reformed.

A large number of the Quakers arrived in 1682, around the time of William Penn's arrival. Abington Monthly Meeting was established in 1683. From 1687 to 1710 it was known as Dublin Monthly Meeting. Gwynedd Monthly Meetings was formed in 1714 out of Radnor Monthly meeting. Horsham Monthly Meeting was formed in 1782 out of Abington Monthly Meeting. The records of Lower Dublin or Pennypack Baptist Church began in 1689. By 1776 there were 10 Lutheran congregations and 8 Reformed congregations in the county.

Many of the abstracts for this volume were made from microfilm or photostat copies. This book does not represent all records of marriages and deaths that have been preserved for the county. It is anticipated that a supplementary volume will be published in the future as translations and records become available. Birth records of Montgomery have been published in Humphrey Publications, Washington, D.C., 1993, *Pennsylvania Birth Montgomery County 1682-1800.*

ABINGTON MONTHLY MEETING MARRIAGES 1685-1800

Richard Worrell, of the Philadelphia Co., brick maker, son of Richard Worrell
of the same county and Rachel May, late of the family of Joseph Phips, both
of Upper Dublin Twp. md. 7th da, 4th mo, 1685.

William Buzby, of Philadelphia Co., husbandman and Sarah Soiry or Soary of
the same place, md. 11th da, 4th mo, 1685.

John Rigors of West Jersey, near the falls of River Delaware, husbandman and
Mary Groom of Southampton Twp., Philadelphia Co. m. 16th da, 7th mo,
1685.

Robert Prossmall of Southampton Twp., Co. of Bucks, husbandman and Mary
Wobor of the family of John Hoart in the Philadelphia Co. md. 3rd da, 4th
mo, 1685.

Morris Roberts, of Gwynedd Twp. and Elizabeth Robins of Abington md. 15th
da, 3rd mo, 1718.

James Shaw of Southampton Twp., Bucks Co., yeomen, son of John Shaw and
Maron Brown, dau of Thomas Brown of Philadelphia Co. md. 11th da, Dec,
1718.

Thomas Kitchon, Sr., of Oxford Twp., Philadelphia Co. and Mary Maco, widow
living near Shoolkill md. 8th da, 10th mo, 1685.

John Eastbourn, of Abington Twp., husbandman and Grace Coltston, dau of
William Coltston of same place md. 16th da, 1st mo, 1721.

Abraham Houlins, of Northampton Twp., husbandman and Esther English of
Byberry Twp., Philadelphia Co. md. 3rd da, 5th mo, 1685.

Thomas Kimber, husbandman, Philadelphia Co. and Elizabeth Chalkey of same
place md. 5th da, 8th mo, 1686.

Edward Eaton of Philadelphia and Ann Kirby of Oxford Twp., md. 18th da, 3rd
mo, 1686.

Honory English and Hannah Wost, both of Byberry Twp., Philadelphia Co. m.
8th da, 4th mo, 1686.

William Hibbs of Byberry Twp. and Hannah Houl, dau of Thomas Houl, of
Southampton Twp., both of Philadelphia Co. md. 2nd da, 12th mo, 1686.

John Wood and Judith Dungworth, both of Oxford Twp., Philadelphia Co. md.
16th da, 9th mo, 1689.

Attwood (Attowoll) Wilmonson of Philadelphia Co. and Hanna Hobson of the
place, widow md. 13th da, 6th mo, 1689.

James Wyatt of Philadelphia and Mary Brodwoll, dau of Mary Brodwoll, widow
of Cheltenham Twp., Philadelphia Co. md. 4th da, 9th mo, 1689.

Isaac Taylor, son of Robart Taylor of Springfield Twp., Chester Co. and Sarah
Broadwoll, dau of Mary Brodwoll, widow Cheltenham Twp., Philadelphia
Co. md. 1st da, 9th mo, 1689.

Edward White and Mary Ashmoat, both of Cheltenham Twp., Philadelphia Co.
md. 1st da, 6th mo, 1689.

Thomas Carby and Sarah Jarvis md. 1st da, 9th mo, 1692.

John Cassoll of Philadelphia Co. and Mary Baldwin, dau of John Baldwin of Oxford Twp., Philadelphia Co. md. 14th da, 1st mo, 1729.

Jacob Duboxoy, and Jane Luke, both of Philadelphia Co. md. 6th da, 9th mo, 1692.

Richard Mason and Abigail Soroy of Philadelphia Co. md. 16th da, 6th mo, 1694.

Peter Davis of Horsham Twp. and Rebekah Michiner, dau of John Michiner md. 15th da, 11th mo, ??

Thomas Ross of Abington Twp. and Elizabeth Colston, dau of William Colson md. 14th da, 2nd mo, 1714.

Thomas Justin and Elizabeth Simm both of Philadelphia Co. md. 4th da, 1st mo, ??

Jack Price, of Philadelphia Co. and Jane Shoemaker md. 4th da, 1st mo, 1696.

Ellis Lowes of Dublin, Philadelphia Co., son of Ellis Lowes and Mary Taylor of Abington Twp. md. 18th da, 10th mo, 1729.

Jack Knight of Philadelphia Co., yeoman and Mary Caruon, dau of John Caruon of the same county md. 2nd da, 4th mo, 1699.

John Worral, son of John Worrall of Oxford Twp., Philadelphia Co. and Hannah Dilworth, dau of James Dillworth, dec'd md. 9th da, 4th mo, 1709.

Lewis Lewis of Chester Twp. and Mary Donoll of Bristol Twp., Philadelphia Co. md. 16th da, 4th mo, 1700.

David Harroy of Radnor Twp. and Lidya Powell, dau of David Powell of Bristol Twp., Philadelphia Co. md. 2nd da, 12th mo, 1690.

Certificate from the Philadelphia Monthly Meeting for Thomas Grodall and his wife, Rebecka dated 29th da, 10th mo, 1710.

Thomas Hodges of Oxford Twp. and Jane Dillworth of Philadelphia Co. md. 8th da, 3rd mo, 1701.

Alexander Mode of Bucks Co. and Ellen Dunkin, dau of William Dunkin md. 5th da, 6th mo, 1702.

Ephraim Horton of Bucks Co., and Sarah Parkon, dau of Humphrey Parkon of Upper Dublin Twp., Philadelphia Co., md. 13th da, 11th mo, 1703.

Benjamin Barrett of Chester Twp. and Mary Hanson, dau of Timothy Hanson of Philadelphia Co. md. 16th da, 2nd mo, 1703.

Gowon Jenkins, the son of William Jenkins of Abington, Philadelphia Co., yeoman and Abigail Pomborton of Bucks Co., md. 14th da, 9th mo, 1704 having consent of parents and guardian.

George Trunk of Oxford Twp., Philadelphia Co., yeoman and Elizabeth Barton late from Shrewsbury, Great Britain, now of said place md. 22nd da, 1st mo, 1726.

Morris Morris, son of Evan Morris of Twp. of Abington, Philadelphia Co., husbandman and Sharon or Shasson Holt, dau of Robert Holt of same place md. 26th da, 8th mo, 1703.

John Phipps, son of Joseph Phipps, and Ann Phillips both of Philadelphia Co. md. 9th da, 3rd mo, 17076.

Samuel Walton, son of Daniel Walton of Twp. of Byberry Twp., husbandman and Mary Watonman, both of Philadelphia Co. md. 15th da, 12th mo, 1709.

John Worth, son of John Worth of Oxford Twp., Philadelphia Co. and Hannah Dillworth, dau of James Dilworth of Bristol Twp., Philadelphia Co. md. 9th da, 4th mo, 1709.

Richard Caurk??, son of John Caurk??, molster of Byberry Twp., Philadelphia Co. and Hannah Bolton, dau of Gabriel Bolton of same place md. 28th da, 8th mo, 1708.

Thomas Canbee and Mary Ollever, both of Abington Twp. md. 2nd da, 4th mo, 1709.

Humphrey Ellis of North Wailes and Sage Morgan of Abington Twp. md. 3rd da, 4th mo, 1712.

Henry English and Hannah Hibbs both of Byberry Twp. md. 23rd da, 8th mo, 1712.

Ishmael Bennett and Rachel Worrell both of Philadelphia Co. md. 5th da, 7th mo, 1712 in Oxford Twp.

Joseph Townsend and Elizabeth Harmer both of Bristol Twp., Philadelphia Co. md. 11th da, 9th mo, 1712 at Abington.

Richard Worrell and Hannah Heath both of Dublin Twp., Philadelphia Co. md. 1st da, 2nd mo, 1711 at Oxford.

Hugh Griffith and Alice Howell both of Philadelphia Co. md. 11 da, 4th mo, 1713 at Horsham Monthly Meeting.

John Buzby and Elizabeth Holyday of Oxford Twp., Philadelphia Co. md. at Horsham 10th da, 1st mo, 1715.

Edward Roberts and Mary Bolton both of Abington Twp., Philadelphia Co. md. 1st da, 12th mo, 1715 at Horsham.

Henry Paul and Ann Gillingham both of Oxford Twp., Philadelphia Co. md. 26th da, 2nd mo, 1716 at the Horsham.

James Paull and Jane Wilmerton, both of Oxford Twp., Philadelphia Co. md. 31st da, 3rd mo, 1716 at the Horsham.

Peter Shoemaker, Jr. and Margaret op do Graeff, both of Gorman Twp., Philadelphia Co. md. 6th da, 2nd mo, 1697 at the Horsham.

Joshua Morris, of Abington Twp., Philadelphia Co., son of Morris Morris of Richland Twp., Bucks Co. and Mary Fletcher, dau of Robert Fletcher, late of Abington Twp., dec'd. md. 26th da, 1st mo, 1745 with surviving parents present at Abington.

Thomas Livezey, son of David Livezey, of Lower Dublin Twp., Philadelphia Co., blacksmith and Mary Shoemaker, of Cheltenham Twp., Philadelphia Co., dau of George Shoemaker, dec'd md. 18th da, 9th mo, 1746.

Samuel Bolton, of Cheltenham Twp., and Mary Livezey, of Lower Dublin Twp., Philadelphia Co., dau of Thomas Livezey of Lower Dublin md. 25th da, 9th mo called Nov, 1746.

Thomas Nedro of the City of Philadelphia, yeoman and Ann Lukins, both of Bristol Twp., Philadelphia Co. md. 3rd da, 10th mo, 1746 at Abington having consent of parents.

Rees Nanney of Gwynedd Twp., Philadelphia Co., widower and Margaret Cadwalder of Warminister Twp., Bucks Co., md. 9th da, 10th mo, 1756 at Abington having consent of parents.

Jacob Edge, son of John Edge of Providence Twp., Chester Co. and Margaret Paul, dau of James Paul of Abington, Philadelphia Co., md. 27th da, 9th mo, 1746 having consent of parents.

Thomas Hallowell of Moreland, Philadelphia Co., yeoman and Margaret Tyson, dau of John Tyson of Abington, Philadelphia Co., yeoman md. 13th da, 10th mo, 1746 at Abington.

John Webster, son of John Webster of Abington Twp., and Sarah Leedom of Southampton, Bucks Co., dau of John Phipps, of Abington md. 28th da, 2nd mo, 1747 at Abington.

Joseph Griffith, son of Evan Griffith of Philadelphia Co. and Rebecca Knight, dau of Isaac Knight of Abington md. 1st da, 3rd mo, 1747 at Abington.

William Buzby, of Oxford Twp., Philadelphia Co., yeoman and Sarah Bristol, dau of Daniel and Hannah Bristel, of same place md. 23rd da, Sept, 1747 at Abington.

Joseph Spencer of Upper Dublin Twp., Philadelphia Co., yeoman and Hannah Lukens, of Bristol Twp. in the aforesaid place md. 5th da, of 9th mo, 1747 at Abington.

John Ider, of Upper Dublin Twp., Philadelphia Co., cordwainer and Mary Burger of Abington Twp., Philadelphia Co. md. 14th da, 12th mo, 1744 at Abington

Benjamin Holt, of Horsham Twp., Philadelphia Co., yeoman and Margaret Pennington of Manor of Moreland Twp., Philadelphia Co. md. 27th da, 9th mo, 1746 at Abington.

Jonathan Livezey, Sr., son of Jonathan Livezey, of Lower Dublin Twp., Philadelphia Co. and Catharine Thomas of Abington Twp., Philadelphia Co. dau of Daniel Thomas, late of Abington, dec'd md. 2nd da, 9th mo, 1747 at Abington

Joseph Waln of Northern Liberties, Philadelphia Co., yeoman and Susannah Paul, dau of James Paul, of Abington Twp., Philadelphia Co. md. 31st da, 10th mo, 1747 at Abington.

Henry Van Oaken of City of Philadelphia, merchant and Rebecca Johnson, of Germantown, Philadelphia Co. md. 15th da, 4th mo, 1748 at Abington.

Rynear Kirk of Abington, Philadelphia Co., son of John Kirk of said place and Mary Michner, dau of John Michner, of Moorland of said place md. 24th da, 8th mo, 1748 at Abington.

Isaac Tyson of Upper Dublin Twp., Philadelphia Co., yeoman, son of Mathias

Tyson, late of Abington and Esther Shoemaker, of Cheltham Twp., Philadelphia Co., dec'd md. 6th da, 3rd mo, 1748 at Abington.

Thomas Livezey, son of Thomas Livezey, of Lower Dublin Twp., Philadelphia Co., yeoman and Martha Knowles, dau of John Knowles, late of said place md. 2nd da, 4th mo, 1748 at Abington.

David Davis of Whitemarsh Twp., Philadelphia Co. and Elizabeth Davis of Horsham Twp., Philadelphia Co., widow, md. 9th da, 4th mo, 1748 at Abington.

Robert Evans, son of Hugh Evans, of Gwynedd, Philadelphia Co. and Elizabeth Knight, dau of Isaac Knight of Abington Twp. md. 17th da, 9th mo, 1748 at Abington.

Isaac Jones of Chelthem Twp., Philadelphia Co., yeoman and Sarah Bristol, of same place md. 1st da, 4th mo, 1749 at Abington.

James Arbuckle, of City of Philadelphia, and Rachel Thomas of Twp. of Byberry Twp., Philadelphia Co. md. 13th da, 12th mo, 1749 at Abington.

John Conrad, Jr., of Horsham in the Philadelphia Co., weaver and Abigail West of Warminster Twp. Philadelphia Co. md. 8th da, 4th mo, 1748 having consent of their parents at Abington.

James Wagstaff of the City of Philadelphia and Mary Hughes, of Abington Twp. md. 6th da, 7th mo, 1750 at Abington.

John Cleaver of Upper Dublin Twp., weaver, son of Peter Cleaver, of said place and Deborah Tyson, of Upper Dublin Twp., seamstress, dau of David Tyson of same place md. 22nd da, 9th mo, 1750 at Abington.

Rynear Tyson of Abington Twp., Philadelphia Co., yeoman and Jane Fletcher of Abington Twp., dau of Robert Fletcher, late of same place, yeoman, dec'd md. 29th da, 3rd mo, 1731 at Abington.

Isaac Cleaver, of Upper Dublin Twp., Philadelphia Co., yeoman and Ann Lukens, spinster of Horsham Twp., Philadelphia Co. md. 18th da, 4th mo, 1751 at Abington.

William Futrell, of the City of Philadelphia, and Sarah Longstreth, of Abington Twp., Philadelphia Co. 10th da, 8th mo, 1750 at Abington.

James Thornton, late of Georgetown, Nottingham, now of Bristol Twp., Bucks Co. and Mary Knight, dau of Joseph Knight of Philadelphia Co. md. 14th da, 9th mo, 1751 at Abington.

John Parry, of Manor of Moorland Twp., Philadelphia Co., and Margaret Tyson, of Upper Dublin Twp., md. 21st da, 9th mo, 1751 at Abington.

Joseph Lukens, of Horsham Twp., Philadelphia Co., blacksmith and Elizabeth Spencer of Upper Dublin Twp., aforesaid Co. md. 9th da, 9th mo, 1751 at Abington.

Jacob Dubro of Manor of Moorland Twp., Philadelphia Co., son of James Dubro of same place, md. Patience Betts, dau of Thomas Betts, of Abington Twp. md. 21st da, 1st mo, 1752 at Abington.

William Hallowell of Abington Twp., Philadelphia Co., son of Thomas

Hallowell of said Twp., yeoman and Margaret Dixson, of said place, dau of
Matthias Tyson, yeoman, dec'd md. 23rd da, 8th mo, 1729 at Abington.

Albrook Bird, of Abington Twp., Philadelphia Co., yeoman and Rachel
Waterman, dau of Thomas Watterman, late of Abington Twp., dec'd md. 7th
da, 5th mo, 1752 at Abington.

Benjamin Hallowell, son of Benjamin Hallowell, yeoman, Abington Twp.,
Philadelphia Co. and Elinor Tyson, dau of Peter Tyson of same place,
seamstress, md. 21st da, 4th mo, 1752 at Abington.

William Shoemaker, son of Abraham Shoemaker of Bristol, sadler and Susanna
Richardson of Cheltenham Twp., dau of Barnaby Richardson, late of said
Twp. md. 26th da, 10th mo, 1752 at Abington.

John Shoemaker, of Cheltenham, Philadelphia Co., miller, of Isaac Shoemaker,
late of same place, dec'd and Elisabeth Livezey, dau of Thomas Livezey of
Lower Dublin Twp., md. 3rd da, 6th mo, 1752 at Abington.

William Davis, of Philadelphia Co., yeoman and Lydia Phipps, of Abington
Twp., spinster md. 14th da, 7th mo, 1752 at Abington.

Richard Roberts, son of Thomas Roberts, of Rockhill Twp., Bucks Co., yeoman
and Rosemaria Tyson, dau of Abraham Tyson of Abington Twp. md. 24th
da, 10th mo, 1752 at Abington.

Leonard Shallcross, of Oxford Twp., Philadelphia Co., and Judith Wood of
Northern Liberties, Co. aforesaid, md. 14th da, 11th mo, 1752 at Abington.

Robert Thomas of Lower Dublin Twp., son of Robert Thomas of same place
and Sarah Austin, dau of Nicholas Austin of Abington Twp. md. 8th da, 7th
mo, 1752 at Abington.

Thomas Potts of Moorland, Philadelphia Co. and Elizabeth Lupton, of Abington
Twp., aforesaid county md. 16th da, 1st mo, 1753 at Abington.

Jonathan Knight of Byberry Twp., Philadelphia Co., son of Jonathan Knight of
same place, dec'd and Ann Paul, dau of James Paul of Abington Twp., same
county md. 7th da, 11th mo, 1752 at Abington.

Benjamin Livezey, son of Jonathan Livezey of Lower Dublin, Philadelphia Co.,
yeoman and Phebe Roberts of Abington, same county, dau of John Roberts,
late dec'd md. 15th da, 2nd mo, 1753 at Abington.

John Spencer, of Upper Dublin Twp., Philadelphia Co. and Elizabeth Kirk, dau
of Joseph Kirk of Abington Twp. md. 21st da, 11th mo, 1752 at Abington.

Robert Tomkins of Warrington Twp., Bucks Co. and Ann Longstreth of
Warrington Twp., Bucks Co. md. 7th da, 6th mo, 1752 at Abington.

John Brock of Solebury Twp., Bucks Co., son of Richard Brock, late dec'd and
Sarah Jenkins of Abington Twp., Philadelphia Co., seamstress, dau of
Phineas Jenkins of aforesaid county md. 4th da, 5th mo, 1752 at Abington.

Daniel Longstreth, of Warrington Twp., Bucks Co. and Grace Mitchner of
Manor of Moorland, Philadelphia Co. md. 22nd da, 8th mo, 1753 at
Abington.

William Loofburrow, of Manor of Moreland, Philadelphia Co., taylor, son of

Nathaniel Loofburrow, dec'd and Mary Kirk, dau of John Kirk of Abington Twp., Philadelphia Co. md. 19th da, 6th mo, 1752 at Abington.

Isaac Jones, son of William Jones of Manor of Moreland, Philadelphia Co., dec'd and Mary Walton of same place, dau of Jeremiah Walton, dec'd md. 15th da, 8th mo, 1753.

Samuel Lloyd of Moorland, Philadelphia Co. and Sarah Walton of same place md. 12th da, 7th mo, 1753 at Abington.

Henry Tomlinson, son of Thomas Tomlinson of Bensalem Twp., Bucks Co. and Jemima Bolton, dau of Isaac Bolton of same county md. 21st da, 11th mo, 1753 at Abington.

Thomas Lloyd of Manor of Moorland, Philadelphia Co., carpenter and Mary Tyson of Upper Dublin Twp., md. 25th da, 12th mo, 1753 at Abington.

Matthew Hallowall, son of William Hallowell of Abington, Philadelphia Co. and Mary Cadwallader of Horsham Twp., aforesaid county, dau of John Cadwallader md. 22nd da, 4th mo, 1753 at Abington.

George Shoemaker, son of Abraham Shoemaker of Bristol Twp, Philadelphia Co., dec'd and Martha Livezey, dau of Jonathan Livezey of Lower Dublin Twp. md 24th da, 3rd mo, 1754 at Abington.

John Hancock, son of William Hancock of Manor of Moreland, Philadelphia Co. and Jane Mitchner, dau of John Mitchner of same place, yeoman, m. 25th da, 4th mo, 1754 at Abington.

Joshua Knight, son of Isaac Knight of Abington Twp, Philadelphia Co. and Sarah Tyson, dau of John Tyson of same place md. 18th da, 12th mo, 1753 at Abington.

Samuel Shoemaker of Manor of Moreland, Philadelphia Co. and Agness Comly of Warminister, Bucks Co. md. 2nd da, 4th mo, 1754 at Abington.

Jacob Lippincott, son of Jacob Lippincott, of Northampton in Burlington Co, NJ and Elizabeth Roberts, widow of Thomas Roberts, late of Abington, Philadelphia Co. dau of John Tyson md. 4th da, 4th mo, 1754 at Abington.

Joseph Livezey, son of Jonathan Livezey of Lower Dublin, Philadelphia Co. and Ann Roberts of Abington Twp. md. 29th da, 12th mo, 1753 at Abington.

William Hallowell of Abington, and Agnes Shoemaker of Germantown, md. 15th da, 1st mo, 1754 at Abington.

Nathaniel Samms, son of John Samms, late of City of Philadelphia and Ann Kirk, dau of Thomas Kirk, late of Manor of Moreland, Philadelphia Co. md. 11th da, 6th mo, 1754 at Abington.

Isaac Shoemaker of Chestertown Twp., Philadelphia Co. and Elizabeth Potts of Upper Dublin Twp., same county md. 4th da, 4th mo, 1754 at Abington.

Richard Clayton of Hatfield Twp., Philadelphia Co., taylor and Margaret Kinderdine of Horsham Twp., md. 1st da, 11th mo, 1754 at Abington.

Jonathan Thomas, son of Robert Thomas of Lower Dublin, Philadelphia Co. and Mary Strickland, dau of John Strickland of Southampton Twp, Bucks Co. md. 11th da, 12th mo, 1753 at Abington.

Barnett Craft of Abington, Philadelphia Co., and Ann Leesom of aforesaid Co., dau of John Leeson, late of Southampton Twp, Bucks Co., dec'd md. 21st da, 11th mo, 1755 at Abington.

Daniel Knight, Jr. of Byberry Twp. in the Philadelphia Co. and Ann Wilson, dau of James Wilson, late of Buckingham, Bucks Co. md. 4th da, 12th mo, 1754 at Abington.

Ezekiel Cleaver, son of Peter Cleaver of Upper Dublin Twp., Philadelphia Co., yeoman and Mary Lewis, dau of Ellis Lewis of aforesaid place md. 4th da, 1st mo, 1757 at Abington.

Bartholomew Mather, son of Richard Mather of Cheltenham, Philadelphia Co., wheelwright and Sarah Livezey, dau of Thomas Livezey of Lower Dublin md. 19th da, 11th mo, 1754 at Abington.

Edward Parry, son of Thomas Parry of Moorland, Philadelphia Co. and Phebe Titus, dau of Silas Titus of Byberry Twp., Philadelphia Co., dec'd md. 10th da, 11th mo, 1753 having consent of surviving parents.

Peter Cleaver, Jr. of Bristol Twp, Philadelphia Co., weaver, son of Peter Cleaver of Bristol Twp., weaver and Elizabeth Potts, of Bristol Twp., seamstress, dau of David and Allice Potts of same place md. 4th da, 8th mo, 1722 having consent of parents.

Robert Merick of Moorland, Philadelphia Co., blacksmith and Jane Waterman of Twp. of Abington, seamstress md. 15th da, 8th mo, 1754 having consent of relations.

Matthew Tyson, son of Matthew Tyson of Upper Dublin, Twp., Philadelphia Co., yeoman and Mary Fitzwater of Whitpain Twp. and aforesaid place m. 1st da, 5th mo, 1755 having consent of parents.

Jonathan Coates, son of Moses Coates of Charlestown, Chester, and Jane Longstreth, dau of Bartholomew Longstreth, of Warminister, Bucks Co., dec'd md. 22nd da, 4th mo, 1755 having consent of surviving parents.

David Davis of Manor of Moreland, Philadelphia Co., mason and Rebecca Pennington, dau of Thomas Pennington of aforesaid place md. 14th da, 5th mo, 1754 having consent of relations.

Aquila Massey, of Boliver Co., Providence of Maryland, tanner, son of Aquila Massey of same place, dec'd and Sarah Bolton, dau of Isaac Bolton of Southampton Twp., Bucks Co. md. 25th da, 11th mo, 1755 having consent of surviving parents.

Nathan Shepherd of Abington, Cumberland Co., late dec'd and Sarah Shoemaker, dau of Isaac Shoemaker of Chelsam Twp., dec'd md. 3rd da, 4th mo, 1755 having consent of surviving parents.

Stephen Parry, son of Thomas Parry, late of Moreland, Philadelphia Co., dec'd and Ester Walmsley, dau of Thomas Walmsley, late of Byberry Twp., aforesaid Co., dec'd md. 10th da, 9th mo, 1755 having consent of relations.

James Robisson of Franconia Twp., Philadelphia Co., yeoman and Mary Kenderine of Northampton Twp., aforesaid Co. md. 11th da, 5th mo, 1756

having consent of parents.

John Tyson, Jr., Abington Twp., Philadelphia Co., yeoman, son of John Tyson of same place and Hannah Cleaver, dau of Isaac Cleaver of Cheltenham, md. 8th da, 5th mo, 1759 having consent of parents.

James Hahurst, of Middleton Twp, Bucks Co., cordwainer and Ann Spencer of Northampton Twp., aforesaid place md. 7th da, 4th mo, 1757 having consent of parents.

Benjamin Walton of Byberry Twp., Philadelphia Co., son of Benjamin Walton, late of same place, dec'd and Abigail Gilbert, dau of Benjamin Gilbert of aforesaid Twp. md. 17th da, 5th mom, 1759 having consent of surviving parents.

Caleb Byrne, of Whitpain Twp., Philadelphia Co. and Mary Davis of Abington, md. 17th da, 5th mo, 1759 having consent of parents.

Henry Walmsly, son of Thomas Walmsly, of Southampton Twp., Bucks Co. and Martha Knight, dau of Daniel Knight of Byberry Twp., Philadelphia Co. md. 21st da, 11th mo, 1759 having consent of parents.

William Pusey of the City of Philadelphia, merchant, son of Joshua Pusey of Long Grove, Chester, yeoman and Mary Jones, dau of John Jones of Germantown, Philadelphia Co., tanner md. 24th da, 10th mo, 1759 having consent of parents.

Jacob Tomkins, of Moreland, Philadelphia Co., sadler and Elizabeth Thomas of same place, seamstress, md. 16th da, 11th mo, 1759 having consent of parents.

Thomas Knight, son of Jonathan Knight, dec'd of Byberry Twp., Philadelphia Co. and Mary Walmsley, dau of William Walmsley, of same place md. 4th da, 11th mo, 1759 having consent of surviving parents.

Thomas Ridge, son of William Ridge of Bensalm, Bucks Co. and Rachel Duncan, dau of William Duncan of same place md. 13th da, 12th mo, 1759 having consent of parents.

John Duncan, son of William Duncan of Bensalem, Bucks Co. and Agness Comly, dau of Isaac Comley, late of Byberry Twp., Philadelphia Co., dec'd md. 5th da, 12th mo, 1759 having consent of surviving parents.

Jacob Jones, of manor of Moreland, Philadelphia Co., yeoman and Priscilla Waterman of Abington Twp. md. 12th da, 12th mo, 1759.

Samuel Griffith of Lower Dublin Twp., Philadelphia Co. and Jane Wood of Northern Liberties, aforesaid Co. md. 15th da, 4th mo, 1760 having consent of parents.

Benjamin Tomkins of Horsham Twp., Philadelphia Co. and Mary Kinderdine, dau of John Kinderdine of same place md. 15th da, 4th mo, 1760.

Peter Lukens, of Horsham Twp., Philadelphia Co., yeoman and Jane Cadawalder, of same place, dau of Isaac Cadwalder, late of Warminister, Bucks Co., yeoman, dec'd md. 17th da, 4th mo, 1760.

John Little John of Moorland, Philadelphia Co. and Sarah Wood, dau of Thomas

Wood of Moorland of aforesaid Co. md. 17th da, 4th mo, 1760 having consent of parents.

Matthew Conard of Cheltenham Twp., Philadelphia Co., sadler, son of Cornelius Conard of Horsham, said Co., yeoman and Mary Roberts, dau of Thomas Robert, late of Bristol Twp., yeoman, dec'd md. 13th da, 4th mo, 1760.

Jacob Kirk of Abington Twp., Philadelphia Co., son of John Kirk of aforesaid place, dec'd and Elizabeth Cleaver, dau of John Cleaver of Bristol Twp., Philadelphia Co. md. 14th da, 5th mo, 1760 having consent of surviving parents.

Rynear Tyson, son of Peter Tyson of Abington Twp., Philadelphia Co., yeoman and Mary Cleaver, dau of Isaac Clever of Cheltenham Twp., aforesaid county, seamstress md. 14th da, 10th mo, 1760 having consent of parents.

Joseph Auston, son of Nicholas Austin of Abington, Philadelphia Co. and Susanna Tyson, dau of John Tyson of same place md. 18th da, 11th mo, 1760 having consent of parents

Thomas Spencer of Northampton Twp., Bucks Co., yeoman, son of William Spencer of same place, dec'd and Mary Hallowell, dau of Thomas Hallowell of manor of Moor Sand, in the aforesaid providence, weaver md. 16th da, 12th mo, 1760 having consent of surviving parents.

Thomas Carington of Lower Dublin, Philadelphia Co., yeoman and Mary Walton, widow, of Manor of Moorland, seamstress md. 21st da, 9th mo, 1745.

Isaac Cadwalder of Moreland, Philadelphia Co., blacksmith and Elizabeth Mitchner, dau of John Mitchner of aforesaid Twp. and Co. md. 5th da, 4th mo, 1761.

David Parry of Manor of Moreland, Philadelphia Co. and son of Thomas Parry, of same place, dec'd and Martha Walmsley of Byberry Twp., dau of Thomas Walmsley, dec'd md. 20th da, 5th mo, 1761 having consent of surviving parents.

James Tyson, of Abington, Philadelphia Co., taylor and Mary James of Manor of Moreland md. 19th da, 5th mo, 1761 having consent of parents.

James Spencer, of Northampton Twp., Bucks Co., son of William Spencer, of same place, dec'd and Sarah Wallen, dau of James Walton of Manor of Moreland md. 23rd da, 5th mo, 1761 having consent of surviving parents.

Everad Conard of Horsham Twp., Philadelphia Co., son of Cornelius Conard of same place and Margaret Cadwalder, dau of Isaac Cadwalder, late of Warminster Twp., dec'd md. 18th da, 6th mo, 1761.

Joseph Paul, of German Twp., Philadelphia Co., miller and Mary Bolton, widow of Samuel Bolton, late of aforesaid Twp. md. 16th da, 7th mo, 1761.

Isaac Shoemaker of Cheltham Twp., Philadelphia Co., widower and Ann Roberts, dau of Thomas Roberts, late of Bristol, dec'd md. 10th da, 6th mo, 1761.

Isaac Comly, of Liberties, Philadelphia Co., husbandman, son of Peter Comley, late of same place, dec'd and Sarah Hudson, dau of John Hudson of Bristol Twp., said Co. md. 14th da, 10th mo, 1761.

Jeremiah Walton, son of Jeremiah Walton, late of Manor of Moreland, Philadelphia Co., yeoman, dec'd and Mary Kirk, dau of Thomas Kirk, late of Manor of Moreland, yeoman, dec'd md. 22nd da. 12th mo, 1761.

Joseph Spencer, Philadelphia Co. and Abigail Conard of Horsham, Philadelphia Co. md. 12th da, 11th mo, 1761 having consent of parents.

Joseph Kinderine, of Horsham, Philadelphia Co., millwright and Sarah Baker, of same place md. 6th da, 5th mo, 1761 having consent of relations.

Jacob Walton, of Manor of Moreland, Philadelphia Co., and Mary Conard, dau of Cornelius Conard of Horsham Twp. md. 25th da, 5th mo, 1762 having consent of parents.

Jonathan Tyson of Upper Dublin, Philadelphia Co., yeoman , son of Derrick Tyson and Sarah Knight of Abington Twp., Philadelphia Co., dau of Isaac Knight, md. 12th da, 10th mo, 1762 having consent of parents.

Daniel Walton, son of Daniel Walton, late of Byberry Twp., dec'd and Ann Knight, dau of Daniel Knight of same place md. 22nd da, 9th mo, 1762 having consent of surviving parents.

Thomas Hallowell, Jr. of Manor of Moreland, Philadelphia Co., son of Thomas Hallowell, weaver of same place and Margaret Tyson, dau of Peter Tyson of Abington, md. 16th da, 11th mo, 1762 having consent of parents.

Rynear Hallowell, of Abington Twp. Philadelphia Co., yeoman, son of William Hallowell of same place, joyner and Margaret Phipps, dau of --- Phipps of aforesaid Twp., dec'd md. 17th da, 2nd mo, 1763 having consent of surviving parents.

Job Walton, son of Jesse Walton of Byberry Twp., Philadelphia Co. and Margaret Powell of same place, dau of John Powel, late of City of Philadelphia, dec'd md. 10th da, 3rd mo, 1763 having consent of surviving parents.

Jeremiah Walton, son of Isaac Walton, late of Moreland, Philadelphia Co., dec'd and Margaret Tyson, dau of Henry Tyson, Twp. of Abington Twp. md. 6th da, 4th mo, 1763 having consent of surviving parents.

Albrick Bird of Abington Twp., Philadelphia Co., yeoman, son of John Bird of same place, dec'd and Abigail Tyson, dau of Isaac Tyson of aforesaid Twp. md. 7th da, 4th mo, 1763 having consent of surviving parents.

Nathan Thomas of Abington, Philadelphia Co., blacksmith, son of Benjamin Thomas, late of Abington, dec'd and Esther Jones, dau of Joseph Jones, late of Manor of Moreland, dec'd md. 12th da, 4th mo, 1763 having consent of surviving parents.

Jacob Comley, son of John Comly of Abington, Philadelphia Co., weaver and Hannah Leedom of Abington, dau of John Leedom of Southampton, Bucks Co., dec'd md. 16th da, 4th mo, 1763 having consent of surviving parents.

Nathan Livezey , son of Jonathan Livezey of Lower Dublin Twp., Philadelphia Co., yeoman and Hannah Williams, dau of Anthony Williams of Bristol, aforesaid Co., yeoman md. 21st da, 4th mo, 1763 having consent of parents.

William Ashbridge, of Byberry Twp., son of George and Jane Ashbridge of Goshen, Chester Co. and Elizabeth Fletcher, dau of Thomas and Susanna Fletcher of Abington Twp., Philadelphia Co. md. 16th da, 5th mo, 1763 having consent of parents.

Isaac Roberts, son of John and Susanna Roberts of Abington Twp., Philadelphia Co. and Agnes Hooper, dau of Robert and Sarah Hooper, he being dec'd, of Northern Liberties, City of Philadelphia md. 24th da, 5th mo, 1763 having consent of surviving parents.

John Roberts of Abington Twp., Philadelphia Co., yeoman and Rebecca Hooper, dau of Robert Hooper of Northern Liberties, City of Philadelphia, yeoman, md. 9th da, 6th mo, 1763 having consent of parents.

John Marshall, of City of Philadelphia, carpenter, son of John Marshall of Darby, Chester Co., dec'd and Margaret Chapman of Abington Twp., Philadelphia Co., dau of Joseph Chapman md. 21st da, 6th mo, 1763 having consent of surviving parents.

Samuel Shoemaker, late of Germantown, Philadelphia Co. and Mary Parry, dau of Thomas Parry, late of Moreland, Philadelphia Co., dec'd md. 16th da, 12th mo, 1753 having consent of surviving parents.

Comly Randal, son of Nicholas Randal of Manor of Moreland, Philadelphia Co. and Mary Phinney, dau of Daniel Phinney, late of same place, dec'd, md. 21st da, 12th mo, 1763 having consent of surviving parents.

Abraham Cadwalder, of Abington Twp., son of Isaac Cadwalder, late of Warminster, Bucks Co., dec'd and Aner Harmor, dau of Joshua Harmor, late of Springfield, Philadelphia Co., dec'd md. 16th da, 2nd mo, 1764 having consent of surviving parents

John Tyson, of Philadelphia Co., widower and Sarah Lewis, of Germantown, md. 1st da, 3rd m o, 1764.

James Tyson of Newton, Philadelphia Co. and Sarah Harper, dau of Robert Harper, of Philadelphia md. 12th da, 4th mo, 1764.

William Walmsley, Jr. of Byberry Twp., Philadelphia Co. and Abigail Knight, dau of Giles Knight of Bensalem, Bucks Co. md. 18th da, 4th mo, 1764 having consent of parents.

William Walmsley, son of Thomas Walmsley of Byberry Twp. and Susanna Comly, widow of Walter Comly of Manor of Moorland, Philadelphia Co. md. 6th da, 5th mo, 1764.

Joseph Janney, of city of Virginia, son of Isaac Janney, of same place and Hannah Jones of Warrington, Bucks Co, dau of John and Rebecca Jones of same place md. 8th da, 9th mo, 1764 having consent of parents.

William Hallowell, Jr. of Abington Twp., joyner, son of William Hallowell of Cheltenham, Philadelphia Co. and Mary Williams, dau of Anthony Williams

of Bristol, in said Co. md. 22nd da, 8th mo, 1764 having consent of parents.
John Sanders of Whitmarsh, in the Philadelphia Co., son of Robert Sanders,
dec'd and Ann Lewis, dau of Ellis Lewis, of Upper Dublin Twp.,
Philadelphia Co. md. 18th da, 1st mo, 1765 having consent of surviving
parents.
James Paul of Lower Dublin Twp., Philadelphia Co. and Susannah Knight, dau
of Giles Knight of Bensalem, Bucks Co. md. 10th da, 4th mo, 1765 having
consent of parents.
Jacob Coffin of Abington Twp., Philadelphia Co. and Lydia Tyson, dau of Isaac
Tyson of same place md. 9th da, 5th mo, 1765.
Joseph Knight, of Byberry Twp., Philadelphia Co. and Elizabeth Jones, dau of
Joseph Jones of Bucks Co. md. 27th da, 5th mo, 1765 having consent of
parents.
Silas Walmsley, of Philadelphia Co. and Martha Comley, dau of Walter Comley
of Manor of Moreland, dec'd md. 5th da, 6th mo, 1765 having consent of
parents.
Edward Bond, of Philadelphia Co., cordwainer and Mary Fox of Abington
Twp., md. 7th da, 6th mo, 1765 having consent of surviving parents.
Isaiah Bell, of the City of Philadelphia, and Barbara Harry of Germantown,
Philadelphia Co. md. 13th da, 7th mo, 1765 having consent of parents.
James Reddick, Philadelphia Co., son of Thomas Reddick and Rebeckah, his
dec'd wife of West Jersey and Hannah Robertson, dau of John Robertson
and Barbara, his wife 21st da, 11th mo, 1765 having consent of surviving
parents.
John Luken, of Horsham Twp., Philadelphia Co., widower and Dorothy Griggs,
of Abington Twp., seamstress md. 5th da, 12th mo, 1765.
John Grimmer, son of John Grimmer, of Abington, Philadelphia Co. and Sarah
Mixander, dau of John Mixander, of same place md. 3rd da, 6th mo, 1765
having consent of parents.
Daniel Thomas, of Manor of Moreland, Philadelphia Co., miller and Rebehah
Iredell of Horsham, aforesaid county md. 24th da, 4th mo, 1765 having
consent of parents.
Enoch Thomas, Philadelphia Co., son of Isaac Thomas, late of Horsham Twp.,
dec'd and Mary Roberts, dau of John Roberts and Barbara, his wife md. 24th
da, 4th mo, 1766 having consent of surviving parents.
Joseph Tyson, Philadelphia Co., yeoman, son of John Tyson of same place and
Abigail Cleaver, dau of Isaac Cleaver of Cheltenham Twp., aforesaid county
md. 13th da, 6th mo, 1766 having consent of parents,
John Engle, of Chester, Burlington Co. yeoman and Mary Thomas, dau of
Jonathan Thomas of Lower Dublin Twp., Philadelphia Co. md. 21st da, 5th
mo, 1766.
William Harmer, of Philadelphia Co. and Mary Tomlinson, dau of Thomas
Tomlinson, late of Bensalem, Bucks Co. md. 22nd da, 5th mo, 1766 having

consent of parents.

Mordecai Thomas, of Manor of Moreland, Philadelphia Co., yeoman, son of Daniel Thomas, dec'd and Susannah, his wife and Elizabeth Garret, dau of John Garrett and Alice, his wife md. 22nd da, 5th mo, 1766 having consent of surviving parents.

Jacob Kirk, son of Timothy Kirk, of Sipeland Twp., Chester Co. and Hannah Davis, dau of Thomas Davis of Germantown Twp., Philadelphia Co. md. 12th da, 11th mo, 1766 having consent of parents.

Henry Atherton, Jr. of Abington Twp., Philadelphia Co., son of Henry Atherton, Sr. and Susanna, his wife of Whiteland, Chester Co. and Hannah Waterman, dau of Humphrey Waterman late of Abington Twp., dec'd and Hannah, his wife 12th da, 11th mo, 1766 having consent of surviving parents.

Isaac Bolton, son of Isaac Bolton of Southampton Twp., Bucks Co, and Sarah Walmsley, dau of William Walmsley of Philadelphia Co. md. 3rd da, 12th mo, 1766 having consent of parents.

William Cowper of Germantown, Philadelphia Co., practitioner in phyick (sic), son of William Cowper, late of Cambridge in Great Brittain, dec'd and Mary Brown of Germantown, aforesaid Co., dau of Thomas Brown of the City of Philadelphia, dec'd 16th da, 1st mo, 1767.

Jonathan Parry, son of Thomas Parry, late of Lower Dublin Twp., Philadelphia Co. dec'd and Rebekah Knight, dau of Giles Knight of Bensalem, Bucks Co md. 22nd da, 4th mo, 1767 having consent of surviving parents,

Thomas Tyson, son of Peter Tyson of Abington Twp., Philadelphia Co., yeoman and Sarah Kirk, dau of Rynear Kirk of Upper Dublin Twp., same place md. 9th da, 6th mo, 1767 having consent of parents.

Samuel Harper, of Oxford, Philadelphia Co., blacksmith and Ann Shoemaker, now of Bristol Twp. md. 9th da, 10th mo, 1767 having consent of parents

Jacob Parry, son of Thomas Parry, late of Manor of Moreland, Philadelphia Co., dec'd and Sarah Cadwalder, dau of Isaac Cadwalder, late of Warminister Twp., Bucks Co, md. 15th da, 10th mo, 1767 having consent of surviving parents.

Jonathan Comley, of Moreland Twp., Philadelphia Co., yeoman and Rachel Thomas, of Lower Dublin Twp., same place, seamstress md. 24th da, 11th mo, 1767 having consent of parents.

Giles Knight, son of Giles Knight of Bensalem, Bucks Co. and Sarah Townsend, dau of Thomas Townsend of Philadelphia Co. md. 25th da, 11th mo, 1767 having consent of parents.

Henry Warrington, Philadelphia Co., Burlington Co. and Rebecca Walton, dau of Benjamin Walton in the Philadelphia Co. md. 17th da, 2nd mo, 1767 having consent of parents.

William Leedom, of Abington Twp., Philadelphia Co., son of John Leedom, late of Southampton, Bucks Co. dec'd and Susanna, his wife and Lydia Richard, dau of Thomas Richard and Mary, his wife, late of same place md. 13th da,

4th mo, 1768 having consent of surviving parents.

George Shoemaker, of Warrington Twp., Bucks Co. weaver, and Edith Spencer, dau of Samuel Spencer of Upper Dublin Twp., Philadelphia Co. md. 19th da, 4th mo, 1768 having consent of parents.

Jacob Holcombe, son of Thomas Holcombe, late of Abington Twp., Philadelphia Co., dec'd and Hannah, his wife and Esther Livezey, dau of Jonathan and Katharine Livezey, of Lower Dublin Twp., same Co. md. 19th da, 5th mo, 1768 having consent of surviving parents.

Cadwalder Roberts, son of Robert Roberts, late of Gwynedd Twp., Philadelphia Co., dec'd and Mary Shoemaker, dau of Richard Shoemaker of Horsham Twp., Philadelphia Co. md. 24th da, 5th mo, 1768 having consent of surviving parents.

Jonathan Roberts, Philadelphia Co., yeoman, son of Thomas Roberts, late of same place, dec'd and Martha Kirk, dau of Thomas Kirk of Upper Dublin Twp., same county, yeoman md. 24th da, 5th mo, 1768 having consent of surviving parents.

Jacob Jeanes, of Moreland, Philadelphia Co. and Leah Harmer of Abington Twp., md. 8th da, 12th mo, 1768 having consent of parents.

William Satterthwaite, of Lower Makesfield, Bucks Co., and Mary Knight, dau of Giles Knight of Bensalem Twp., md. 21st da, 12th mo, 1768 having consent of parents.

Nathan Lukens, of Bensalem Twp., Philadelphia Co. and Jane Comley of same place md. 11th da, 4th mo, 1768 having consent of parents.

Moses Sheppard, of Abington Twp., Philadelphia Co. and Hannah Fletcher, dau of Thomas Fletcher of aforesaid Twp. and Co., yeoman md. 12th da, 4th mo, 1769 having consent of parents.

Daniel Ashbridge, of Philadelphia Co., son of George Ashbridge and Jane, his wife of Goshen, Chester Co. and Hannah Pauls, dau of John Pauls and Mary, his wife of Lower Dublin Twp., Philadelphia Co. 3rd da, 5th mo, 1769 having consent of parents.

Isaac Bond, of Moorland, Philadelphia Co., cooper and Jane Williams of Horsham Twp., same county md. 12th da, 5th mo, 1769 having consent of parents.

Jonathan Radcliffe, of Warminister Twp., Bucks Co. son of John Radcliffe and Rebecca, his wife and Gainor Lukens, dau of Abraham Lukens and Rachel, his wife of Horsham Twp., Philadelphia Co. md. 5th da, 5th mo, 1769 having consent of parents.

David Parry, son of Thomas Parry, late of Manor of Moreland, Philadelphia Co., dec'd and Martha Comly, dau of Robert Comley of Horsham Twp., same county md. 6th da, 6th mo, 1769 having consent of surviving parents.

Joseph Paul, son of James Paul and Mary, his wife, of Warrington Twp., Bucks Co., and Hannah Paul, dau of James Paul, late of Abington Twp., dec'd and his wife, Sarah md. 8th da, 6th mo, 1769 having consent of surviving parents.

Joshua Walton, son of Isaac Walton, late of Manor of Moreland, Philadelphia Co., dec'd and Elizabeth Shoemaker, dau of Isaac Shoemaker, of Upper Dublin Twp., Philadelphia Co. md. 15th da, 3rd mo, 1770 having consent of surviving parents.

William Nichols, of State of Virginia, farmer and Sarah Spencer, dau of Samuel Spencer of Upper Dublin Twp., Philadelphia Co. md. 22 da, 3rd mo, 1770 having consent of parents.

Isaac Mather, of Cheltenham Twp., Philadelphia Co., millwright, son of Richard Mather of aforesaid Twp. and Co., yeoman and Mary Morris, dau of Joshua Morris of Abington Twp., in same place md. 17th da, 5th mo, 1770 having consent of parents.

Joseph Roberts, son of Robert Roberts of Gwynedd in Philadelphia Co., dec'd and Sarah Shoemaker, dau of Richard Shoemaker of Horsham Twp., md. 22nd da, 5th mo, 1770 having consent of surviving parents.

William Buckman, son of William Buckman of Newton, Bucks Co. yeoman and Hannah Dilworth, dau of Joseph Dilworth of Warminister, Bucks Co, cooper, md. 23rd da, 5th mo, 1770 having consent of parents.

John Heston, son of Labolun Heston and Elizabeth, his wife of Upper Mansfield, Bucks Co, and Hannah Garrett, dau of John Garrett and Alice, his wife of Horsham Twp., Philadelphia Co. md. 24th da, 5th mo, 1770 having consent of parents.

Benjamin Cutter, son of Horsham Twp., Bucks Co. and Susannah Dixon, dau of Ralph Dixon of Byberry Twp., Philadelphia Co. md. 25th da, 7th mo, 1770 having consent of parents.

James Lloyd, son of Thomas Lloyd of Manor of Moreland, Philadelphia Co. and Mary, his wife and Sarah Thomas, dau of Benjamin Thomas of Abington Twp., aforesaid place and Hannah, his wife, both dec'd md 5th da, 7th mo, 1770 having consent of surviving parents.

John Johnson, Jr. of Germantown, Philadelphia Co., son of John Johnson of same place and Rachel Livezey, dau of Thomas Livezey, Abington Twp. md. 15th da, 11th mo, 1770 having consent of parents.

Isaac Longstreth, of Manor of Moreland, Philadelphia Co., tanner, son of Bartholomew Longstreth, dec'd and Anne, his wife and Martha Thomas, dau of Daniel Thomas, dec'd and Susannah, his wife md. 15th da, 11th mo, 1770 having consent of surviving parents.

Charles Iredell, of Horsham Twp., Philadelphia Co. and Phebe Cadwalder of same place md. 27th da, 12th mo, 1770 having consent of parents.

Henry Simmons, son of John Simmons of Middletown Twp., Bucks Co, and Sarah Dunn, dau of Ralph Dunn of Byberry Twp. Twp., Philadelphia Co. md. 27th da, 3rd mo, 1771 having consent of parents.

Isaac Walton, of Warminister Twp., Bucks Co.., son of Job Walton of Byberry Twp., Philadelphia Co. and Susannah Kirk, dau of Thomas Kirk md. 2nd da,

4th mo, 1771 having consent of parents.

Joshua Gilbert, son of Benjamin Gilbert of Byberry Twp., Philadelphia Co. and Mary Randle, dau of Nicholas Randle of Manor of Moreland, Philadelphia Co. md. 13th da, 4th mo, 1771 having consent of parents.

Robert Harper, son of John Harper, dec'd of Northern Liberties, Philadelphia Co. and Hannah Thomas, dau of Jonathan Thomas of Lower Dublin Twp., Philadelphia Co. md. 24th da, 4th mo, 1771 having consent of surviving parents.

Thomas Knight, son of Daniel Knight of Byberry Twp., Philadelphia Co. and Sarah Walton, dau of Benjamin Walton, dec'd of Byberry Twp., same place md. 1st da, 5th mo, 1771 having consent of surviving parents.

Robert Fletcher, son of Thomas Fletcher, Abington Twp., Philadelphia Co., yeoman and Susanna, his wife and Priscilla Roberts, dau of Thomas Roberts, late of Abington Twp., dec'd and Elizabeth, his wife md. 24th da, 6th mo, 1771 having consent of surviving parents.

Robert Morris of Bristol Twp., Philadelphia Co., miller, son of Daniel Morris, late of Upper Dublin Twp., and Mary Tyson, dau of Renior Tyson, late of Abington Twp. in said place, md. 12th da, 11th mo, 1771 having consent of parents.

William Walton, son of Benjamin Walton, late of Byberry Twp., Philadelphia Co., dec'd and Lydia Thornton, dau of James Thornton, of aforesaid Twp. and place md. 27th da, 11th mo, 1772 having consent of surviving parents.

William Walton, son of Isaac Walton, dec'd of Byberry Twp., Philadelphia Co. and Rachel Atkinson, widow, dau of Benjamin Gilbert of same place md. 1st da, 1st mo, 1772 having consent of surviving parents.

Joseph Longstreth, of Southampton Twp., Bucks Co, yeoman and Susanna Morris, dau of Joshua Morris of Abington, Philadelphia Co. md. 16th da, 4th mo, 1772 having consent of parents.

Jonathan Shoemaker, Philadelphia Co. and Martha Shoemaker of Upper Dublin Twp., Philadelphia Co. md. 7th da, 5th mo, 1772 having consent of parents.

John Roberts, son of John Roberts of Whitepain Twp., Philadelphia Co. and Elizabeth Cleaver, dau of Peter Cleaver of Upper Dublin Twp., same county md. 9th da, 6th mo, 1772 having consent of parents.

Thomas Paul, son of John Paul of Lower Dublin Twp., Philadelphia Co. and Hannah Shalcross, dau of Leonard Shalcross of Oxford in the aforesaid place md. 16th da, 6th mo, 1773 having consent of parents.

Samuel Conard, of Horsham Twp., Philadelphia Co., yeoman, son of Cornelius Conard, late of aforesaid place, yeoman, dec'd and Hannah Kenderdine, widow of Jacob Kinderdine, late of aforesaid place, dec'd md. 6th da, 11th mo, 1773.

Anthony Williams, son of Anthony Williams of Bristol, Philadelphia Co. and Rachel Garret, dau of John Garret, dec'd of Horsham, said county md. 25th da, 11th mo, 1772 having consent of surviving parents.

Isaac Tyson, son of Isaac Tyson, dec'd of Abington Twp., Philadelphia Co. and
Sarah Cleaver, dau of Isaac Cleaver of Cheltenham in said place md. 22 da,
12th mo, 1773 having consent of surviving parents.

Thomas Townsend of Byberry Twp., Philadelphia Co. and Mary Chapman, late
of Wrightstown, Bucks Co, widow, but now of Byberry Twp., dau of
Benjamin Mason of Northern Liberties, Philadelphia Co. md. 4th da, 3rd mo,
1773 having consent of parents.

Francis Jones, son of Robert Jones, late of Merion, dec'd and Margaret, his wife
and Elizabeth Roberts, dau of Thomas Roberts and Rachel, his wife md. 6th
da, 5th mo, 1773 having consent of surviving parents.

Samuel Carver, of Byberry Twp., Philadelphia Co. and Susannah Conard, dau
of Cornelius Conard of Horsham Twp. and aforesaid place, dec'd. md. 13th
da, 10th mo, 1774 having consent of surviving parents.

Jonathan Thomas, of Upper Dublin Twp., Philadelphia Co., joyner, son of
Daniel Thomas dec'd and Susannah, his wife and Alice Garret, of Horsham
Twp., aforesaid place, dau of John Garret, dec'd and Alice, his wife md. 14th
da, 10th mo, 1773 having consent of surviving parents.

William Garret, of Horsham Twp., Philadelphia Co., son of John Garret, late of
same place, dec'd. and Ann Lukens, of Bristol Twp., Philadelphia Co., dau
of John Lukens of Philadelphia md. 22nd da, 10th mo, 1773 having consent
of surviving parents.

Joshua Hallowell, of Cheltenham Twp., Philadelphia Co., yeoman, son of
William Hallowell of same place and Hannah Trump, dau of Michael
Trump, of Upper Dublin Twp., Philadelphia Co. md. 19th da, 11th mo, 1773
having consent of parents.

Mathew Fitzwater of Upper Dublin Twp., Philadelphia Co., son of John
Fitzwater of Horsham Twp., yeoman and Sarah Bawley, dau of Nathan
Bewley, late of Abington Twp., yeoman, dec'd md. 25th da, 11th mo, 1773
having consent of surviving parents.

John Wood, son of Thomas Wood, late of Manor of Moreland, Philadelphia Co.,
dec'd and Elizabeth Kinard, dau of Joseph Kinard, late of same place, also
dec'd md. 17th da, 2nd mo, 1774 having consent of surviving parents.

Cephas Child, son of Cephas Child, late of Plumsted, Bucks Co, dec'd and Mary
Cadwalder, dau of Isaac Cadwalder, late of Warminister in aforesaid place,
dec'd md. 24th da, 3rd mo, 1774 having consent of surviving parents.

Thomas Leeach, of Abington Twp., Philadelphia Co., and Hannah Tyson of
same place md. 31st da, 3rd mo, 1774 having consent of parents.

Samuel Spencer, son of Jacob Spencer of Moreland Twp., Philadelphia Co. and
Mary Fitzwater, dau of John Fitzwater of Upper Dublin Twp., Philadelphia
Co. md. 14th da, 4th mo, 1774 having consent of parents.

John Fitzwater, of Upper Dublin Twp., Philadelphia Co., mason, son of John
Fitzwater of same place and Hannah Lukens, dau of Rynear Luken, md. 21st
da, 4th mo, 1774 having consent of parents.

Thomas Roberts, of Bristol Twp., Philadelphia Co., yeoman, son of Thomas
Roberts, late of same place, dec'd and Susannah Kirk, dau of Rynear Kirk of
Upper Dublin Twp., same place md. 12th da, 5th mo, 1774 having consent
of surviving parents.

Joseph Woollen, of Lower Dublin Twp., Philadelphia Co., son of Joseph
Woollen, dec'd and Rebecca Cleaver, dau of John Cleaver, of Upper Dublin
Twp., aforesaid place md. 27th da, 10th mo, 1774 having consent of
surviving parents.

Thomas Pennington, son of William Pennington of Chester Co, and Susannah
Heaton, dau of Robert Heaton of Byberry Twp., Philadelphia Co., dec'd md.
2nd da, 11th mo, 1774 having consent of surviving parents.

Henry Paul, of Oxford, Philadelphia Co., son of Joseph Paul of Northern
Liberties of City of Philadelphia and Ruth Harper, dau of Robert Harper, late
of Northern Liberties, dec'd md. 15th da, 11th mo, 1774 having consent of
surviving parents.

Jonathan Roberts, of Byberry Twp., Philadelphia Co., yeoman, son of Thomas
Roberts, late of same place, yeoman and Mary Spencer, dau of Samuel
Spencer of Upper Dublin Twp. md. 15th da, 11th mo, 1774 having consent
of parents.

Elijah Walton, Bucks Co, yeoman, son of Job Walton and Rebecca Briggs, dau
of Edmond Briggs, md. 22nd da, 11th mo, 1774 having consent of parents.

Ephraim Howell, of Southampton Twp., Bucks Co. Co, and Esther Walton, dau
of Richard Walton of Byberry Twp., Philadelphia Co. md. 1st da, 3rd mo,
1775 having consent of parents.

David Parry, of Bensalum Twp., Bucks Co, son of Thomas Parry, dec'd and
Isabel Heaton, dau of Robert Heaton of Byberry Twp., Philadelphia Co. md.
5th da, 4th mo, 1775 having consent of surviving parents.

Thomas Fletcher, son of Thomas Fletcher and Susanna, his wife of Abington
Twp., Philadelphia Co., yeoman and Hannah Ashbridge, widow, dau of John
Paul and Mary, his wife, yeoman, md. 6th da, 4th mo, 1775 having consent
of parents.

Abel Fitzwater, son of George Fitzwater, late of Upper Dublin Twp.,
Philadelphia Co., dec'd and Hannah Hochdale, dau of William Hochdale,
late of Wrightstown Twp., Bucks Co, dec'd md. 7th da, 4th mo, 1775 having
consent of surviving parents.

David Evans, of the City of Philadelphia, cabinet maker, son of Evan Evans, late
of same place, dec'd and Elizabeth, his wife and Sarah Roberts, dau of John
Roberts, of Bristol Twp., Philadelphia Co. md. 22nd da, 11th mo, 1775
having consent of surviving parents.

Benjamin Lloyd, of Manor of Moreland, Philadelphia Co., son of John Lloyd
and Susanna, his wife and Sarah Child, dau of John Child and Sarah, his wife
md. 15th da, 6th mo, 1775 having consent of parents.

Arnold Mitchener, of Bristol Twp., Philadelphia Co. and Martha Tyson, dau of

Rynear Tyson, of Abington Twp., Philadelphia Co. md. 20th da, 6th mo, 1776 having consent of parents.

Jesse Trump, son of Michael Trump of Upper Dublin Twp., Philadelphia Co. and Grace, his wife and Margaret Loosbourrow, dau of William Loosburrow and Mary, his wife md. 24th da, 10th mo, 1776 having consent of parents.

John Jones, of Bristol Twp., Philadelphia Co., yeoman, son of Joseph Jones of same place and Priscilla Hallowell of Manor of Moreland, in same place, dau of Thomas Hallowell of same place md. 22nd da, 11th mo, 1776 having consent of parents.

David Lukens, Horsham Twp., Philadelphia Co., son of William Lukens of same place and Sarah Lloyd of Manor of Moreland, same place, dau of Samuel Lloyd of same place md. 20th da, 12th mo, 1776 having consent of parents.

David Jones, son of Joseph Jones of Bristol Twp., Philadelphia Co. and Mary Shalcross, dau of Joseph Shalcross of Lower Dublin Twp. md. 24th da, 12th mo, 1776 having consent of parents.

Jonathan Lukens, of Horsham Twp., son of William Lukens of same place and Mary Conard of aforesaid Twp. and place, dau of Dennis Connard of same place md. 24th da, 4th mo, 1777 having consent of parents.

John Child, son of Henry Child of Cheltenham, Philadelphia Co. and Mary Phips, dau of Peter Phips of Abington Twp. md. 5th da, 6th mo, 1777 having consent of parents.

Nicholas Randell, son of Nicholas Randell of Manor of Moreland, Philadelphia Co. and Hannah Townsend, dau of Thomas Townsend of Byberry Twp. aforesaid place md. 4th da, 9th mo, 1777 having consent of parents.

Benjamin Stemple, son of Leonard Stemple of Gwynedd Twp., Philadelphia Co. and Sarah Menely, dau of Thomas Menley md. 19th da, 12th mo, 1777 having consent of parents.

Benjamin Bond, of Horsham Twp., Philadelphia Co., son of Joseph Bond, late of North Carolina, dec'd and Mary Walton, dau of Thomas Walton of Manor of Moreland md. 17th da, 4th mo m 1778 having consent of surviving parents.

Jonathan Garret, of Warminister, Bucks Co, son of Jacob Garret of Horsham, dec'd and Hannah Mather, dau of Richard Mather, dec'd of Cheltenham, Philadelphia Co. md. 21st da, 5th mo, 178 having consent of surviving parents.

Benjamin Mather, son of Richard Mather, dec'd of Cheltenham, Philadelphia Co. and Ann Thomas, dau of Jonathan Thomas of Lower Dublin Twp., aforesaid county md. 7th da, 6th mo, 1778 having consent of surviving parents.

Caleb Hallowell, of Cheltenham Twp., Philadelphia Co., farmer, son of William Hallowell of same place and Priscilla Tyson, dau of Ryner Tyson of Abington Twp. md. 15th da, 10th mo, 1778 having consent of parents.

Thomas Parry, son of John Parry of Manor of Moreland, Philadelphia Co. and Elizabeth Child, dau of John Child of Bristol in the aforesaid place md. 16th da, 11th mo, 1778 having consent of parents.

Thomas Beal of New Brittain Twp., Bucks Co, son of William Beal of same place, dec'd and Alice Heston of Manor of Moreland, Philadelphia Co. md. 24th da, 3rd mo, 1778 having consent of surviving parents.

Isaac Shoemaker, son of John Shoemaker of Cheltenham Twp., Philadelphia Co., miller and Sarah Mather, dau of Joseph Mather of Germantown, in the aforesaid place md. 5th da, 5th mo, 1779 having consent of parents.

Emanuel Kinard of Manor of Moreland, Philadelphia Co., son of Joseph Kinard lately of Horsham, dec'd and Mary Brown, of same place, dau of Samuel Deal, dec'd, of Kentown, NJ md. 4th da, 6th mo, 1778 having consent of surviving parents.

Thomas Mather, son of Bartholomew Mathers of Cheltenham Twp., Philadelphia Co., miller and Rachel Leech, dau of Isaac Leah, dec'd of aforesaid place and place md. 21st da, 7th mo, 1778 having consent of surviving parents.

John Hallowell, son of Thomas Hallowell, of Manor of Moreland, Philadelphia Co. and Lydia Trump, dau of Michael Trump of Lower Dublin Twp. md. 22nd da, 8th mo, 1778 having consent of parents.

Moses Grubb, son of William Grubb of Fincastle, DE, dec'd and Grace Thomas, dau of Jonathan Thomas, Lower Dublin Twp. Philadelphia Co. md. 29th da, 11th mo, 1778 having consent of parents.

Jesse Roberts, son of John Roberts, dec'd of Abington Twp., Philadelphia Co. and Mary Wilson, dau of John Wilson late of Bristol Twp., Bucks Co., dec'd md. 4th da, 11th mo, 1778 having consent of surviving parents.

Jesse James of Byberry Twp., Philadelphia Co., son of Samuel Jones, late of Chester Co., dec'd and Phebe Townsend, dau of Thomas Townsend, of Byberry Twp., aforesaid county md. 11th da, 11th mo, 1778 having consent of surviving parents.

Jonathan Shoemaker, of Cheltenham Twp., Philadelphia Co., blacksmith and Hannah Lukens, dau of Joseph Lukens, of Horsham Twp., same place md. 19th da, 11th mo, 1779 having consent of parents.

Ezra Comley of Warminister Twp., Bucks Co., and Hannah Iredell, of Horsham Twp., Philadelphia Co. md. 20th da, 5th mo, 1779 having consent of parents.

John Wood, son of Thomas and Ann Wood, late of Manor of Moreland, Philadelphia Co., dec'd and Mary Sammons, dau of Nathaniel and Ann Samons of same place md. 21st da, 4th mo, 1780 having consent of surviving parents.

William Webster, son of William Webster, dec'd of Abington Twp., Philadelphia Co. and Sarah Alberson, dau of Benjamin Alberson of Abington Twp., same place md. 4th da, 5th mo, 1780 having consent of surviving parents.

John Edwards, son of Robert Edwards, of Horsham Twp., Philadelphia Co. and
Ellen Stephens, dau of Cornelius Stephens, late of aforesaid place, dec'd md.
5th da, 5th mo, 1780 having consent of surviving parents.

Cadwalder Foulks, of Upper Dublin Twp., Philadelphia Co., weaver, son of
Edward Foulke, dec'd and Sarah Hallowell of Cheltenham Twp. of aforesaid
place, dau of William Hallowell of same place md. 18th da, 5th mo, 1780
having consent of surviving parents.

Absolom Mitchener of Bristol Twp., Philadelphia Co., son of John Mitchener,
of same place and Priscilla Kirk, dau of Isaac Kirk of Upper Dublin Twp.,
same place md. 25th da, 5th mo, 1780 having consent of parents.

John Shalcross of Oxford Twp., Philadelphia Co., son of Leonard Shalcross of
same place and Mary Paul of Lower Dublin Twp., same place, dau of John
Paul of same place md. 7th da, 8th mo, 1780 having consent of parents.

Christopher Smith, of Northern Liberties, City of Philadelphia, sailor, son of
Joseph and Margaret Smith of Yorkshire, Great Britain and Susanna
Comley, dau of John Comley, late of Northern Liberties, of City of
Philadelphia, dec'd and Hannah, his wife md. 15th da, 6th mo, 1780 having
consent of surviving parents.

John Edwards, of Toamencin Twp., Philadelphia Co., son of Rowland Edwards,
dec'd and Sarah Mitchener, dau of John Mitchener of Bristol Twp.,
Philadelphia Co. md. 11th da, 10th mo, 1780 having consent of surviving
parents.

William Stapler, son of Thomas Stapler, Bensalem Twp., Bucks Co., and Mary
Mitchel, dau of Joseph Mitchel of Manor of Moreland, Philadelphia Co. md.
1st da, 11th mo, 1780 having consent of parents.

Peter Robinson, son of Jonathan Robinson of Whitemarsh Twp., Philadelphia
Co., miller and Martha Livezey, dau of Thomas Livezey of Foxborrow Twp.,
same place, miller md. 15th da, 11th mo, 1780 having consent of parents.

Abraham Cadwalder, of Abington Twp., Philadelphia Co., carpenter and Martha
Deaves, dau of Abraham Deaves of Germantown Twp., aforesaid place md.
16th da, 11th mo, 1780 having consent of parents.

John Mitchel, of Manor of Moreland, Philadelphia Co., and Tacy Tyson of
Upper Dublin Twp., aforesaid place md. 24th da, 11th mo, 1780 having
consent of parents.

Thomas Ross, son of John Ross, of Solebury Twp., Bucks Co., millwright and
Rachel Longstreth, dau of Daniel Longstreth of Warminister, same place,
yeoman md. 30th da, 3rd mo, 1781 having consent of parents.

John Stackhouse, son of John Stackhouse of Middletown Twp., Bucks Co., and
Sarah Knight, dau of Jonathan Knight of Byberry Twp., Philadelphia Co.
md. 16th da, 5th mo, 1781 having consent of parents.

Thomas Albertson of Abington Twp., Philadelphia Co., son of Benjamin
Albertson of same place and Priscilla Bird, dau of Alberah Bird of Fasuink??
Twp., aforesaid place md. 17th da, 5th mo, 1781 having consent of parents.

James Shoemaker, son of Isaac Shoemaker of Upper Dublin Twp., Philadelphia Co. and Hannah, his wife and Phebe Walton, dau of William Walton and Phebe, his wife, late of same place, dec'd md. 1st da, 6th mo, 1781 having consent of surviving parents.

Bartholomew Fussell of Manor of Moreland, Philadelphia Co., son of William Fussell of Charlestown, Chester Co. and Rebekah Bond, dau of Joseph Bond, of Southampton, Bucks Co. md. 6th da, 6th mo, 1781 having consent of parents.

Daniel Knight, son of Jonathan Knight of Byberry Twp., Philadelphia Co. and Rachel Walton, dau of Daniel Walton, of same place md. 14th da, 11th mo, 1781 having consent of parents.

Benjamin Adams, son of Jediah Adams of Bristol Twp., Bucks Co., and Mary Ridge, dau of Thomas Ridge, of Bensalem and same place md. 19th da, 12th mo, 1781 having consent of parents.

John Parry, son of John Parry of Manor of Moreland, Philadelphia Co. and Elizabeth Roberts, dau of John Roberts, dec'd of Abington Twp., aforesaid place md. 18th da, 4th mo, 1782 having consent of surviving parents.

David Garret, son of John Garret, late of Horsham Twp., Philadelphia Co., dec'd and Rebekah Cadwalder, dau of Jacob Cadwalder of Warminister Twp., Bucks Co., md. 8th da, 5th mo, 1782 having consent of surviving parents.

Nathan Harper, of Oxford Twp., Philadelphia Co., son of Robert Harper, dec'd. and Mary Kirkner, dau of Jacob Kirkner of same place, yeoman md. 14th da, 5th mo, 1782 having consent of surviving parents.

John Shallcross, son of Joseph Shallcross, of Lower Dublin Twp., Philadelpha Co. and Mary Livezey, dau of Joseph Livezey, same place md. 16th da, 8th mo, 1782 having consent of parents.

John Jones, son of Jonathan Jones of Warrington Twp., Bucks Co., and Sarah Waterman, dau of John Waterman of Abington Twp., Philadelphia Co. md. 16th da, 5th mo, 1782 having consent of parents.

Isaac Stackhouse, son of Isaac Stackhouse, of Middletown Twp., Bucks Co., and Elizabeth Townsend, dau of Thomas Townsend of Byberry Twp., Philadelphia Co. md. 5th da, 6th mo, 1782 having consent of parents.

Isaac Tyson, son of Isaac Tyson, of Abington Twp., Philadelphia Co., yeoman and Lydia Tomkins of Manor of Moreland md. 20th da, 6th mo, 1782 having consent of parents.

Joseph Tyson of Abington Twp., Philadelphia Co., son of Rynear Tyson of same place and Sarah Hallowell, dau of Benjamin Hallowell, of aforesaid place md. 17th da, 10th mo, 1782 having consent of parents.

Abner Lukens of Upper Dublin Twp., Philadelphia Co., son of Joseph Lukens of same place and Sarah Fitzwater, dau of John Fitzwater of aforesaid Twp. and county md. 10th da, 4th mo, 1782 having consent of parents.

Jacob Taylor, son of Jesse Taylor and Ann, his wife, the latter dec'd of

Newlinton Twp., Chester Co., and Elizabeth Jones, dau of Joseph Jones and Mary, his wife, the latter dec'd of Cheltenham Twp., Philadelphia Co. md. 18th da, 6th mo, 1782 having consent of surviving parents.

Edward Ambler of Montgomery Twp., Philadelphia Co. and Ann Mather of Germantown Twp., aforesaid place md. 18th da, 7th mo, 1783 having consent of parents.

Hugh Evans, son of Thomas Evans of Gwynedd Twp., Philadelphia Co. and Sarah Shoemaker, dau of Joseph Mather of Germantown Twp., same place md. 16th da, 12th mo, 1783 having consent of parents.

Jesse Cleaver, son of John Cleaver of Upper Dublin Twp., Philadelphia Co. and Elizabeth Kirk, dau of Isaac Kirk of aforesaid Twp. and place md. 22nd da, 1st mo, 1784 having consent of parents.

Dennis Conrad, son of Dennis Conrad, Horsham Twp., Philadelphia Co. and Margaret Peters, dau of John Peters, late of Abington Twp., Philadelphia Co., dec'd md. 18th da, 3rd mo, 1784 having consent of surviving parents.

Amos Jones, son of John Jones of Cheltenham Twp., Philadelphia Co. and Ann Phipps, dau of Peter Phipps of Abington Twp. and aforesaid providence md. 20th da, 5th mo, 1784 having consent of parents.

John Clayton of Cheltenham Twp., Philadelphia Co., son of Richard Clayton, dec'd and Mary Hallowell, dau of Rynear Hallowell md. 18th da, 11th mo, 1784 having consent of surviving parents.

John Samms of Manor of Moreland, Montgomery Co., son of Nathaniel and Ann Samms of same place, and Sarah Blair of Cheltenham Twp., aforesaid place, dau of William and Elizabeth Blair, both dec'd md. 9th da, 12th mo, 1784 having consent of surviving parents.

Charles Shoemaker, of Cheltenham Twp., Philadelphia Co., miller, son of John Shoemaker, of same place and Elizabeth Paul, dau of John Paul, late of Germantown Twp., Philadelphia Co., dec'd md. 15th da, 3rd mo, 1785 having consent of surviving parents.

Thomas Shoemaker, Jr. of Cheltenham Twp., Montgomery Co., son of Isaac Shoemaker, late of Cheltenham Twp., dec'd and Mary Shoemaker, dau of Benjamin Shoemaker, of same place. 8th da, 9th mo, 1785 having consent of surviving parents.

Jonathan Roberts of Bristol Twp., Philadelphia Co., yeoman, son of Thomas Roberts late of same place, yeoman and Mary Jones, dau of Joseph Jones of Cheltenham Twp., Montgomery Co., yeoman md. 7th da, 10th mo, 1785 having consent of parents.

Thomas Lancaster of Whitemarsh Twp., son of Thomas Lancaster, late of Richland, Bucks Co., dec'd and Martha Lloyd of Abington Twp., dau of John Lloyd and Elinor, his wife, late of Horsham Twp., Philadelphia Co., dec'd md. 13th da, 10th mo, 1785 having consent of surviving parents.

Nathan Walton, son of Benjamin Walton, of Byberry Twp. Philadelphia Co. and Ann Roberts, dau of Lewis Roberts, of Abington Twp., Montgomery Co., md 17th da, 11th mo, 1785 having consent of parents.

Thomas Hallowell, son of Rynear Hallowell, Cheltenham Twp., Montgomery Co., and Dorathea Clayton, dau of Richard Clayton, dec'd of same place md. 15th da, 6th mo, 1786 having consent of surviving parents.

John Tyson, of Abington Twp., Montgomery Co., son of John Tyson, late of same place, dec'd and Mary Kirk, dau of Rynear Kirk, of Upper Dublin Twp., aforesaid place md. 16th da, 11th mo, 1786 having consent of surviving parents.

Elijah Lukens, of Upper Dublin Twp., Montgomery Co., son of Joseph Lukens of same place and Rebecah Tyson, of Abington Twp., aforesaid place, dau of John Tyson late of same place, dec'd md. 14th da, 12th mo, 1786 having consent of surviving parents.

Leonard Shallcross, son of Leonard Shallcross of Oxford Twp., Philadelphia Co., yeoman and Mary Livezey, dau of Jonathan Livezey, of Lower Dublin Twp., aforesaid place, yeoman md. 3rd da, 4th mo, 1787 having consent of parents.

Abel Cadwallader of Horsham Twp., Montgomery Co. , son of John Cadwallader and Christiana, his wife of same place and Jane Cadwallader, dau of Isaac Cadwallader and Elizabeth, his wife, of Manor of Moreland of same place md. 5th da, 10th mo 1787 having consent of parents.

Thomas Parker, Bristol Twp., Philadelphia Co., miller, son of Thomas Parker, late of City of Philadelphia, dec'd and Elizabeth, his wife and Mary Harper, dau of Samuel Harper of aforesaid place md. 6th da, 4th mo, 1787 having consent of surviving parents.

Thomas Hallowell, son of William Hallowell of Abington Twp., Philadelphia Co. and Latitia Shoemaker, dau of George Shoemaker of Lower Dublin Twp. md. 4th da, 3rd mo, 1756 having consent of parents.

John Wilson, son of Samuel Wilson and Mary, his wife of Bristol Twp., Philadelphia Co. and Sarah Livezey, dau of Nathan Livezey and Hannah, his wife of Lower Dublin Twp., aforesaid place md. 10th da, 4th mo, 1788 having consent of parents.

Henry Child, son of John Child of Bristol Twp. Philadelphia Co. and Sarah Kirk, dau of Isaac Kirk of Upper Dublin Twp., Montgomery Co., md. 22nd da, 5th mo, 1788 having consent of parents.

Jonathan Knight, son of Jonathan Knight, of Byberry Twp., Philadelphia Co. and Elizabeth Thomas, dau of Jonathan Thomas, of Lower Dublin Twp. aforesaid place md. 15th da, 6th mo, 1788 having consent of parents.

John Shoemaker, of Cheltenham, Montgomery Co., miller, son of John Shoemaker of same place, miller and Jane Ashbridge of Abington Twp., aforesaid place, dau of Daniel Ashbridge, late of Bensalem Twp., Bucks Co.. md. 16th da, 10th mo, 1788 having consent of parents.

Joseph Kirkbride, son of Stacy Kirkbride, of Haverford Twp., Chester Co., yeoman and Mary Paul, dau of John Paul, late of Germantown Twp.,

Philadelphia Co. dec'd md. 16th da, 1st mo, 1789 having consent of surviving parents.

Rynear Lukens, son of Joseph Lukens of Upper Dublin Twp., Montgomery Co., and Tacy Hallowell, dau of Benjamin Hallowell, of Abington Twp. aforesaid place, md. 19th da, 3rd mo, 1789 having consent of parents.

Thomas Watson, son of Thomas Watson, Buckingham, Bucks Co., dec'd and Mary Veree, dau of Robert Veree, of Lower Dublin Twp., Philadelphia Co. md. 23rd da, 4th mo, 1789 having consent of surviving parents.

Nathan Thomas, of Abington Twp., Montgomery Co., blacksmith and Sarah Shallcross, dau of Joseph Shallcross late of Lower Dublin Twp., Philadelphia Co. dec'd md. 14th da, 5th mo, 1789 having consent of surviving parents.

Thomas Hooton, Jr. of Philadelphia, son of Thomas Hooton of Evesham, West Jersey, Burlington Co., and Ann Wynn, Jr., dau of John Wynn, late of Germantown, Philadelphia Co., dec'd. md. 15th da, 5th mo, 1789 having consent of surviving parents.

William Bailey, of Falls Twp., Bucks Co., yeoman and Tacy Livezey, dau of Nathan Livezey, of Lower Dublin Twp., Philadelphia Co. md. 19th da, 11th mo, 1789 having consent of parents.

David Michener, son of John Michener, of Bristol Twp., Philadelphia Co. and Rebecca Wilson, dau of John Wilson, late of Bucks Co., md. 26th da, 11th mo, 1789 having consent of parents.

James Veree, son of Robert Veree, of Lower Dublin Twp., Philadelphia Co. and Ann, his wife and Susannah Ashbridge, dau of William Ashbridge, Oxford Twp., same county md. 6th da, 4th mo, 1790 having consent of parents.

William Thomas, son of Nathan Thomas of Abington Twp., Montgomery Co. and Judith Griffith, dau of Samuel Griffith, of Lower Dublin Twp., Philadelphia Co. md. 7th da, 5th mo, 1790 having consent of parents.

Joseph Phipps, son of Peter Phipps and Mary, his wife of Abington Twp., Montgomery Co. and Mary Eastburn of same place, dau of Joseph Eastburn, dec'd and Mary, his wife of Solebury, Bucks Co., md. 20th da, 5th mo, 1790 having consent of surviving parents.

George Crafts, son of Bunard Craft, of Abington Twp., Montgomery Co., and Rebecca Tyson, dau of Joseph Tyson, late of Abington Twp. md. 10th da, 6th mo, 1790 having consent of parents.

Caleb Lownes, of the City of Philadelphia, son of John Lownes of said city and Agnes, his wife, dec'd and Margaret Robeson, dau of Jonathan and Catharine Robeson of Whitemarsh Twp., Montgomery Co. md. 11th da, 9th mo, 1790 having consent of surviving parents.

Jesse Foulke, son of William Foulke and Priscilla, his wife, of Richland, Bucks Co., and Sarah Phipps, dau of Peter Phipps and Mary, his wife of Abington Twp., Montgomery Co. md. 17th da, 10th mo, 1790 having consent of parents.

Thomas Jones, son of Joseph Jones of Cheltonham Twp., Montgomery Co. and

Mary Righter of Abington Twp., dau of Peter Righter of Roxborough Twp., Philadelphia Co. md. 21st da, 10th mo, 1790 having consent of parents.

Benjamin Hallowell, son of Benjamin Hallowell of Abington Twp., Montgomery Co. and Abigail Waterman, dau of Isaac Walterman of same place md. 7th da, 11 mo, 1790 having consent of parents.

Enoch Thomas, son of Enoch Thomas of Cheltenham Twp., Montgomery Co. and Rebeckah Hallowell, dau of Thomas Hallowell of Abington Twp., same place md. 8th da, 11th mo, 1790 having consent of parents.

George Roberts, of Oxford Twp., Philadelphia Co., son of John Roberts of same place, merchant and Rebecca, his wife and Mary Ashbridge, dau of William Ashbridge, late of same place, dec'd, miller and Elizabeth, his wife md. 5th da, 11th mo, 1790 having consent of surviving parents.

John Righter, son of Peter Righter, Philadelphia Co. and Elizabeth Phipps, dau of Peter Phipps, of Abington Twp. md. 15th da, 9th mo, 1790 having consent of parents.

Robert Field, of Abington Twp., Montgomery Co., and Priscilla Roberts, of same place, dau of Abraham Roberts, of Bucks Co., md. 29th da, 9th mo, 1791 having consent of parents.

Solomon Miller of York Co., son of Robert Miller, dec'd and Hannah Jenkins of Abington Twp., Montgomery Co., dau of Joshua Litler, dec'd. md. 3rd da, 11th mo, 1791 having consent of surviving parents.

Thomas Walton, son of Thomas Walton of Manor of Moreland, Montgomery Co., and Hannah Child, dau of John Child of Bristol Twp., Philadelphia Co. md. 18th da, 11th mo, 1791 having consent of parents.

Joseph Livezey, Jr., son of Joseph Livezey of Lower Dublin Twp., Philadelphia Co. and Deborah Lloyd, dau of John Lloyd, late of Horsham, dec'd md. 15th da, 12th mo, 1791 having consent of surviving parents.

John Iredell, son of Robert and Hannah Iredell, of Horsham Twp., Philadelphia Co. and Mary Paul, dau of Jacob and Jane Paul of Abington Twp. md. 29th da, 3rd mo, 1792 having consent of parents.

John Michener, son of William Michener of Moreland Twp., Montgomery Co., and Martha Hallowell, dau of Benjamin Hallowell of Abington Twp., aforesaid place md. 19th da, 4th mo, 1792 having consent of parents.

Isaac Walton, son of Jeremiah Walton of Bayberry Twp., Philadelphia Co. and Sarah Roberts, dau of Isaac Roberts of Moreland Twp, Montgomery Co. md. 24th da, 5th mo, 1792 having consent of parents.

Joseph Marshall, son of John Marshall of Lower Dublin Twp., Philadelphia Co. and Agness Hallowell, dau of Rynear Hallowell, of late of Cheltenham Twp., Montgomery Co., dec'd md. 7th da, 6th mo, 1792 having consent of surviving parents.

Cabel Hallowell, of Abington Twp., Montgomery Co., son of William Hallowell of Cheltenham Twp., same place and Mary Waterman, dau of Isaac Waterman, of Abington Twp. md. 26th da, 11th mo, 1792 having consent of parents.

Isaac Lukens, son of John Lukens, of Towamensin Twp., Philadelphia Co. and Hannah Marshall of Lower Dublin Twp., Philadelphia Co. dau of John Marshall of same place md. 15th da, 11th mo, 1792 having consent of parents.

Josiah Pryor, son of Thomas Pryor, dec'd, late of City of Burlington, NJ and Elizabeth Roberts, dau of John Roberts of Oxford Twp., Philadelphia Co. md. 4th da, 12th mo, 1792 having consent of surviving parents.

Joseph Mitchell, of Moreland Twp., Montgomery Co., and Hannah Shallcross of Lower Dublin Twp., Philadelphia Co. md. 24th da, 4th mo, 1793 having consent of parents.

Jesse Walton, of Borough of Bristol, Bucks Co., tanner, son of Jeremiah Walton, late of Moreland, Philadelphia Co., dec'd and Mary, his wife and Ann Love, dau of Benjamin Love of Village of Frankford, Philadelphia Co. md. 14th da, 5th mo, 1793 having consent of surviving parents.

Anthony Hallowell of Abington Twp., Montgomery Co., son of William Hallowell of same county and Jane Shoemaker, dau of Benjamin Shoemaker, of Cheltenham Twp., same county md. 6th da, 6th mo, 1793 having consent of parents.

Daniel Thomas, Jr., son of Daniel Thomas of Germantown Twp., Philadelphia Co. and Agness Johnson, dau of Anthony Johnson of same place md. 10th da, 10th mo, 1793 having consent of parents.

Jonathan Roberts, son of Jonathan Roberts of Bristol Twp., Philadelphia Co. and Tacy Morris, dau of Robert Morris, of same place md. 14th da, 1st mo, 1794 having consent of parents.

Thomas Harding of Moreland Twp., Montgomery Co., son of Thomas Harding, late of Southampton, Bucks Co., dec'd and Tacy Roberts, dau of Isaac Roberts of Moreland Twp., Montgomery Co., md. 13th da, 3rd mo, 1794 having consent of surviving parents.

Aaron Clark of City of Philadelphia, house carpenter, son of Isaac Clarke of Windsor, Middlesex Co., NJ and Elizabeth Lukens, dau of Rynear Lukens, late of Upper Dublin Twp, Montgomery Co., dec'd md. 1st da, 4th mo, 1794 having consent of surviving parents.

Benjamin Harper, of Northern Liberties of City of Philadelphia, flour merchant, son of Robert Harper, late of said Liberties and Sarah, his wife, both dec'd and Rachel Conrad of City of Philadelphia, dau of Matthew Conrad, late of said city and Mary, his wife, also dec'd md. 13th da, 5th mo, 1794 having consent of surviving parents.

Moses Gillingham, son of Yemen Gillingham of Oxford Twp., Philadelphia Co. and Martha Kirkner, dau of Jacob Kirkner, of Concord Twp., Delaware Co, md. 2nd da, 9th mo, 1794 having consent of parents.

Watson Playter of Bayberry Twp., Philadelphia Co., son of George Playter, of Kingston in Fontenac, Province of Upper Canada and Priscilla Waterman, dau of Isaac Waterman of Abington Twp., Montgomery Co. md. 4th da, 12th mo, 1794 having consent of parents.

William Shoemaker of Cheltenham Twp., Philadelphia Co. and Hannah Tomkins of Abington Twp., aforesaid commonwealth md. 9th da, 7th mo, 1795 having consent of parents.

Benjamin Love, of Oxford Twp., Philadelphia Co., son of Andrew Love, formerly of Plunstead Twp., Bucks Co., dec'd. and Elizabeth Whitelock, dau of James McHarry, late of Borough of Lancaster, dec'd, md. 22nd da, 9th mo, 1795 having consent of surviving parents.

Thomas Knight, son of Jonathan Knight of Bayberry Twp., Philadelphia Co. and Mary Worrell, dau of Isaiah Worrell, of Oxford Twp., aforesaid county md. 13th da, 10th mo, 1795 having consent of parents.

Joseph Shaw, of Abington Twp., Montgomery Co., son of Jonathan Shaw and Sarah, his wife, the former dec'd of Plumstead Twp., Bucks Co. and Elizabeth Tyson, dau of Jonathan Tyson and Sarah, his wife of Abington Twp. md. 12th da, 11th mo, 1795 having consent of surviving parents.

Samuel Sholfield, of City of Philadelphia, son of Samuel Scholfield and Edith, his wife of Solebury Twp., Bucks Co. and Rebecca Tyson, dau of Jonathan Tyson and Sarah, his wife of Abington Twp., Montgomery Co., md. 12th da, 11th mo, 1795 having consent of parents.

Mark Watson, of Lower Dublin Twp., Philadelphia Co., son of Amos and Phebe Watson, dec'd and Priscilla Livezey, dau of Joseph and Ann Livezey of same place md. 17th da, 3rd mo, 1795 having consent of surviving parents.

Benjamin Fell, son of Thomas and Grace Fell of Buckingham Twp., Bucks Co. and Jane Jeans, dau of Jacob and Leah Jeans of Moreland Twp., Philadelphia Co. md. 7th da, 4th mo, 1796 having consent of parents.

John Harvey of Cheltenham Twp., Montgomery Co., son of William Harvey, dec'd and Elizabeth Thomas, dau of Enoch Thomas and Mary, his wife of Cheltenham Twp., aforesaid place md. 12th da, 5th mo, 1796 having consent of surviving parents.

Jonathan Tyson, son of James Tyson of Darby in Delaware Co, and Sarah, his wife and Rachel Jones, dau of Jonathan Jones of Bedford Twp., Philadelphia Co. and Hannah, his wife md. 17th da, 5th mo, 1796 having consent of parents.

John Waterman, son of John and Hannah Waterman of Abington Twp., Philadelphia Co., dec'd and Mary Livezey, dau of Benjamin Livezey of Radnor Twp., Chester Co., aforesaid dec'd and Phebe his wife md. 30th da, 9th mo, 1796 having consent of surviving parents.

Atkinson Rose of City of Philadelphia, son of John Rose of Wrightstown Twp., Bucks Co., and Rebeckah Shoemaker, dau of Benjamin Shoemaker of Cheltenham, Montgomery Co., md. 6th da, 10th mo, 1796 having consent of parents.

Richard Roberts of Abington Twp., Philadelphia Co., son of Thomas Roberts, late of Bucks Co, dec'd and Tacy Shoemaker, dau of George Shoemaker of Cheltenham Twp., aforesaid place md. 17th da, 11th mo, 1796 having consent of surviving parents.

Ruhamah John Alsop of City of Philadelphia, merchant, son of Scrivener Alsop and Mary, his wife, late of City of London in Great Britain, both dec'd and Elizabeth Jeanes, dau of Jacob Jeanes of Moreland Twp., Montgomery Co., and Leah, his wife md. 11th da, 5th mo, 1797 having consent of surviving parents.

John Bewley, of Upper Dublin Twp, Montgomery Co., son of Isaac Bewley, late of Abington Twp., aforesaid place, dec'd. and Rachel Tyson, dau of Rynear Tyson, of Abington Twp. md. 8th da, 6th mo, 1797 having consent of surviving parents.

Thomas Shoemaker, Jr. of Cheltenham Twp., Montgomery Co., son of Isaac Shoemaker, late of aforesaid Twp., dec'd. and Hannah Thomson, dau of John Thomson of same place md. 5th 10th mo, 1797 having consent of surviving parents.

John Richards, of City of Philadelphia, currier, son of Samuel Richards, of aforesaid city and Mary, his wife, dec'd and Rachel Henry, dau of Robert Henry and Elizabeth, his wife, late of Camden, Kent Co., DE, both dec'd md. 5th da, 1st mo, 1798 having consent of surviving parents.

Isaac Thomas, of City of Philadelphia, merchant, son of Nathan Thomas and Esther Thomas, the latter dec'd of Abington Twp., Montgomery Co. and Sarah Hallowell, dau of William and Mary Hallowell, of same place md. 15th da, 11th mo, 1798 having consent of surviving parents.

Anthony Livezey, son of Nathan Livezey, of Lower Dublin Twp., Philadelphia Co. and Esther Bailey of same place md. 4th da, 4th mo, 1799 having consent of parents.

Isaac Hallowell of Abington Twp., Montgomery Co., son of John Hallowell, late of same place and Martha, his wife and Elizabeth Fletcher, dau of Robert and Priscilla Fletcher of same place md. 16th da, 5th mo, 1799 having consent of parents.

John Brumfield, of Lower Dublin Twp., Philadelphia Co., son of Solomon Brumfield, of Amith Twp., Berks Co, dec'd and Margaret Hallowell, dau of William Hallowell, Sr. of Abington Twp., Montgomery Co. md. 6th da, 6th mo, 1799 having consent of surviving parents.

George Hallowell, of Abington Twp., Montgomery Co., son of William Hallowell, Sr. of same place and Sarah Walton, dau of Jeremiah Walton, of Abington Twp. md. 13th da, 6th 1mo, 1799 having consent of parents.

Joseph Pryor, of City of Philadelphia, soon of Thomas Pryor of City of Burlington, NJ, dec'd. and Hannah, his wife and Sarah Tyson, dau of Thomas Tyson of Abington Twp., Montgomery Co. and Sarah, his wife md. 17th da, 4th mo, 1800 having consent of surviving parents.

Joseph Williams, son of Anthony Williams and Rachel, his wife, of Cheltenham

Twp., Montgomery Co. and Ann Hallowell, dau of John Hallowell, of Abington Twp., aforesaid place, dec'd and Martha, his wife md. 15th d, 5th mo, 1800 having consent of surviving parents.

Ely Welding of Frankford, Philadelphia Co., son of Watson Welding, of Wrighttown, Bucks Co, and Sarah Jones, dau of Jonathan Jones of Cheltenham, Montgomery Co., md. 14th da, 11th mo, 1800 having consent of parents.

DEATHS OF GWYNEDD MONTHLY MEETING

Katherine, dau of John and Janes Jones, d. 22nd da, 11th mo, 1715.

Hugh Roberts of Dublin bur. 8th da, 8th mo, 1717.

Anne, wife of Thomas Evans bur. 26th da, 5th mo, 1716.

Mary, wife of Rowland Roberts bur. 4th da, 12th mo, 1716.

William, son of Evan Evans and Elizabeth, his wife bur. 9th da, 10th mo, 1716.

Richard, son of Meredith Davies and Gwen, his wife bur. 15th da, 12th mo, 1716.

John, son of John and Ellin Evans, d. 11th da, 12th mo, 1727 age 3 yr, 7 mo.

Samuel, son of Samuel and Margaret Thomas, d. 16th da, 2nd mo, 1727.

Hannah, dau of Evan and Elizabeth Evans bur. 12th mo, 1720.

Owen Evans, bur. 7th da, 10th mo, 1727 age 64 years.

Evan Evans, bur. 7th da, 5th mo, 1728, age 44 years.

Samuel Evans, son of Evan Evans, bur. 14th da, 8th mo, 1728.

Edward Evans, son of Thomas Evans and Elisabeth, his wife bur. 7th da, 8th mo, 1728.

Josiah Jones, son of Robert and Ann Jones bur. 23rd da, 14th da, 1728.

Mary Thomas, dau of Samuel and Margaret Thomas, d. 11th mo, 1728.

Abram Dawes, d. 26th da, 12th mo, 1730.

John Dawes, d. 4th da, 3rd mo, 1731.

Ellin, wife of Edward Foulk bur. 5th mo, 1733.

Elizabeth Evans, wife of Owen Evans was bur. 5th mo, 1733.

Ruth, dau of John and Jane Jones bur. 7th da, 7th mo, 1733.

Catherine, wife of Thomas Evans, bur. 21st da, 11th mo, 1732.

Ruth, dau of John and Jane Jones bur. 3rd da, 7th mo, 1732.

Cadwalader, dau of Richard and Gwen Morris bur.1731.

Margaret, dau of Thomas and Gwen Foulke, bur. 23rd da, 9th mo, 1731.

William, son of William and Rebecca Arwyn, bur. 12th da, 11th mo, 1735.

Samuel, son of Abraham and Mary Dawes bur. 24th da, 9th mo, 1737.

Richard Morris bur. 6th da, 22nd mo, 1737.

Robert Humphrey bur. 30th da, 6th mo, 1736

Margaret, dau of Robert Humphrey 22nd da, 6th mo, 1736.

Elizabeth, dau of Robert and Margaret Humphrey bur. 23rd da, 6th mo, 1736.

Ann, dau of Robert and Margaret Humphrey bur. 15th da, 6th mo, 1736.

Benjamin, son of John and Jane Jones bur. 13th da, 8th mo, 1736

Gwen, wife of Richard Morris bur. 3rd da, 8th mo, 1736.

Cabel, son of Thomas and Gwen Foulke, bur. 7th da, 7th mo, 1736

William, son of William and Rebecca Arwyn, bur. 1738.

Rees David of Upper Dublin bur. 2nd da, 10th mo, 1739.

David, son of Joshua and Elizabeth Dickinson bur. 4th da, 8th mo, 1740.

Priscilla, dau of John and Jane Jones of Montgomery, wife of Evan Jones of Meirion, bur. at Meirion 25th da, 10th mo, 1742.

Gainor, wife of Edward Foulke bur. 14th da, 7th mo, 1741.

Daniel, son of Edward Foulke bur. 19th da, 7th mo, 1741.

Margaret, dau of Edward Foulke bur. 27th da, 7th mo, 1741.

Thomas William bur. 17th da, 8th mo, 1741.

Susannah William, dau of Thomas William bur. 18th da, 8th mo, 1741.

Sarah, wife of Thomas William bur. 17th da, 8th mo, 1741.

Katherine, dau of John and Jane Jones 26th da, 9th mo, 1741.

Margaret, dau of William and Hannah Foulk, 1st da, 11th mo, 1741.

Richardson, son of Benjamin and Elisabeth ?? Bur. 6th da, 7th mo, 1748.

Mary Roberts, widow of William Roberts bur. 16th da, 6th mo, 1748 in Frederick County, Virginia.

Katherine Williams bur. 17th da, 10th mo, 1748.

Cadawalder, son of John and Jane Roberts bur. 1st da, 4th mo, 1745.

Evanson, son of Thomas and Gwen Foulke, bur. 11th da, 7th mo, 1745.

Sarah, dau of William and Hannah Foulke bur. 9th da, 7th mo, 1748.

Margaret Evans, wife of John Evans bur. 6th da, 3rd mo, 1748 in her 72nd year.

Elinor Evans, widow of John Evans bur. 29th da, 4th mo, 1765.

Doctor Cadawalder Evans bur. 30th da, 6th mo, 1749.

Sarah, dau of Jeptha and Ann Lewis bur. 9th da, 9th mo, 1749.

Margaret, dau of Benjamin and Ann Davids bur. 21st da, 7th mo, 1749.

Rachel, dau of John and Jane Hubbard bur. 23rd da, 9th mo, 1751.

Judah, son of William and Hannah Foulke bur. 9th da, 2nd mo, 1754.

Joshua Dickinson bur. 20th da, 4th mo, 1752.

Rowland Hugh bur. 31st da, 3rd mo, 1752.

Phebe, dau of Ellis and Hannah Hughs bur. 1753.

John, son of Israel and Sarah Jacobs bur. 22nd da, 7th mo, 1756.

Jane, wife of John Jones bur. 14th da, 5th mo, 1758.

Margaret Davis bur. 30th da, 5th mo, 1758.

Joshua, son of John and Margaret Carpenter bur. 31st da, 5th mo, 1758.

Richard Davies's mother bur. 5th da, 6th mo, 1758.

Gainor Jones bur. 16th da, 7th mo, 1758.

Child of John Davis bur. 25th da, ?, 1758.

Eli Humphrey bur. 6th da, 12th mo, 1758.

Hugh Griffith bur. 12th da, 1st mo, 1758.

Sarah Calander bur. 24th da, 1st mo, 1758.

Child of John Lukens bur. 16th da, 2nd mo, 1758.

Sarah, dau of Benjamin and Ann Davids bur. 20th da, 5th mo, 1758.

Hugh Jones bur. 5/8/1759.

Sarah, dau of Robert and Ruth Evans bur. 6th da, 8th mo, 1759.

Child of John Miller bur. 21st da, 8th mo, 1759.

Patience Philips bur. 24th da, 8th mo, 1759.

Ann, dau of George and Susannah Evans bur. 30th da, 9th mo, 1759.

Amos, son of George and Susannah Evans bur. 12th da, 10th mo, 1759.

Hannah, wife of Elias Hughs bur. 12th da, 5th mo, 1759 aged 33 years, 4 mo, 9 days.

Child of William Arwnyn bur. 3rd da, 3rd mo, 1760.

Elizabeth, wife of Edward Roberts bur. 21st da, 5th mo, 1760.

Thomas Evans, Sr. bur. 22nd da, 5th mo, 1760.

Margaret, wife of Evan Griffith bur. 5th da, 6th mo, 1760.

Hannah, wife of Thomas Evans bur. 22nd da, 6th mo, 1760.

Child of John Hubbs, bur. 29th da, 7th mo, 1760.

Gwen, wife of Thomas Foulke bur. 6th da, 12th mo, 1760.

John Morris, a shoemaker, bur. 3rd da, 5th mo, 1760.

Jane, wife of John Roberts bur. 9th da, 10th mo, 1760.

Thomas Foulke, bur. 10th da, 10th mo, 1762.

Evan Roberts, bur.23rd da, 6th mo, 1761.

Ann Roberts, bur. 5th da, 7th mo, 1761.

Ellis Pugh, bur. 25th da, 8th mo, 1761.

Evan Ellis, bur. 30th da, 8th mo, 1761.

Jonah, son of John and Jane Roberts bur. 16th da, 9th mo, 1761.

Amos, son of George and Jane Morris, bur. 5th da, 10th mo, 1761.

Hannah, wife of Jacob Jones bur. 5th da, 12th mo, 1764.

Grace Thomas, bur. 17th da, 4th mo, 1762.

John Jones, a carpenter, bur. 5th da, 1st mo, 1775.

Amos Griffin, bur. 31st da, 3rd mo, 1775.

Winifred Davenport, bur. 25th da, 12th mo, 1779.

John Davis, bur. 5th mo, 12th da, 1780.

Child of Owen Hughes bur. 10th da, 12th mo, 1780.

Joseph Jones of Plymouth, bur. 31st da, 1st mo, 1781.

Job Lukens's wife, bur. 4th da, 2nd mo, 1781.

Rachel, dau of John and Mary Thomas, bur. 30th da, 10th mo, 1783.

Ellin, wife of Joseph Shoemaker, bur. 26th da, 9th mo, 1784.

Ezekiel Cleaver bur. 20th da, 4th mo, 1785 aged 36 years.

Gainor, wife of John Evans 12th da, 12th mo, 1785.

Mary, dau of Ellis and Elizabeth Cleaver bur. 30th da, 1st mo, 1797 aged 3 years, 9 mo, 20 days.

Phebe, wife of Amos Griffith bur. 11th da, 5th mo, 1786

Sarah, dau of Amos Griffith bur. 31st da, 10th mo, 1790.

William, son of Isaac and Hannah Jacobs bur. 6th da, 6th mo, 1795.

Rachel, dau of Isaac and Hannah Jacobs bur. 4th mo, 1796.

Jane, wife of Thomas Williams bur. 22nd da, 12th mo, 1731.

Jane, wife of Evan Griffith bur. 12th da, 9th mo, 1730.

Lowery, wife of John Rich?? bur. 18th da, 9th mo, 1730.

John Nailor bur. 31st da, 4th mo, 1724.

Cadawalder Evans bur. the 1st da, 4th mo, 1745.

Jane, the wife of William Jones, dau of Thomas and Elizabeth Evans bur. 4th da, 5th mo, 1745.

Elisabeth, dau of Thomas Evans and Elisabeth, his wife was bur. 4th da, 5th mo, 1745.

Margaret, dau of Rees and Mary Harvey bur. 7th da, 6th mo, 4th da, 5th mo, 1745.

Mary, dau of John and Mary Dawes bur. 10th da, 6th mo, 1745.

Mary, wife of Abraham Griffith, bur. 10th da, 6th mo, 1745.

Nathan, son of John and Mary Davies bur. 11th da, 6th mo, 1745.

Catherine, wife of Theophilus Williams bur. 1745.

Anne, dau of John and Mary Davies bur. 1745.

Robert Jones' little children all three bur. the 13th da, 6th mo, 1745.

Hannah, dau of John and Mary Roberts bur. 14th da, 6th mo, 1745.

Robert, son of Robert and Jane Hugh bur. 16th da, 6th mo, 1745.

Mary, dau of Robert Evans ?? 16th da, 6th mo, 1745.

Ellis, son of Robert and Jane Hugh bur. 18th da, 6th mo, 1745.

Rebecah, dau of Owen and Mary Evans bur. 20th da, 6th mo, 1745.

Ellin, dau of Robert and Jane Hugh bur. 20th da, 6th mo, 1745.

Son of Ruth Osborn bur. 22nd da, 5th mo, 1745.

Son of Aubrey and Ellin Roberts, bur. 22nd da, 5th mo, 1745.

Son to John Starkey, bur. 24th da, 5th mo, 1745.

Child to Jenkin and Ellen Morris, bur. 25th da, 5th mo, 1745.

Evan Foulke bur. 25th da, 5th mo, 1745.

John, son of Owen and Jane Roberts bur. 26th da, 5th mo, 1745.

Elisabeth Roberts, widow bur. 27th da, 5th mo, 1745.

Edward, son of William Roberts and Anne, his wife bur. 27th da, 5th mo, 1745.

Margaret, dau of John and Jane Jones bur. 28th da, 5th mo, 1745.

Child of Samuel Sanders, bur. 28th da, 5th mo, 1745.

Edward, son of Evan and Ellin Foulk bur. 29th da, 5th mo, 1745.

Dau of Evan and Anne Foulk bur. 29th da, 5th mo, 1745.

William, son of Evan and Elizabeth Evan, 3rd da, 5th mo, 1745.

Son of Aubrey and Ellin Robert, bur. 22nd da, 5th mo, 1745.

Son of John Starkey, bur. 22nd da, 5th mo, 1745

Child of Jenkin and Ellin Morris bur. 24th da, 5th mo, 1745

John, son of Owen and Jane Roberts bur. 26th da, 5th mo, 1745

Elisabeth Roberts, widow bur. 27th da, 5th mo, 1745

Margaret, dau of John and Jane Jones bur. 28th da, 5th mo, 1745

Child of John and Jane Jones, bur. 28th da, 5th mo, 1745

Edward, son of Evan and Ellin Foulk, bur. 29th da, 5th mo, 1745

Dau of Evan and Anna Foulk bur. 29th da, 5th mo, 1745

William, son of Evan and Elisabeth Evans bur. 30th da, 5th mo, 1745

Evan, son of Thomas and Mary Evans, bur. 30th da, 5th mo, 1745

Sarah, dau of Hugh and Margaret Evans bur. 30th da, 5th mo, 1745

Child of Paul Osbourn, bur. 30th da, 5th mo, 1745

Child of Grace Robert, bur. 30th da, 5th mo, 1745

Child of Moses Peters, bur. 30th da, 6th mo, 1745

Mordecai, son of John and Elizabeth Roberts, bur. 3rd da, 6th mo, 1745

Ellen, dau of Evans and Ann Foulk, bur. 5th da, 6th mo, 1745.

A son of Robert and Rachel Davies, bur. 6th da, 6th mo, 1745.

Abraham, son of Robert and Rachel Davies, bur. 7th da, 6th mo, 745.

A dau of Thomas and Edward Beward bur. 8th da, 6th da, 1745.

Child of Isaac Jones and Elisabeth, his wife bur. 8th da, 6th, 1745.

Son of John Forman bur. 8th da, 6th mo, 1745.

Jane, dau of John and Mary Foulk bur. 9th da, 6th mo, 1745.

Child of Joseph Lukens bur. 9th da, 6th mo, 1745.

Wife of John Roberts Cadawalder 7th da, 6th mo, 1745.

A child of Hugh David bur. 12th da, 6th mo, 1745.

A daughter of Evan Foulk bur. 13th da, 6th mo, 1745.

Mary, dau of Hugh and Mary Evans 13th da, 6th mo, 17

Widow of Starkey bur. the 15th da, 6th mo, 1745.

George, son of Isaac and Elisabeth Jones, bur. 15th da, 6th mo, 1745.

A child of Moses Peters bur. 15th da, 6th mo, 1745.

Elizabeth, dau of William Williams Taylor bur. 15th da, 6th mo, 1745.

A child of Wm. Macgee bur. 18th da, 6th mo, 1745.

Catherine William, widow bur. 18th da, 6th mo, 1745.

Hannah, dau of Edward and Ellis Evans bur. 18th da, 6th mo, 1745.

Martha, dau of William Williams Taylor, bur. 20th da, 6th mo, 1745.

A child of Hugh David bur. 23rd da, 6th mo, 1745.

Sarah, dau of William Williams Taylor bur. 24th da, 6th mo, 1745.

A child of Hugh Jones bur. 24th da, 6th mo, 1745.

Hannah Foulke bur. 12th da, 1st mo, 1798 at Gwynedd, 85 years of age, widow
of Wm. Foulke, dau of John Jones.

Jessie Maris bur. 25th da, 6th mo, 1792 aged 27 years 9 mos from Philadelphia.

Jonathan Maris bur. 28th da, 2nd mo, 1797, aged 31 years 2 mos from
Gwynedd.

Rachel Thomas bur. 30th da, 10th mo, 1783 aged 22 years from Montgomery,
dau of John and Mary Thomas.

Margaret Coleman bur. 6th da, 11th mo, 1789 from Montgomery, formerly of

Philadelphia.

Elizabeth Moore bur. 29th da, 12th mo, 1795, 81 years lately from Philadelphia, wife of Mordecai Moore.

Thomas Moore bur. 27th da, 8th mo, 1799 age 75 years from Philadelphia.

Joseph Butler bur. 28th da, 11th mo, 1793 age 59 years of Gwynedd, formerly of Upper Dublin.

Mary Shoemaker bur. 14th da, 5th mo, 1796 aged 64 years from Gwynedd, wife of Thomas Shoemaker.

Jane Roberts bur. 7th da, 10th mo, 1762 aged 48 years from Gwynedd from Whitepain, wife of John Roberts Cadwalder.

Ellen Roberts, 2nd wife of John Roberts Cadwalder bur. 12th da, 12th mo, 1796.

Elizabeth Evans bur. 10th da, 8th mo, 1794 aged 54 years from Whitepain, wife of Thomas Evans, widow of John Roberts Cadwalder.

Frances Hobson bur. 29th da, 9th mo, 1792 age 72 from Providence, formerly Limerick.

Deborah Hobson bur. 11th da, 3rd mo, 1777 age 33 from Providence, formerly Limerick, dau of Frances Hobson.

Anna Hall bur. 20th da, 9th mo, 1784 age 31 years from Providence, late of Charlestown late Coates.

Rachel Coates bur. 25th da, 11th mo, 1795 age 27 years from Providence formerly Charlestown, dau of James Wood.

Margaret Cox bur. 11th da, 2nd mo, 1789 age 42 years from Providence formerly Charlestown.

Elizabeth Cox bur 5th da, 1st mo, 1792 age 68 years from Providence formerly Charlestown.

Edward Thomas bur. 2nd mo, 1795 age 21 years from Providence formerly Charlestown, son of David and Mary Thomas.

Evan Edwards bur. 15th da, 1st mo, 1778 from Gwynedd.

Joseph Lukens bur. 15th da, 11th mo, 1777 from Gwynedd.

Mary Evans bur. 12th da, 2nd mo, 1778 aged 43 years from Gwynedd, dau of John Lukens.

Susanna Pawling bur. 26th da, 11th mo, 1786 aged 31 years from Gwynedd, dau of John Lukens.

Joseph Lukens bur. 15th da, 3rd mo, 1786 from Gwynedd, Towaminain, son of John and Rachel Lukens.

Cadawalder Lukens bur. 1st da, 4th mo, 1786, age 27 years from Gwynedd, Towaminain, son of John and Rachel Lukens.

Rachel Lukens bur. 13th da, 6th mo, 1790 aged 65 years from Gwynedd, Towaminain.

John Martin bur. 16th da, 8th mo, 1777 aged 46 years Plymouth, Roseborough.

Mary Roberts bur. 25th da, 12th mo, 1795 age 52 from Horsham, wife of Cadawalder Roberts.

Jane Jones bur. 15th da, 11th mo, 1777.

Peter Shoemaker bur. 13th da, 4th mo, 1797 age 13 years, Plymouth, son of Peter and Hannah Shoemaker.

GWYNEDD MONTHLY MEETING MARRIAGES

Edward Jones, son of John Evan, late of Radnor, County of Chester, dec'd and Sarah Evans, dau of Thomas Evans of Gwynedd, Philadelphia Co. md. 11th da, 6th mo, called August, 1715 having consent of parents.

William Roberts, son of Edward Roberts late of Meirion, Philadelphia Co., dec'd and Anne Evans, dau of Robert Evans of Gwynedd, Philadelphia Co., yeoman md. 25th da, 6th mo, 1715 having consent of parents.

Isaac Williams of Whitemarsh twp, Philadelphia Co., batchelor, and Elizabeth Marle of the aforesaid place, spinster md. 10th da, 6th mo, 1715 having consent of parents.

Thomas Edward, son of Alexander of Montgomery, Philadelphia Co., dec'd and Mary Price of Gwynedd, same county, spinster md. 23rd da, 7th mo, 1715 having consent of parents.

Robert Rogers of Norinton, Philadelphia Co. and Jane Roberts of Gwynedd, aforesaid county md. 4th da, 11th mo, 1763 having consent of parents.

Hugh Evans, eldest son of Evans Pugh of Gwynedd, Philadelphia Co., batchelor and Mary Roberts, dau of Robert John of Meirion, dec'd md. 25th da, 3rd mo, 1716 having consent of parents.

Cephas Child, son of Cephas Child of Johnsisted, Bucks County, and Priscilla Naylor, dau of Joseph Naylor of Montgomery, Philadelphia Co. md. 16th da, 2nd mo, 1751 having consent of parents.

Benjamin Dickinson, son of Joshua Dickinson of Whitpain, Philadelphia Co. and Iozabel Wright, dau of John Wright of Hatfield, aforesaid county md. 23rd da, 10th mo, 1755 having consent of parents.

Benjamin Mendenhall, son of Benjamin Mendenhall of Concord, Chester Co. and Lydia Roberts, dau of Owen Roberts of Gwynedd?, yeoman, dec'd. md. 13th da, 9th mo, 1717 having consent of parents.

Nicholas Roberts, son of Robert Cadwaller of Gwynedd, dec'd and Margaret Foulke, dau of George Foulke 23rd da, 3rd mo, 1717 having consent of parents.

John Roger, son of Roger Roberts of Meirion, County of Philadelphia, and Ellin Pugh, dau of Robert Pugh 21st da, 4th mo, 1717.

Richard William of Gwynedd, County of Philadelphia, barber and Margaret Eaton, widow 10th da, 7th mo, 1717.

Robert Jones of Gwynedd, taylor and Anne Coultone, dau of William Coultone, yeoman 22nd da, 8th mo, 1717.

John Shiers of the Northern Liberties, city of Philadelphia, yeoman and Sarah Williams, of Plymouth, Philadelphia Co., widow md. 19th da, November, 1717 having consent of parents.

William Harmer, son of William Harmer, Philadelphia Co., yeoman and Elinor Richardson, dau of Joseph Richardson of Perquioinany, Philadelphia Co. md. 14th da, 9th mo, 1717 having consent of parents.

Robert Hugh, son of Hugh Griffith of Gwynedd, Philadelphia Co. and Catherine Gomis, dau of Evan Pugh md. 21st da, 12th mo, 1718 having consent of parents.

William Lewis of Howtown, Chester Co, and Lowry Jones of Gwynedd, Philadelphia Co. md. 7th da, 5th mo, 1718 having consent of parents.

Jenkins Evans of Montgomery, Philadelphia Co., batchelor and Alie Morgan, dau of Edward Morgan md. 17th da, 8th mo, 1718 having consent of parents.

Daniel Morgan, son of Edward Morgan of Gwynedd, Philadelphia Co. and Elizabeth Roberts, dau of Robert Cadwallader md. 21st da, 9th mo, 1718 having consent of parents.

Humphrey Jones, son of John Humphrey, of Gwynedd, Philadelphia Co. and Catherine Jones, md. 23rd da, 2nd mo, 1719 having consent of relatives.

Rees David of Upper Dublin, Philadelphia Co., widower and Margaret Morgan of Montgomery, said county, widow md. 9th da, 3rd mo, 1719 having consent of relatives.

Cadwalader Jones, son of John Cadwalader, late of Wanfaior, Meirionwith Shire, North Wales in Great Brittain, dec'd and Martha Thomas, dau of David Thomas of Radnor, Chester Co., yeoman md. 12th da, 4th mo, 1719 having consent of parents.

Cadwallader Foulk, son of Edward Foulk of Gwynedd, yeoman and Mary Evans, dau of Robert Evans of Gwynedd, said county md. 13th da, 4th mo, 1719 having consent of parents.

Hugh Evans, son of Robert Evans of Gwynedd, Philadelphia Co., yeoman and Margaret Robert, dau of Edward Robert of Gwynedd, yeoman md. 23rd da, 8th mo, 1719.

William Heald of Remmett twp, Chester Co., son of Samuel Heald of said place, yeoman and Elizabeth Potts, spinster, dau of Jonas Potts of Perqueoman Creek, Philadelphia Co. md. 15th da, 8th mo, 1719 having consent of parents.

Joseph Burson of Gilbert Maner, Philadelphia Co., batchelor and Rachel Potts, dau of Jonas Potts of the same place md. 15th da, 8th mo, 1719 having consent of parents.

William Morris, son of Morris Richard, late of Meirioneth Shire, North Wales, Great Brittain, dec'd and Catherine Pugh, dau of Richard Pugh, late of Montgomery twp, Philadelphia Co., dec'd md. 26th da, 8th mo, 1719 having consent of parents.

John Webb of Philadelphia Co. and Mary Boone, dau of George Boone of same place md, 13th da, 7th mo, 1720 having consent of parents.

Squire Boone, son of George Boone of Philadelphia Co., yeoman and Sarah Morgan, dau of Edward Morgan of said county md. 23rd da, 7th mo, 1720

having consent of parents.

Thomas Williams of Montgomery, Philadelphia Co., widower and Jane Morris, dau of Morris Richard, late of Meirioneth Shire, North Wales, Great Brittain, dec'd md. 14th da, 8th mo, 1720 having consent of parents.

David Jones of Plymouth, Philadelphia Co. and Ruth Dickinson, dau of William Dickinson md. 12th da, 2nd month called April, 1721 having consent of parents.

Conrad Conrad of Germantown, Philadelphia Co. and Anne Burson of Peiqicommoid, said county md. 12th da, 8th mo, 1720 having consent of parents.

William Coulstone of Whitpain twp, Philadelphia Co., widower and Mary Davies of the same place md. 15th da, 1st mo, 1721/2 having consent of parents.

Samuel Stanfield of East Caln, Chester Co. And Mary Martin, dau of George Martin of Charleston, aforesaid county md. 1st da, 12th mo, 1756 having consent of parents.

Joseph Shair of Wilmington, New Castle County, Del and Rebecca Jacobs of Peirquicommd, Philadelphia Co. md. 29th da, 12th mo, 1756 having consent of parents.

Robert Easttown, son of John Easttown of Noriten, Philadelphia Co. and Esther Frank, dau of George Frank, late of said county md. 22nd da, 5th mo, 1755 having consent of parents.

Enos Rogers, son of Robert Rogers of Norristown, Philadelphia Co. and Margaret Evans, dau of Cadalawader?? Evans, dec'd md. 17th da, 10th mo, 1757 having consent of parents.

Samuel Spencer of Horsham, Philadelphia Co., yeoman and Mary Dawes, dau of Abraham Dawes, of Whitemarsh twp, said county, yeoman md. 18th da, 4th mo, called June 1723 having consent of parents.

John Roberts, son of John Roberts of Abington, Philadelphia Co., yeoman and Mary Dawes, dau of Francis Dawes of Montgomery, said county md. 15th da, 6th mo, 1723 having consent of parents.

John Harris of Gwynedd, Philadelphia Co., yeoman and Gainor Hugh, dau of John Hugh of Gwynedd, md. 5th da, 10th mo, 1723 having consent of parents.

Richard Thomas, son of Abel Thomas of Meirion, Philadelphia Co. and Margaret Owens, dau of Owen Owens of Plymouth, same county md. 22nd da, 5th mo, 1722/3 having consent of parents.

Eldad Roberts, son of Rowland Roberts of Montgomery, Philadelphia Co. and Jane Jones, dau of Isaac Jones of same place 18th da, 10th mo, 1763 having consent of parents.

George Harmer, son of William Harmer of Upper Dublin, Philadelphia Co., yeoman and Anne Williams, dau of Evan William, late of said county md. 6th da, 1st mo, 1724 having consent of parents.

Charles Crusey of Whitepain, Philadelphia Co. and Mary Davies, dau of William Davies of same place, dec'd md. 15th da, 8th mo, 1724 having consent of parents.

John Williams, son of William Williams of Philadelphia Co. and Jane Naylor, dau of Joseph Naylor of said county md. 25th da, 1st mo, 1740 having consent of parents.

William Luken, son of Abraham Lukens, of Tawamencian, Philadelphia Co. and Cathrine Evans, dau of Edward Evans late of the same place, dec'd md. 20th da, 10th mo, 1762 having consent of parents.

Joseph Martin of Roxbury, Philadelphia Co., single man and Lydia Trotter of Plymouth, said county, single md. 9th da, 6th mo, 1757 having consent of parents.

Evan Evans, son of Cadwalader Evans of Whitepain, Philadelphia Co., dec'd and Cathrine Morris, dau of Edward Morris of the City of Philadelphia md. 23rd da, 11th mo, 1762 having consent of parents.

Edward Reese, son of John Rees of Plymouth, Philadelphia Co., yeoman and Elizabeth Thomas, dau of Othinor? Thomas, late of City of Philadelphia md, 17th da, 11th mo, 1726 having consent of parents.

Joseph Jones, son of Hugh Jones of Plymouth, Philadelphia Co. and Elizabeth Samuel, dau of William Samuel late of said county, dec'd md. 22nd da, 4th mo, 1726 having consent of parents.

Samuel Richards, son of Rowland Richards, late of Free Dissrin?, Philadelphia Co., dec'd and Elizabeth Evans, dau of Owen Evans, late of Gwynedd md. 21st da, 2nd mo, 1726 having consent of parents.

Mathias Rhodes of Gwynedd twp, Philadelphia Co. and Hannah Hardy of Horsham twp, said county md. 3rd da, 7th mo, 1759 having consent of parents.

Richard Jacobs, son of John Jacobs of Periquomia, Philadelphia Co., yeoman and Barbara Woolrush of the same place, widow md. 24th da, 9th mo, 1746 having consent of parents.

Thomas Evans of Gwynedd, Philadelphia Co. and Mary Brooke, of Limerick twp, said county md. 9th da, 10th mo, 1764 having consent of parents.

Abel Walker of Gwynedd, Philadelphia Co. and Lena Pugh of Philadelphia Co. md. 13th da, 4th mo, 1727 having consent of parents.

Robert Tuckness of the City of Philadelphia, hatter, son of Henry Tuckness, late of the City of Burlington, New Jersey, cordwainer, dec'd and Mary Daws, dau of Abraham Daws of Whitpain twp, Philadelphia Co. md. 17th da, 5th mo, 1764 having consent of parents.

Abraham Shoemaker of Germantown twp, Philadelphia Co., shopkeeper, son of Abraham Shoemaker, late of Bristol twp, said county, yeoman, dec'd and Lydia Daws, dau of Abraham Daws of Whitpain twp, said county md. 3rd da, 6th mo, 1762 having consent of parents.

John Worrall, of Chester Co., and Mary Taylor of Montgomery, Philadelphia

Co. md. 2nd da, 7th mo, 1727 having consent of parents.

Job Spencer, son of William Spencer of Northern twp, Bucks Co, and Hannah Kinderdine of Horsham twp, Montgomery Co., md. 7th da,, 10th mo, 1725 having consent of parents.

Ellis Pugh, son of Ellis Pugh of Plymouth, Philadelphia Co., dec'd and June Longworth, dau of   John Longworthy, late of Treddyfinn??, Chester County md. Marriage record gave no dates.

Amos Ellis of Whitepain, Montgomery Co., son of Isaac Ellis, of the same place and Hannah Roberts, dau of Joseph Roberts of Nortowon??, Montgomery Co. Md. 17th da, 11th mo, 1785 having consent of parents.

Lewis Lewis, son of Ellis Lewis of Upper Dublin, Philadelphia Co., yeoman and Anne Lord, dau of Henry Lord, late of said county, dec'd md. 19th da, 2nd mo, 1728 having consent of parents.

John Davies, son of Meredith Davies late of Gwynedd, Philadelphia Co., dec'd and Mary Bennet, dau of Henry Bennet late of Abington, said county, dec'd md. 17th da, 8th mo, 1728 having consent of parents.

Benjamin Wilson of Wilmington, New Castle, New Jersey, miller and Rachel Byrne, dau of Daniel Byrne of Philadelphia Co., yeoman md. 19th da, 10th mo, 1769 having consent of parents.

William Coulstone, son of William Coulstone, late of Plymouth, Philadelphia Co., dec'd and Ann Rodes, dau of Jacob Roads, of said county md. 24th da, 9th mo, 1729 having consent of parents.

Abraham Daws, son of Abraham Daws, of Horsham, Philadelphia Co. and Mary Harry, dau of David Harry of said twp md. 20th da, 8th mo, 1731 having consent of parents.

Daniel Jones, son of Isaac Jones of Montgomery, Philadelphia Co. and Margaret Moore, dau of Mordica Moore of Abington twp, Philadelphia Co. md. 10th da, 1st mo, 1765 having consent of parents.

Peter Jones, son of Peter Jones of Meirion, Philadelphia Co. and Cathrine Evans, dau of Robert Evans, of Northwales, same county md. 14th da, 3rd mo, 1740 having consent of parents.

Enoch Morgan, son of Edward Morgan of Philadelphia Co. and Sarah Kinderdine, dau of Richard Kinderdine of same place md. 14th da, 3rd mo 1741 having consent of parents.

Ezekiel Shomaker, son of Richard Thomas of Horsham, Philadelphia Co. and Ann Williams, dau of John Williams of same place md. 10th da, 11th mo, 1761 having consent of parents.

Ellis Lewis, Philadelphia Co. and Ellin Evans, dau of John Evans of Gwynedd, dec'd md. 18th da, 12th mo, 1764 having consent of parents.

Thomas Head and Dianna Fleisling?? Md. 20th da, 11th mo, 1730/1 having consent of parents.

Evan Meredith, son of David Meredith of Philadelphia Co., dec'd and Susan Day, dau of William Day late of Radnor twp, Chester Co. Md. 19th da, 12th mo, 1765 having consent of parents.

John Robeson, son of James Robeson of Trancon, Philadelphia Co., dec'd and
Mary Edward, dau of John Edward of Tawamen, Philadelphia Co. md. 17th
da, 11th mo, 1761 having consent of parents.

Edward Philips of Richland twp, Bucks Co., and Elizabeth Davies of
Montgomery, Philadelphia Co. md. 25th da, 2nd mo, 1729 having consent of
parents.

Benjamin Dickensian of Plymouth in Philadelphia Co. and Elizabeth Haler of
said county md. 4th da, 9th mo, 1761.

William Lewis, son of William Lewis of Newton twp, Chester Co., dec'd and
Ruth Jones, dau of Evan Jones, late of Meirion twp, Philadelphia Co., dec'd
md. 20th da, 11th mo, 1764 having consent of parents.

William Morgan of Montgomery, Philadelphia Co. and Catherine Robeson,
Meirion, Philadelphia Co. md. 9th da, 10th mo, 1731 having consent of
parents.

Edward Amblerson, son of Joseph Amblerson of Montgomery, Philadelphia Co.
and Ellin Foulke, dau of Edward Foulke, of same place me. 14th da, 5th mo,
1767 having consent of parents.

William Wamlsby of Plymouth, Philadelphia Co. and Rose Rees, dau of John
Rees of same place md. 6th da, 2nd mo, 1733 having consent of parents.

Isaac Daws of the City of Philadelphia and Mary Evans of Philadelphia Co. md.
12th da,, 9th mo, 1732 having consent of parents.

James Morris of Upper Dublin twp, Philadelphia Co., son of Joseph Morris of
the City of Philadelphia, merchant and Elisabeth Daws, dau of Abraham
Daws, of Whitspain twp, Philadelphia Co. md. 1st da, 10th mo, 1772 having
consent of parents.

George Burson of Providence twp, Philadelphia Co., yeoman and Sarah Cox of
the said twp and county md. 9th da, 7th mo, 1731 having consent of parents.

Edward Roberts, son of Robert Roberts of Gwynedd, Philadelphia Co. and Ellin
Lewis, dau of Enos Lewis of the same place md. 4th da, 10th mo, 1764
having consent of parents.

Daniel Williams of Northwales, Philadelphia Co. and Sarah Meredith, dau of
Meredith Davis of Plymouth, Philadelphia Co. md. no date. The record has
no date for this marriage.

John Roberts, son of John Roberts of Whitpain, Philadelphia Co. and Ellen
Williams, dau of Thomas Williams, late of Montgomery, Philadelphia Co.,
dec'd md. 11th mo, 10th da, 1764 having consent of parents

William Spencer, son of Samuel Spencer, late of Horsham, Philadelphia Co.,
dec'd and Elisabeth Lewis, dau of Ellis Lewis of Upper Dublin twp,
Philadelphia Co. md. 24th da, 3rd mo, 1733 having consent of parents.

John Jones, son of Robert Jones of Gwynedd, Philadelphia Co. and Gainor
Humphrey, dau of Robert Humphrey of said place md. 7th da, 4th mo, 1788
having consent of parents.

Joseph Potts, son of John Potts of Duglas twp, Philadelphia Co. and Mary Morris, dau of John Morris of Whitemarsh twp, said county md. 14th da, 8th mo, 1764 having consent of parents.

Abraham Road, son of Jacob Road of Darby, Chester Co. and Ellin Rees, dau of John Rees of Whitpain, Philadelphia Co. md. 24th da, 7th mo, 1733 having consent of parents.

Peter Shoemaker, son of Isaac Shoemaker of Upper Dublin, Philadelphia Co. and Hannah Stephens, dau of John Stephens, late of Upper Merion twp, aforesaid county md. 20th da, 10th mo, 1768 having consent of parents.

Thomas Williams of Montgomery, Philadelphia Co., widower and Sarah Hank of Gwynedd, same county md. 6th da, 5th mo, 1733 having consent of parents.

Aquila Jones, son of Griffith Jones, late of the City of Philadelphia, dec'd and Margaret Evans, dau of Rowland Evans of Gwynedd, Philadelphia Co., dec'd md. 25th da, 10th mo, 1759 having consent of parents.

Thomas White Pryor, son of Thomas Pryor of the City of Burlington, West Jersey and Susannah Edge, dau of Jacob Edge of Whitemarsh, Montgomery Co., dec'd md. 12th da, 5th mo, 1785 having consent of parents.

Moses Peter, son of Garet Peter of Montgomery Co., and Martha Thomas, dau of Robert Thomas of same place md. 17th da, 3rd mo, 1788 having consent of parents.

Thomas Lewis, son of Richard Lewis of Montgomery Co. and Hannah Morgan, dau of Edward Morgan, same place md. 17th da, 8th mo, 1734 having consent of parents.

William Foulk, son of Thomas Foulke of Philadelphia Co. and Hannah Jones, dau of John Jones of Montgomery Co. md. 15th da, 8th mo, 1735 having consent of parents.

Robert Ellis, son of Theodor Ellis of Gwynedd, Philadelphia Co. and Sarah Davis, dau of Meredith Davis of same place md. 1734 having consent of parents. No day or month in record.

George Maris of Gwynedd, Philadelphia Co., son of George Maris of Springfield, Chester Co. And Jane Foulke, dau of William Foulke of Gwynedd, Philadelphia Co. md. 6th da, 12th mo, 1757 having consent of parents.

David Davies of Whitemarsh, Philadelphia Co., widower and Mary Woodward of same place md. 13th da, 9th mo, 1735 having consent of parents.

Edward Evans of Philadelphia Co., yeoman and Elisabeth Griffith, dau of Evan Griffith of same place md. 20th da, 3rd mo, 1735 having consent of parents.

Robert Lloyd of Gwynedd, Philadelphia Co. and Catherine Humphrey, dau of Robert Humphrey of same place md. 21st da, 6th mo, 1735 having consent of parents.

John Jones, Jr., son of John Jones of Germantown, Philadelphia Co., tanner and Tacy Daws, dau of Abraham Daws of Whitpain, Philadelphia Co., yeoman md. 2nd da, 12th mo, 1762 having consent of parents.

Griffith Ellis, son of Theodor Ellis of Gwynedd, Philadelphia Co. and Jane Lewis of same place md. 9th da, 7th mo, 1735 having consent of parents.

John Forman, son of Alexander Forman of New Brittain, Philadelphia Co. and Elizabeth Naylor, dau of Joseph Naylor md. 20th da, 8th mo, 1735 having consent of parents.

William Erwin of Gwynedd, Philadelphia Co. and Rebecca Roberts, dau of Cadawaller Roberts, dec'd md. 13th da, 11th mo, 1735/6 having consent of parents.

Thomas Paxoin of Great Swamp, Bucks Co., and Catherin Fonet, dau of Arthur Fonet of the same place md. No date on record.

William Roberts, son of John Roberts of Lower Milford twp, Bucks Co. And Rebecca Pennington, dau of Paul Pennington of Baltimore, Md md. 1st da, 11th mo, 1785 having consent of parents.

Samuel Davis of Plymouth, Philadelphia Co. and Jane Rees, dau of John Rees of Whitpain, Philadelphia Co. md. 24th da, 3rd mo, 1736 having consent of parents.

Enos Lewis, son of William Lewis, late of Newtown, Chester Co., dec'd and Jane Lewis, dau of Elis Lewis of Upper Dublin, Philadelphia Co. md. 15th da, 4th mo, 1736 having consent of parents.

Richard Rickeson of New Providence, Philadelphia Co. and Mary Star of Charlestown, Chester Co. Md. 12th da, 6th mo, 1736 having consent of parents.

Joseph Jones of Plymouth, Philadelphia Co. and Sarah Morris of Whitemarsh, Philadelphia Co., widow md. 25th da, 6th mo, 1736 having consent of parents.

William Roberts of Philadelphia Co. and Mary Pugh of Gwynedd, same county, widow md. 16th da, 9th mo, 1736 having consent of parents.

John Roberts of Montgomery, Philadelphia Co. and Jane Hank, dau of John Hank of Whitemarsh of same county md. 30th da, ?, 1736 having consent of parents.

Evan Griffith of Gwynedd, Philadelphia Co. and Margaret Owen of the same place md. 3rd da, 9th mo, 1736 having consent of parents.

David Norman, son of Robert Norman of Whitpain, Philadelphia Co. and Mary Stevenson, dau of John Stevenson late of Norinton, same county, dec'd md. 24th da, 5th mo, 1764 having consent of parents.

Joseph Penrose, son of Joseph Penrose and Sarah Wily, dau of Joseph Wily both of Maiden Creek, Philadelphia Co. md. 21st da, 3rd mo, 1735 having consent of parents.

Jonathan Paul of Germantown, Philadelphia Co., son of Joseph Paul late of the same place, dec'd and Edith Daws, dau of Abraham Daws of Whitpain twp, Philadelphia Co. md. 19th da, 5th m o, 1768 having consent of parents.

John Ball, son of John Ball of Great Swamp and Rebecca Heuling of the same place md. 24th da, 4th mo, 1736 having consent of parents.

John Lewis, son of Ellis Lewis of Upper Dublin twp, Philadelphia Co. and Hannah Shoemaker, dau of Jacob Shoemaker of Whitemarsh twp, Philadelphia Co. md. 5th da, 11th mo, 1772 having consent of parents.

Thomas Lee, son of Antony Lee of Oly, Philadelphia Co. and Ruth Roberts (she according to the custom of marriage assuming the name of her husband). No date on record.

Nathan Cleaver, son of Peter Cleaver of Upper Dublin twp, Philadelphia Co. and Ruth Roberts, dau of John Roberts of Whitepain twp, Philadelphia Co. md. 24th da, 5th mo, 1768 having consent of parents.

John Wells of Philadelphia Co. and Susanna Martin, of same place md. 19th da, 2nd mo, 1734 having consent of parents.

Edward Edward, son of John Edward of Philadelphia Co. and Elizabeth Robeson, dau of James Robeson of same place md. 7th da, 5th mo, 1741 having consent of parents.

John Hamer, son of John Hamer of Plymouth, Philadelphia Co. and Rebecca Jones md. 2nd da, 10th mo, 1736 having consent of parents.

Samuel Morris of Whitemarsh twp, son of Daniel Morris late of Upper Dublin, Philadelphia Co., dec'd and Rachel Dawes, dau of Abraham Dawes of Whitpain twp, said county md. 14th da, 5th mo, 1772 having consent of parents.

Owen Roberts, son of William Roberts of Philadelphia Co. and Jane Williams, dau of John Williams of Gwynedd, said county, dec'd md. 15th da, 9th mo, 1737 having consent of parents.

Isaac Jones, of Warrington twp, Bucks Co., yeoman, son of John Jones of same place and Ann Ambler, dau of Joseph Ambler of Montgomery twp, Philadelphia Co. md. 14th da, 10th mo, 1766 having consent of parents.

William Martin of Gwynedd, Philadelphia Co. and Mariam Morgan, dau of Edward Morgan late of Gwynedd, dec'd md. 25th da, 3rd mo, 1738 having consent of parents.

John Jones, son of David Jones of Plymouth, Philadelphia Co. and Catherine Williams, widow md. 8th da, 4th mo, 1738 having consent of parents.

William Edward, son of John Edward of Millford, Bucks Co. And Martha Foulke, dau of Hugh Foulke of Richland, same county md. 24th da, 8th mo, 1738 having consent of parents.

Owen Williams, son of John Williams of Gwynedd, Philadelphia Co., dec'd and Mary Meredith, dau of Meredith David of Plymouth, same county, also dec'd md. 22nd da, 10th mo, 1738 having consent of parents.

Evan Jones of Meirion, Philadelphia Co. and Priscilla Jones, dau of John Jones of Montgomery, Philadelphia Co. md. 20th da, 3rd mo, 1740 having consent of parents.

Peter Jones, son of Peter Jones of Meirion, Philadelphia Co. and Catherine Evans, dau of Robert Evans of Gwynedd md. 15th da, 3rd mo, 1740 having consent of parents.

Jacob Jones, son of David Jones late of Blochly?, Philadelphia Co., dec'd and Ellin Humphrey, dau of Robert Humphrey of Gwynedd md. 18th da, 8th mo, 1739 having consent of parents.

Joseph Jarret, of Horsham twp, Montgomery Co., joiner, son of --- Jarret, dec'd and Alice, his wife and Rachel Edge of Whitemarsh twp, Philadelphia Co., dau of Jacob Edge, dec'd and Margaret, his wife md. 23rd da, 11th mo, 1787 having of surviving relations.

David Morris, son of Cadwalader Morris of Philadelphia Co., and Jane Roberts, of same place md. 20th da, ? mo, 1741 having consent of parents.

Sam Nixon of Millford, Bucks Co. and Margaret Evans, dau of William Evans of Limerick, said county md. 19th da, 9th mo, 1742 having consent of parents.

John Roberts, son of William Roberts of Worcester, Philadelphia Co. and Ann Hughs, dau of Rowland Hughs of same place md. 20th da, 3rd mo, 1742 having consent of parents.

William Stony of Philadelphia Co. and Catherine Morgan of the same place md. 17th da, 6th mo, 1742 having consent of parents.

Joseph Hallowell of Philadelphia Co. and Sarah Nanney, dau of Rees Nanney of same place md. 19th da, 3rd mo, 1742 having consent of parents.

John Roberts, son of Thomas Roberts of Buckland and Martha Roberts, dau of Edward Roberts md. 1742 having consent of parents. No month or day in record.

John Lloyd of Horsham twp, Philadelphia Co. and Ellin Foulke, dau of Hugh Foulke of Richland, Bucks Co, md. 21st da, 8th mo, 1742 having consent of parents.

Robert Roberts, son of Cadwalder Roberts of Gwynedd, Philadelphia Co. and Sarah Ambler, dau of Joseph Ambler, of same place md. 11th da, 11th mo, 1742/3 having consent of parents.

David Humphrey, son of Robert Humphrey of Gwynedd, Philadelphia Co. and Elizabeth Roberts of Gwynedd, same county md. 12th da, Apr, 1743 having consent of parents.

James Pugh, son of John Pugh, late of East Nantmell, Chester Co., dec'd and Ann Hilles, dau of Hugh Hilles of Richland twp, Bucks Co. Md. 19th da, 4th mo, 1768 having consent of parents.

Henry Cunrad of Upper Dublin, Philadelphia Co. and Jane Jones of Whitemarsh, same county md. 18th da, 9th mo, 1742 having consent of parents.

Nathan Cook of Upper Meirion, Philadelphia Co., bachelor and Elizabeth Butterwack? of Whitemarsh, Philadelphia Co. md. 17th da, 6th mo, 1734 having consent of parents.

David Pugh, son of Ellis Pugh of Radnbor, Chester Co. and Sarah Morgan, dau of William Morgan late of Montgomery, Philadelphia Co., dec'd md. 5th da,

4th mo, 1744 having consent of parents.

David Shoemaker, son of Jacob Shoemaker of Whitemarsh twp, Philadelphia Co., yeoman and Jane Roberts, dau of John Roberts of the same place md. 22nd da, 10th mo, 1776 having consent of parents.

John Bell of Norriton, Philadelphia Co. and Hannah Rees, dau of John Rees of Whitpain, Philadelphia Co. md. 14th da, 3rd mo, 1745 having consent of parents.

William Robert, son of William Roberts of Gwynedd, Philadelphia Co. and Ann Roberts, dau of William Roberts of Worcester, same county md. 17th da, 4th mo, 1746 having consent of parents.

Edward Evans of Dublin, Philadelphia Co. and Elizabeth Jones, dau of Humphrey Jones, of same place md. 22nd da, 3rd mo, 1746 having consent of parents.

Daniel Roberts of Upper Dublin, Philadelphia Co. and Mary Namey of the same place md. 10th da, 4th mo, 1746 having consent of parents.

John Reese, son of John Reese of Whitpain, Philadelphia Co. and Cathrine Evans, dau of Cadwalder Evans, same place md. 11th da, 9th mo, 1746 having consent of parents.

Nathan Evans, son of Evan Evans, late of Gwynedd, Philadelphia Co. and Ruth Morgan, dau of Daniel Morgan of same place md. 1746 having consent of parents. No day or month in the record.

Rowland Edwards, son of John Edwards of towamenein, Philadelphia Co. and Mary Robeson, dau of James Robeson of same place md. 11th da, 10th mo, 1746 having consent of parents.

Joshua Richard, son of John Richard, late of the Philadelphia Co. and Mary Dickinson, dau of Joshua Dickinson of the same place md. 21st da, 3rd mo, 1747 having consent of parents.

William Jones, son of Robert Jones of Philadelphia Co. and Rebecca Trotter, dau of William Trotter of the same place md. 12th da, 3rd mo, 1748 having consent of parents.

Robert Jones of Lower Meirion, Philadelphia Co. and Margaret Evans of same place md. The date was unreadable on record.

Hugh Ellis of Limerick, Philadelphia Co. and Ann Evans, dau of William Evans md. 16th da, 4th mo, 1748 having consent of parents.

John Cunrade of Springfield, Philadelphia Co. and Elizabeth Shoemaker, dau of George Shoemaker of Bucks Co. Md. 17th da, 6th mo, 1748 having consent of parents.

Jacob Jones of Gwynedd, Philadelphia Co. and Hannah Bennet of the same place md. 17th da, June, 1748 having consent of parents.

Rowland Evans, son of John Evans of Gwynedd, Philadelphia Co. and Susanah Foulke, dau of Thomas Foulke of the same place md. 15th da, Nov, 1748 having consent of parents.

Joseph Ambler, son of Joseph Ambler of Montgomery, Philadelphia Co. and

Mary Naylor, dau of Joseph Naylor of the same place md. 17th da, 8th mo, 1748 having consent of parents.

Jesse Evans, son of Hugh Evans, late of Gwynedd, Philadelphia Co., dec'd and Catherine Jones, dau of John Jones of Horsham, same county md. 8th da, 4th mo, 1750 having consent of parents.

Edward Foulke of Gwynedd, Philadelphia Co. and Margaret Griffith of the same place md. 25th da, 8th mo, 1750 having consent of parents.

Herman Yerkas of Plymouth, Philadelphia Co. and Mary Frouds?, dau of Edward Frouds md. 22nd da, 3rd mo, 1750 having consent of parents.

John Robeson, son of William Robeson of Whitpain, Philadelphia Co., dec'd and Mary Evans, dau of Samuel Evans of Norton??, same county md. 24th da, 3rd mo, 1750 having consent of parents.

Thomas Holt, son of Benjamin Holt of Horsham twp, Philadelphia Co. and Sarah Morgan, dau of Enoch Morgan of Gwynedd tp, same count md. 13th da, 2nd mo, 1781 having consent of parents.

William Hallowell, son of Joseph Hallowell of Whitemarsh twp, Philadelphia Co., dec'd and Mary Roberts, dau of John Roberts of Whitpain twp, same county md. 17th da, 6th mo, 1777 having consent of parents.

Jacob Albertson of Cheltenham twp, Philadelphia Co., son of Benjamin Albertson and Mary Roberts of Whitemarsh twp, Philadelphia Co., dau of Robert Roberts, dec'd md. 21st da, 11th mo, 1782 having consent of parents.

Thomas Evans, son of Thomas Evans, late of Gwynedd twp, Philadelphia Co. and Mary Roberts, dau of John Roberts of Whitpain twp, Philadelphia Co. md. 19th da, 11th mo, 1765 having consent of parents.

Thomas Shoemaker, son of George Shoemaker, Warrington twp, Bucks Co., and Mary Ambler, dau of Joseph Ambler of Montgomery, Philadelphia Co. md. 11th da, 10th mo, 1757 having consent of parents.

Joshua Foulke, son of Edward Foulke of Gwynedd, Philadelphia Co. and Catharine Evans, dau of Thomas Evans of the same place md. 20th da, 12th mo, 1765 having consent of parents.

Jarret Spencer, son of Jacob Spencer of the Manor of Moorland, Philadelphia Co. and Hannah Evans, dau of Thomas Evans of Gwynedd, Philadelphia Co. md. 22nd da, 11th mo, 1774 having consent of parents.

Reese Nanna of Upper Dublin, Philadelphia Co., cooper and Ann Trotter, dau of Richard Bevan and widow of Joseph Trotter, late of Plymouth, Philadelphia Co. md. 7th da, 4th mo, 1761 having consent of parents.

Jehu Evans, son of Edward Evans, late of Tonamenan twp, Philadelphia Co. and Mary Lawrence, dau of Daniel Lawrence of Haverford twp, Chester Co. Md. 19th da, 11th mo, 1776 having consent of parents.

Daniel Thomas of the Manor of Moreland, Philadelphia Co., miller and Ann Paul of Germantown twp, same count md. 11th da, 11th mo, 1773 having consent of parents.

Israel Roberts, son of John Roberts of Bristol twp, Philadelphia Co., yeoman

and Martha Rakestraw, dau of William Rakestraw of the City of
Philadelphia, house carpenter md. 21st da, 5th mo, 1772 having consent of
parents.

Daniel Evans of the City of Philadelphia, blacksmith, son of Evan Evans of
Gwynedd twp, Philadelphia Co. and Eleanor Rittenhouse, dau of Matthias
Rittenhouse of Worcester Twp, said county md. 14th da, 4th mo, 1763
having consent of parents.

Joseph Ambler, son of John Ambler of Montgomery twp, Philadelphia Co. and
Elizabeth Forman, dau of John Forman of New Britain twp, Bucks Co md.
8th da, 10th mo, 1776 having consent of parents.

Joseph Jones of Plymouth, Philadelphia Co. and Hannah Bell of Whitemarsh
twp, Philadelphia Co. md. 8th da, 9th mo, 1774 having consent of parents.

Morgan Morgan, son of Edward Morgan of Whitpain twp, Philadelphia Co. and
Ann Roberts, dau of John Roberts of same place md. 21st da, 4th mo, 1774
having consent of parents.

John Evans, son of John Evans of Gwynedd, Philadelphia Co. and Margaret
Foulke, dau of Evan Foulke of the same place, dec'd md. 19th da, 11th mo,
1754 having consent of parents.

Jesse Holt, son of Benjamin Holt of Horsham twp, Philadelphia Co. and Sarah
Thomas, dau of John Thomas of Montgomery twp, Philadelphia Co. md.
21st da, 11th mo, 1780 having consent of parents.

HORSHAM MONTHLY MEETING BOOK MARRIAGES.

Moses Comfort, son of Stephen Comfort of Middletown Twp, Bucks Co., and
Elizabeth Mitchell, dau of Joseph Mitchel of the same place, md. 20th da,
11th mo, 1782 having consent of parents.

Israel Knight, son of Giles Knight, of Bensalem Twp, Bucks Co., and Sarah
Tyson, dau of Isaac Tyson of Upper Dublin Twp., same county md. at
Horsham Monthly Meeting 26th da, 11th mo, 1782 having consent of
parents.

Thoms Lukens, of Horsham Twp, Philadelphia Co., son of William Lukens, of
same place and Jane Parry of Manor of Moorland Twp, dau of Stephen
Parrry, dec'd of the same place md. at Horsham and Byberry Monthly
Meeting, 6th da, 12th mo, 1782 having consent of parents.

Nicholas Austin of the Manor of Moorland Twp, Philadelphia Co., and Susanah
Tomkins, of the same place md. at Horsham 18th da, 4th mo, 1783.

Thomas Samms, of the City of Philadelphia, son of Nathaniel and Ann Samms,
and Mary Carver, dau of John and Rachel Carver of Byberry Twp.,
Philadelphia Co., md. 23rd da, 4th mo, 1783.

Amos Harmer, of the City of Philadelphia, carpenter and Mary Heaton of the
Manor of Moorland Twp, Philadelphia Co., md. at Horsham 10th da, 10th
mo, 1783 having consent of parents.

John Evans, son of John Evans, of the Gwynedd Twp, Philadelphia Co., and Gaynor Iredell, dau of Robert Iredell, of Horsham Twp., said county md. at Byberry and Horsham Monthly Meeting 14th da, 11th mo, 1783 having consent of parents.

Jacob Tomkins, of Manor of Moorland Twp, Philadelphia Co., sadler and Sarah Lloyd of Warminster Twp, Bucks Co., widow md. 7th da, 11th mo, 1783 having consent of parents.

Seneca Fell, son of John Fell of Buckingham, Bucks Co., and Grace Holt, dau of Benjamin Holt of Horsham Twp, Philadelphia Co., md. at Horsham, 19th da, 12th mo, 1783 having consent of parents.

Joseph Nailer, of Upper Dublin Twp., Philadelphia Co., blacksmith and Lydia Tomkins, dau of Jacob Tomkins of Manor of Moorland Twp, same county, md. at Horsham Monthly Meeting 5th da, 3rd mo, 1784 having consent of parents.

Abraham Lukens, son of Joseph Lukens, of Whitemarsh Twp, Philadelphia Co., and Martha Lukens, dau of William Lukens, of Horsham Twp, same county md. at Horsham Monthly Meeting 7th da, 5th mo, 1784 having consent of parents.

Benjamin Walton, of Byberry Twp., Philadelphia Co., and Hannah Wilson, dau of Jonathan Wilson of same place, md. at Horsham and Byberry Monthly Meeting 12th da, 11th mo, 1784 having consent of parents

Benjamin Kite, son of Thomas Kite, of the City of Philadelphia, and Rebekah Walton, dau of Benjamin Walton, of Byberry Twp., said county md. at Horsham and Byberry Monthly Meeting 6th da, 10th mo, 1784 having consent of parents.

Silas Walton, son of Thomas Walton, of Manor of Moorland Twp, Montgomery Co., and Phebe Parry, dau of John and Margaret Parry of the same place md. Horsham Monthly Meeting 18th da, 11th mo, 1784 having consent of parents.

William Cumming of the City of Philadelphia, copper smith, son of David Cumming of Philadelphia, and Sarah, his wife, dec'd and Mary Parry, dau of Stephen Parry, dec'd and Esther, his wife of Philadelphia Co. md at Horsham Monthly Meeting 6th da, 11th mo, 1784.

William Paxson, son of Thomas Paxson of Middletown Twp, Bucks Co., and Elizabeth Walton, dau of Jeremiah Walton and Mary, his wife of Moorland Twp, Philadelphia Co., md. at Horsham Monthly Meeting 12th da, 11th mo, 1784 having consent of parents.

Jesse Hallowell, of the Manor of Moorland Twp, son of Thomas Hallowell, of the same place and Sarah Lukens, dau of William Lukens, of Horsham Twp., md. at Horsham Monthly Meeting 26th da, 11th mo, 1784 having consent of parents.

Izor Lukens of Horsham Twp., son of William Lukens, late of Horsham Twp., Philadelphia Co., and Ann Cunnard of the same place, dau of Jonathan

Cunnard, md. at Horsham Monthly Meeting 19th da, 11th mo, 1784 having consent of parents.

Abraham Trump, of the Upper Dublin Twp., Montgomery Co., son of Michael Trump and Grace, his wife of the same place and Jemima Heaton, dau of Thomas Heaton, late of Cheltenham Twp, same county md. at Horsham Monthly Meeting 8th da, 4th mo, 1785 having consent of parents.

John Cleaver, son of Peter and Elizabeth Cleaver, late of the Upper Dublin Twp., Philadelphia Co., dec'd and Hannah Walton, dau of William and Phebe Walton, late of the same place, dec'd md. at Horsham Monthly Meeting , Montgomery Co. 6th da, 5th mo, 1785.

William Pennington, son of Thomas Pennington, dec'd and Anna Walton, dau of Jacob Walton, both of the Manor of Moorland Twp md. at Horsham Monthly Meeting 7th da, 6th mo, 1785 having consent of parents.

Daniel Shoemaker, son of Isaac and Hannah Shoemaker, of Upper Dublin Twp., Montgomery Co., and Phebe Walton, dau of Thomas and Mary Walton of Manor of Moorland Twp, same county md. at Horsham Monthly Meeting 18th da, 11th mo, 1785 having consent of parents.

Ezra Townsend, son of John Townsend of Bensalem Twp, Bucks Co., and Elizabeth Paul, dau of James Paul of Lower Dublin Twp., 17th da, 5th mo, 1786 having consent of parents.

Robert Croasdale, son of Robert Croasdale, dec'd of Middletown Twp, Bucks Co., and Tace Knight, dau of Jonathan Knight of Byberry Twp., Philadelphia Co., md. at Horsham Monthly Meeting 12th da, 6th mo, 1786 having consent of parents.

Jacob Wilson, son of Jonathan Wilson of Bensalem Twp, Bucks Co., and Rebecca Thomas dau of David Thomas, dec'd of Byberry Twp., Philadelphia Co., md. at Horsham Monthly Meeting 18th da, 10th mo, 1786 having consent of parents.

Robert Comfort, son of Stephen Comfort, dec'd of Middletown Twp, Bucks Co., and Mary Parry, dau of Edward Parry of Byberry Twp., Philadelphia Co., md. at Byberry Monthly Meeting 10th da, 12th mo, 1786 having consent of parents.

Joseph Kinderdine, of the Northern Liberties, City of Philadelphia, son of Jacob Kinderdine, late of Horsham, dec'd and Christiana Morrison, dau of Murdock Morrison of York County, md. at Horsham Monthly Meeting 7th da, 3rd mo, 1787 having consent of parents.

Thomas Ackly, of the Manor of Moorland, Montgomery Co., son of Thomas Ackly of the same place and Rachel Walton, dau of Jeremiah Walton of the same place md. at Horsham Monthly Meeting 18th da, 4th mo, 1787 having consent of parents.

John Miller, of Middletown Twp, Bucks Co., son of Jacob Miller of Moorland, Montgomery Co., dec'd and Sarah Mitchel, dau of Joseph Mitchel of the Manor of Moorland, Montgomery Co. md. at Horsham Monthly Meeting

13th da, 6th mo, 1787 having consent of parents.

Thomas Parry, son of Edward Parry of Byberry Twp, Philadelphia Co., and Elizabeth Playter, dau of George Playter, of Byberry Twp, Philadelphia Co., at Horsham Monthly Meeting md. 16th da, 5th mo, 1787 having consent of parents.

Jesper Scott, of Baltimore County, MD, son of Abraham Scott and Elizabeth, his wife and Rebecca Jones, dau of Jonathan Jones and Jane, his wife of Warrington Twp, Bucks Co., md. at Horsham 7th da, 11th mo, 1787 having consent of parents.

Abraham Harmer of Cheltenham Twp, Montgomery Co., son of Elias Harmer, dec'd and Hannah Mitchel, dau of Joseph Mitchel of Moreland Twp, md. 5th da, 7th mo, 1787 having consent of parents.

Benjamin Griffith, son of Samuel Griffith of Lower Dublin Twp., Philadelphia Co., and Elizabeth Comley, dau of Robert Comely of Bucks Co., md. at Horsham Monthly Meeting 18th da, 1st mo, 1788 having consent of parents.

James Spencer of the Upper Dublin Twp., Montgomery Co., son of William Spencer, dec'd and Elizabeth Marpole, dau of William Lukens, of Horsham Twp, same county md. at Horsham Monthly Meeting 16th da, 5th mo, 1788 having consent of parents.

Matthew Hallowell, son of Matthew Hallowell and Mary, his wife, of Morelands Twp, Montgomery Co. and Martha Gummore, dau of John Gummore and Sarah, his wife md. 11th da, 4th mo, 1788 having consent of parents.

Henry Butler, son of Thomas Butler of the City of Philadelphia, and Ann Mitchell, dau of Joseph Mitchell, of the Manor of Moreland, Philadelphia Co., md. at Horsham Monthly Meeting 11th da, 6th mo, 1788 having consent of parents.

Joseph Lukens, son of Joseph Lukens, dec'd of Horsham Twp, Montgomery Co. and Elizabeth Kirk, dau of Jacob Kirk, of Abington, same county md. at Horsham Monthly Meeting 14th da, 11th mo, 1788 having consent of parents.

Nathan Bewley of Upper Dublin Twp., Montgomery Co., blacksmith, son of Isaac Beweley and Rachel, his wife, dec'd and Hannah Robinson of the same place, dau of John Robinson and Mary, his wife md. at Horsham Monthly Meeting 13th da, 11th mo, 1788 having consent of parents.

William Walton, son of Jacob Walton and Mary, his wife of Buckingham Twp, Bucks Co., and Hannah Shoemaker, dau of Isaac Shoemaker and Hannah, his wife md. at Horsham and Byberry mm, Montgomery Co. md. 21st da, 11th mo, 1788 having consent of parents.

Isaac Longstreth, son of Daniel Longstreth of Warminister Twp, Bucks Co. and Jane Vanderin, dau of Godfrey Vanderin of Southampton Twp, same county md. at Horsham Monthly Meeting 10th da, 2nd mo, 1789 having consent of parents.

Samuel Gourley of Moorland, Montgomery Co., son of John and Elizabeth
Gourley of Wrights Town, Bucks Co., and Priscilla Walton, dau of Jacob
and Mary Walton of the same place md. at Horsham Monthly Meeting md.
23rd da, 10th mo, 1789 having consent of parents.

Jeremiah Walton, son of Thomas Walton of Moorland Twp, Montgomery Co.
and Rachel Lukens, dau of William Lukens, of Horsham Twp, same county
md. at Horsham 13th da, 11 mo, 1789 having consent of parents.

George Christian, son of Christian Christine, of Horsham Twp, Montgomery
Co. and Joanna Holt, dau of Benjamin Holt, of the same place md. at
Horsham Monthly Meeting 18th da, 12th mo, 1788 having consent of
parents.

Oliver Hough of Upper Makefield, Bucks Co., son of Isaac Hough, late of
Warminster, dec'd and Phebe Cadwallader, dau of Jacob Cadwallader, of
Warminster, Bucks Co., md. at Horsham Monthly Meeting 7th da, 4th mo,
1790 having consent of parents.

David Davis, of the Manor of Moorland Twp , son of David Davis of the same
place, dec'd and Joanna Homer, dau of William Homer of Upper Dublin
Twp. md. at Horsham Monthly Meeting 21st da, 5th mo, 1790 having
consent of parents.

Job Quimby, son of Isaiah Quimby, of Amwell Twp, Hunterdon Co. NY and
Martha Cadwallader, dau of Edward Cadwallader, of Moorland Twp,
Montgomery Co. md. at Horsham Monthly Meeting 8th da, 10th mo, 1790
having consent of parents.

James Barns, son of John Barnes, dec'd of Horsham Twp, Philadelphia Co., and
Sarah Palmer, dau of John Palmer, dec'd of the same place md. at Horsham
Monthly Meeting 22nd da, 4th mo, 1790 having consent of parents.

William Gregory of the Northern Lights, of the City of Philadelphia, son of
Bennoni Gregory, late of Chesterfield Twp, Burlington Co., NJ, dec'd and
Susanna Lukens of Horsham Twp, Montgomery Co. md. at Horsham
Monthly Meeting 12th da, 11th mo, 1790 having consent of parents.

Jesse Wilson, son of Thomas Wilson of Southampton Twp, Bucks Co., and
Amy Parry, dau of Isaac Parry of Horsham Twp, Philadelphia Co., md. at
Horsham Monthly Meeting 19th da, 11th mo, 1790 having consent of
parents.

Isaac Clark, of the Manor of Moorland, Philadelphia Co., and Amy Walton, dau
of Thomas Walton of the same place md. at Horsham Monthly Meeting 6th
da, 11th mo, 1790 having consent of parents.

Thomas Mitchener, of the Manor of Moorland, Philadelphia Co., son of John
Mitchener, dec'd and Ann Walton, dau of Jeremiah Walton, of the same
place md. 20th da, 5th mo, 1791 having consent of parents.

Jonathan Knight of Byberry Twp, Philadelphia Co., son of Jonathan Knight,
dec'd and Martha Lloyd, dau of Samuel Lloyd of Moorland Twp,
Montgomery Co., dec'd md. at Horsham Monthly Meeting 5th da, 4th mo,

1791 having consent of surviving parents.

Jonathan Thomas, son of Mordecai Thomas of the Twp of Moorland, Montgomery Co. and Sarah Spencer, dau of John Spencer of Upper Dublin Twp., same county md. 21st da, 10th mo, 1791 having consent of parents.

John Thomson of Gwynedd Twp, Montgomery Co., son of John Thomson, late of the same place, dec'd and Margaret, his wife and Mary Hallowell of Horsham Twp, same county, dau of Thomas Hallowell of the same place md. at Horsham Monthly Meeting 18th da, 11th mo, 1791 having consent of parents.

William Worthington, Jr. of the Buckingham Twp, Bucks Co., son of William Worthington of the same place and Margaret Spencer, dau of Thomas Spencer of Northampton Twp, md. at Horsham Monthly Meeting 16th da, 12th mo, 1791 having consent of parents.

Joseph Clark, of the City of Philadelphia, Schoolmaster, son of Richard Clark and Ann, his wife of London, Middle sex Co., England, the latter dec'd and Edith Shoemaker, widow, dau of Samuel Spencer and Mary, his wife of Upper Dublin Twp., Montgomery Co. md. at Horsham and Byberry Monthly Meeting 9th da, 12th mo, 1791 having consent of parents.

Samuel Dean, of Lower Makefield Twp, Bucks Co., son of Samuel Dean, dec'd and Rachel Atkinson, dau of Ezekiel Wineson, late of Upper Makefield, Bucks Co., md. at Horsham Monthly Meeting 4th da, 1st mo, 1792 having consent of parents.

Daniel Lukens, son of William Lukens of Horsham Twp, Montgomery Co., and Mary Shoemaker, dau of Isaac Shoemaker of Upper Dublin Twp., same county md. at Horsham Monthly Meeting 20th da, 4th mo, 1792 having consent of parents.

Nathan Shoemaker, of Moorland Twp, Montgomery Co., son of Benjamin Shoemaker, of Cheltenham, same county and Sarah Miller, dau of Solomon Miller of Abington, same county md. at Horsham Monthly Meeting 18th da, 5th mo, 1792 having consent of parents.

Jonathan Iredell, son of Robert and Hannah Iredell, of Horsham Twp, Montgomery Co., and Hannah Kirk, dau of Rayner and Elizabeth Kirk, of Upper Dublin Twp. md. at Horsham Monthly Meeting 5th da, 10th mo, 1792 having consent of parents.

Jacob Kirk, son of Jacob Kirk and Elizabeth, his wife of Abington Twp, Montgomery Co. and Rebeckah, dau of Charles Iredell, dec'd and Phebe, his wife of Horsham Twp, same county md. 12th da, 10th mo, 1792 having consent of parents.

Jeremiah McIlvain, son of John and Lydia McIlvain, said John dec'd of Ridley Twp, Delaware Co. and Elizabeth Spencer, dau of John and Elizabeth Spencer, of Upper Dublin Twp., Montgomery Co. md. at Horsham Monthly Meeting 1st da, 11th mo, 1792 having consent of parents.

Richard Mather, son of Bartholomew Mather, of Cheltenham Twp,

Montgomery Co. and Sarah Thomas, dau of Jonathan Thomas, late of Lower Dublin Twp., Philadelphia Co., md. at Horsham Monthly Meeting 15th da, 11th mo, 1792 having consent of parents.

Isaac Walton, son of Jacob and Margaret Walton, of Warwick Twp, Bucks Co., and Mary Spencer, dau of Thomas and Mary Spencer of Northampton Twp, same county md. at Horsham and Byberry Monthly Meeting 16th da, 11th mo, 1792 having consent of parents.

George Shoemaker, of Gwynedd Twp, Montgomery Co., son of Thomas and Mary Shoemaker of the same place and Sarah Hallowell, of Horsham Twp, same county, dau of Thomas and Margaret Hallowell of the same place md. at Horsham and Byberry Monthly Meeting 23 da, 11th mo, 1792 having consent of parents.

Benjamin Atkinson of Byberry Twp, Philadelphia Co., son of Ezekiel Atkinson, late of Upper Makefield, Bucks Co., dec'd and Jane Adams, dau of Jedediah Adams, late of Bristol Twp, Bucks Co., also dec'd md. at Horsham Monthly Meeting 3rd da, 4th mo, 1793 having consent of parents.

David Parry, son of David Parry of the Manor of Moorland, Montgomery Co. and Elizabeth Thomas, dau of Mordecai Thomas of the same place md. at Horsham Monthly Meeting 17th da, 5th mo, 1793 having consent of parents.

Joseph Bolton, of Byberry Twp, Philadelphia Co., son of Isaac Bolton, dec'd and Jane Knight, dau of Jonathan Knight, of the same place md. at Horsham Monthly Meeting 16th da, 10th mo, 1793 having consent of parents.

William Walmsley, son of Silas Walmsley, of Byberry Twp, Philadelphia Co., and Phebe Knight, dau of Giles Knight of Bensalum, Bucks Co. Md. at Horsham Monthly Meeting 25th da, 12th mo, 1793 having consent of parents.

James Playter, of Byberry Twp., Philadelphia Co., son of George Playter of Kingston in Upper Canada and Margaret Bolton, dau of Isaac Bolton, late of Southampton, Bucks Co., dec'd md. Horsham Monthly Meeting 12th da, 3rd mo, 1794 having consent of parents.

Joseph Lukens, son of William and Elizabeth Lukens of Horsham Twp., Montgomery Co. and Ann Webster, dau of Naylor and Martha Webster of the same place md. Horsham Monthly Meeting 12th da, 9th mo, 1794 having consent of parents.

Thomas Phipps of Abington , Montgomery Co., son of Peter Phipps of the same place and Mary, his wife and Sarah Walmsley, dau of William Walmsley of Byberry Twp., Philadelphia Co. md. 15th da, 10th mo, 1794 having consent of parents.

Jesse Walmsley, son of Silas Walmsley, Byberry Twp., Philadelphia Co. and Mary Paul, dau of James Paul of Lower Dublin Twp , same county md. Horsham Monthly Meeting 5th da, 11th mo, 1794 having consent of parents.

Nathan Marshall, of Lower Dublin Twp , Philadelphia Co., son of John Marshall of the same place and Margaret, his wife and Elizabeth Parry, dau of

Jonathan Parry, of Byberry Twp. and Rebecca, his wife md. Horsham Monthly Meeting 12th da, 11th mo, 1794 having consent of parents.

Isaiah Walton, of Moorland Twp, Montgomery Co., son of Jacob Walton of the same place and Mary Harding, dau of Thomas Harding, late of Southampton Twp., Bucks Co., dec'd md. at Horsham Monthly Meeting 14th da, 11th mo, 1794 having consent of parents.

Amos Cooper, son of William Cooper of Northampton Twp, Bucks Co., and Hannah Lloyd, dau of John Lloyd of Horsham Twp, Montgomery Co. md. 12th da, 12th mo, 1794 having consent of parents.

Thomas Wilson, son of Thomas Wilson, of Bristol Twp, Bucks Co., and Phebe Gilbert, dau of Joshua and Mary Gilbert of Byberry Twp., Philadelphia Co. md. at Horsham Monthly Meeting 14th da, 10th mo, 1795 having consent of parents.

Asa Knight, son of Giles Knight of Bensalem Twp, Bucks Co. and Elizabeth Paul, dau of Joseph Paul, late of Lower Dublin Twp , Philadelphia Co. md. at Horsham Monthly Meeting 11th da, 7th mo, 1795 having consent of parents.

Joseph Stackhouse, son of Thomas Stackhouse, Bensalem Twp, Bucks Co., and Phebe Parry, dau of Jonathan Parry of Byberry Twp., Philadelphia Co. md. at Horsham Monthly Meeting 9th da, 3rd mo, 1796 having consent of parents.

Samuel Paul, son of Robert Paul of the Northern Liberties of Philadelphia and Rachel Knight, dau of Giles Knight of Bensalem Twp, Bucks Co. Md. at Horsham Monthly Meeting 18th da, 5th mo, 1796 having consent of parents.

Evan Knight, son of Giles Knight of Bensalem Twp, Bucks Co. and Martha Comley, dau of Isaac and Asenath Comley of Byberry Twp., Philadelphia Co. Md. at Horsham Monthly Meeting 14th da, 12th mo, 1796 having consent of parents.

Peter Yarnall, of Moreland Twp, Montgomery Co., son of Mordecai Yarnall, late of Springfield, decd. and Hannah Thornton of Byberry Twp., Philadelphia Co., dau of Edmund Haines, late of Evesham, NJ md. at Horsham Monthly Meeting 15th da, 2nd mo, 1797 having consent of parents.

John Jarrett, of Moreland Twp, Montgomery Co., son of John Jarret and Priscilla, his wife, of Upper Dublin Twp, same county and Hannah Lukens, dau of John Lukens and Rachel, his wife, late of City of Philadelphia, dec'd md. at Horsham Monthly Meeting 19th da, 5th mo, 1797 having consent of parents.

Benjamin Olden, of the City of Philadelphia, son of John and Mary Oldden, dec'd and Mary Townsend of Byberry Twp., Philadelphia Co., dau of Benjamin and Margaret Mason, dec'd md. at Horsham Monthly Meeting 7th da, 6th mo, 1797 having consent of friends.

Thomas Samms, of Byberry Twp., Philadelphia Co., son of Nathaniel Samms, dec'd and Anna, his wife and Elizabeth Knight, dau of Giles Knight of

Bensalem, Bucks Co. and Elizabeth, his wife, dec'd md. at Horsham Monthly Meeting 15th da, 11th mo, 1797 having consent of parents.

Joseph Hallowell, of Moreland Twp, Montgomery Co., son of Thomas Hallowell, of the same place, dec'd and Rachel Homer, dau of William Homer of Upper Dublin Twp, same county md. at Horsham Monthly Meeting 8th da, 12th mo, 1797 having consent of parents.

James Walton, son of William Walton of Byberry Twp., Philadelphia Co. and Lydia, his wife, and Achsah Crosdale, dau of Ezra Croasdale, dec'd of Southampton Twp, Bucks Co., and Mary, his wife md. at Horsham Monthly Meeting 13th da, 12th mo, 1797 having consent of parents.

Amos Knight of Byberry Twp., Philadelphia Co., son of Thomas Knight and Sarah, his wife and Rebecca Dubre, dau of Jacob Dubre and Rebecca, his wife md. 7th da, 12th mo, 1797 having consent of parents.

Jesse Worthington, of Buckingham Twp, Bucks Co., son of William Worthington of the same place and Martha Walton, dau of Jacob Walton of Moorland Twp., Montgomery Co. md. at Horsham Monthly Meeting 14th da, 12th mo, 1798 having consent of parents.

David Comfort of Middle Town Twp., Bucks Co., son of Stephen Comfort and Sarah, his wife and Beulah Walton of Byberry Twp., Philadelphia Co., dau of William Walton and Lydia, his wife md. at Horsham Monthly Meeting 13th da, 3rd mo, 1799 having consent of parents.

Samuel Robinson, of Upper Dublin Twp., Philadelphia Co., carpenter, son of John Robinson and Mary, his wife of same place and Rachel Shoemaker of the same place, dau of George Shoemaker, late of Abington , dec'd and Edith, his wife md. at Horsham Monthly Meeting 8th da, 3rd mo, 1799 having consent of parents.

Jonathan Fell, son of Joseph Gill of Upper Makefield, Bucks Co., dec'd and Sarah Baldenton, dau of Jonathan Balderton of Moreland Twp, Montgomery Co. md. at Horsham Monthly Meeting 15th da, 3rd mo, 1799 having consent of parents.

Edward Farmer, of Horsham Twp, Montgomery Co., son of Edward Farmer and Hannah, his wife and Sarah Samms of Byberry Twp., Philadelphia Co., dau of Nathaniel Samms and Ann, his wife md. at Horsham Monthly Meeting 7th da, 3rd mo, 1799 having consent of parents.

Walter Mitchell, of Middle Town Twp, Bucks Co., son of Samuel Mitchel and Ann, his wife and Hannah Comley of Moorland Twp, Philadelphia Co., dau of Joshua Comley and Catherine, his wife md. at Horsham Monthly Meeting 15th da, 5th mo, 1799 having consent of parents.

Thomas Thompson, of Cheltenham Twp, Montgomery Co., son of John Thompson and Abigail, his wife of the same place and Jane Jarret, dau of William Jarret and Ann, his wife md. at Horsham Monthly Meeting 17th da, 5th mo, 1799 having consent of parents.

William Webster, of Horsham Twp, Montgomery Co., son of Naylor Webster

and Martha, his wife of the same place and Sarah Wollen, dau of Joseph
Wollen and Rebecca, his wife of Lower Dublin Twp , Philadelphia Co. md.
15th da, 10th mo, 1799 having consent of parents.

Samuel Maulsby, son of Morchant Maulsby, dec'd of Whitemarsh and Susanna
Thomas, dau of Jonathan Thomas of Upper Dublin Twp, both of
Montgomery Co., md. at Horsham Monthly Meeting md. 15th da, 11th mo,
1799 having consent of parents.

Isaac Walton of Manor of Moorland Twp, Montgomery Co., son of Jeremiah
Walton, dec'd and Martha Lloyd of Horsham Twp, same county, dau of John
Lloyd and Sarah, his wife of same place md. at Horsham Monthly Meeting
15th da, 11th mo, 1799 having consent of parents.

Benjamin Albertson of Abington, Montgomery Co., son of Benjamin Alberton
and Susanna, his wife of the same place and Ann Knight, dau of Jonathan
Knight of Byberry Twp., Philadelphia Co., and Ann, his wife, dec'd md. at
Horsham Monthly Meeting 20th da, 7th mo, 1799 having consent of parents.

Nathan Marshall of Lower Dublin Twp , Philadelphia Co., son of John Marshall
of the same place and Margaret, his wife and Mary Bolton, dau of Isaac
Bolton, dec'd late of Southampton Twp, Bucks Co., and Sarah, his wife md.
14th da, 5th mo, 1800 having consent of parents.

John Townsend of Byberry Twp. Twp, Philadelphia Co., son of Evan Townsend
and Abi, his wife and Asanath Carver, of the same place, dau of John Carver
and Mary, his wife md. at Horsham Monthly Meeting 21st da, 5th mo, 1800
having consent of parents.

John Shoemaker of Cheltenham Twp, Montgomery Co., and Martha Parry of
Horsham Twp, widow of David Parry of Moreland Twp, same county, md.
at Horsham Monthly Meeting md. 22nd da, 5th mo, 1800 having consent of
parents.

Thomas Shoemaker of Upper Dublin Twp, Montgomery Co., son of Isaac
Shoemaker, dec'd and Eleanor Hallowell of Horsham Twp, dau of Thomas
Hallowell of the same place md. at Horsham Monthly Meeting 10th da, 10th
mo, 1800 having consent of parents.

Abel Thomas, son of David Thomas, dec'd and Mary, his wife of Providence
Twp, Montgomery Co. and Sarah Paul, dau of Joseph Paul, dec'd and
Hannah, his wife of Warrington Twp, Bucks Co. md. at Horsham Monthly
Meeting 17th da, 4th mo, 1800 having consent of parents.

Abraham Shoemaker of Horsham Twp, Montgomery Co., son of George
Shoemaker, dec'd and Martha Webster of Horsham Twp, same place, dau of
Naylor Webster and Martha, his wife of the same place md. at Horsham
Monthly Meeting 17th da, 10th mo, 1800 having consent of parents.

Thomas Preston of Londonwine, Chester Co., son of William Preston and
Deborah, his wife and Anna Samms of Byberry Twp, Philadelphia Co., dau
of Nathaniel Samms, and Ann, his wife md. at Horsham Monthly Meeting
1st da, 11th mo, 1800 having consent of parents.

Joseph Comley of Byberry Twp., Philadelphia Co., son of Isaac Comley and Assenath, his wife and Abigail Parry of the same place, dau of Jonathan Parry and Prebeua, his wife md. at Horsham Monthly Meeting 17th da, 12th mo, 1800 having consent of parents.

LOWER DUBLIN OR PENNIPACK BAPTIST CHURCH

Elizabeth, wife of Richard Collet d. 1717.
Eleanor Crispin md. John Hart 9.25.1708.
Sarah Crispin md. John Evans Oct 26, 1762, by P. P. Vanhorn.
James David md. Margaret Thomas Nov. 1720 at Montgomery.
David Davis died and was buried in Dublin twp, Philadelphia Co. 11.5.1699.
Daniel Dungan md. Martha Langhlen Feb 4, 1762 by P. P. Vanhorn.
Elizabeth, widow of Thomas Dungan, d. and was buried at Cold Spring in Bucks Co, 169-
Sarah Dungan md. Benjamin Fisher Oct 27, 1761, by P. P. Vanhorn.
Wm. Dungan d. 1713.
Alex. Edwards md. Ann Edwards Jul 23, 1737.
Alex. Edwards md. Elizabeth Morgan Nov 5, 1772.
Ann, wife of Alex. Edwards, d. Sep 7, 1771.
Martha Edwards md. Joseph Todd 4.20/1703 at Southampton, Bucks Co.
Mary, wife of Allen Foster d. and was buried at Pennipack 5.30, 1702.
Sarah, wife and a child of Thomas Foster buried 6 mo. 1702.
Richard Hall md. Susannah Edge Aug 22, 1745.
Susannah, wife of Joseph Hall, buried. 1706/7.
John Hart md. Eleanor Crispin 9.25.1708.
Susanna Hart d. Mar 30, 1733.
John, son of John Hart, Jr. d. Jun 11, 1743.
Wm. Hart d. Oct 6, 1714.
Silas Hart d. Oct 30, 1740.
Joseph, son of John Hart d. 1714.
John Hart d. 1714, Susannah, his wife d. 12.27.1724/5.
Mary Hart d. 1721.
Joseph Hart md. Sarah Stout, 2.2.1713.
Joseph Hart md. Elizabeth Collet Oct 9, 1740.
Susannah Hart d. and was buried in Pequeston, 1725.
Henry Jones md. Eleanor --- 1714.
Samuel Jones md. Katharine --- 12.2.1697.
Samuel Jones d. 1722, buried at Pennipack 3.1721/2.
John James and dau, Rachel died and buried at Pennipack 10.1712.
Griffith Miles, d. 1719.
Mary Swife md. Evan Morgan 7.29.1705.

Frances Swift, wife of John d. 1716/7.
John Watts of Dublin Twp, Philadelphia Co. md. Sarah --- 12.28.1687.
Sarah Watts md. Anthony Yerkes 7.9.1705.
John Watts died and was buried at Pennipack 6.27.1702 aged 42 years.
Anthony Yerkes md. Sarah Watts 7.9.1705.
Joseph Todd md. Martha Edwards at Southampton, Bucks Co. 4.20.1703.
Joseph Todd d. Dec 1721.
The widow Todd d. Apr. 30, 1748.
Margaret Thomas md. James David Nov 1720 at Montgomery.
Nathaniel West died near Burlington in W. N. Jersey and was buried at Cold
    Springs in Bucks Co. about 169-.
Elizabeth, widow of Nathaniel West d. Near Burlington and was buried at Cold
    Springs 169-.

TRINITY CHURCH AT OXFORD - MARRIAGES

Sarah Allen, widow md. Richard Mowey, Jun 2, 1746.
Richard Allen md. Elizabeth Boore, widow, Jan 7, 1748/9.
Isaac Asheton md. Sarah Renshaw oct 21, 1743.
Isaac Ashton md. Mary Hall, widow Jun 16, 1749.
Jacob Ashton of Northern Liberties md. Mary Stephens of Roxborough Twp.
    Sept 15, 1754.
Joseph Comley md. Eliner Hall May 17, 1763.
Abigail Comley, widow md. Richard Walton May 10, 1763.
Phebe Cumly md. John Swift Feb 21, 1764.
Hannah Cotman, widow of Somerset Co, Md md. Apr. 16, 1751 James
    Treheam, Somerset Co, Md.
Isaac Delworth md. Sarah Burby Dec 12, 1768.
Andrew Hannie md. Mary Wright Apr. 2, 1765.
Rebecca Dilworth of Philadelphia Co. md. Jacob Armitage of Philadelphia Co.
    Jan 1, 1761.
Charles Dilworth md. Mary Taylor Jan 27, 1765.
Samuel Dungen of Byberry md. Elizabeth Walton of Byberry Apr. 6, 1758.
Mary Finney md. John Bringhurst Apr. 3, 1750.
Sarah Bringhurst of Gtn. md. George Palmer of Gtn Jan 23, 1749/50.
George Bringhurst of Gtn md. Sarah Trump of White Marsh Oct 14, 1760.
Sarah Foster md. William Tillier Apr. 26, 1750.
Mary Foster md. Daniel Street Apr. 9, 1752.
Mary Foster md. Jeremiah Northropp of Lower Dublin Twp May 31, 1763.
Thomas Foster md. Mary Tillyer Nov 30, 1758.
Rebecca Foster md. Elias Yerkes md. Mar 18, 1755.
John Green md. Anna Sevela Delgin Oct 8, 1754.

Elizabeth Harding md. Henry Knight Nov 25, 1748.

Mary Harding md. Amos Strickland Mar 31, 1766.

Rebecca Hartley md. Matthies Aspden Mar 28, 1749.

Elinor Hall md. Joseph Comley May 17, 1763.

Elisah Hall of MD md. Ruth Hall of Cheltenham md. May 27, 1746.

Hannah Hall md. George Rice Dec 23, 1762.

Jacob Hall md. Rebecca Ingles Jan 5, 1764.

John Hall md. Sarah Parry May 28, 1747.

Mary Hall md. Joseph Street Jul 23, 1743.

Mary Hall, widow md. Isaac Aston Jun 16, 1749.

Mary Hall md. Jacob Laughlin Jan 20, 1763.

Susannah Hall md. John Ayres Mar 26, 1722.

Susannah Hall, Oxford twp md. Enoch Holme of Oxford Twp Apr. 30, 1761.

Esther Harvey, widow md. George Clift Apr. 23, 1751.

Benj. Harvey, Bucks Co. md. Margaret Lowdermore, Bucks Co. May 14, 1751.

Joyce Harvey, spinster, Philadelphia md. James Ham of Philadelphia Apr. 16, 1754.

John Knight of Philadelphia md. Susanna Paschall of Philadelphia Apr. 12, 1746.

Henry Knight md. Elizabeth Harding Nov 25, 1748.

Joseph Knight of Bucks Co. md. Rachel Townsend of Philadelphia Jul 20, 1761.

John Knowles md. Mary Wilkinson Sep 13, 1744.

Mary Linton md. James Macky, Jr. Nov 21, 1747.

John Lucken md. Jane Scull Jan 16, 1745.

Joseph Mather md. Elizabeth Barge, widow Sep 2, 1756.

Catharine Matthews of Abington Twp md. Samuel Waterman of Abington Twp Apr. 25, 1754.

Edward Milner, Jr. md. Susanna Martin, widow Feb 14, 1750/1.

Hester Noble md. Thomas White Mar 13, 1744.

Sarah Parry md. John Hall May 28, 1747.

Elijah Pearson of Bucks Co. md. Hannah Morris of Frankford, Philadelphia, Pa, Mar 2, 1761.

Samuel Penrose md. Ann Fleeson Apr. 3, 1766.

Ann Roberts, md. Morris Gwin Dec 6, 1747.

Susannah Roberts md. George Rumbley Jun 25, 1747.

William Roberts md. Rebecka McVah Aug 15, 1765.

Gertrude Ross, New Castle md. Thomas Till, Sussex Co. Jun 18, 1752.

Joseph Rush md. Mary Street Jul 26, 1746.

Witneth Rush, widow, Lower Dublin Twp md. Daniel Steward, widower, Oxford Twp Jul 31, 1755.

Isabella Shute md. Thomas Renshaw Apr. 6, 1752.

Joseph Stackhouse md. Catharine Dodamead Sept 29, 1780.

Joseph Shallcross of Oxford md. Mary Simmins of Oxford Twp May 29, 1758.

Benjamin Street md. Elizabeth Collins Jun 7, 1746.

Daniel Street md. Mary Forster Apr. 9, 1752.

Joseph Street md. Mary Hall Jul 23, 1743.

Mary Street md. Joseph Rush Jul 26, 1746.

Elizabeth Swift md. Jacob Leech Mar, 1766.

John Swift md. Phebe Cumly Feb 21, 1764.

Mary Swift md. Matthias Keen Sep 1, 1743.

Sarah Swift md. John Keen May 8, 1762.

Isaac Taylor md. Sarah Stone Jan 7, 1747/8.

Elizabeth Taylor md. John Addis Nov 21, 1750.

Mary Taylor md. Charles Dilworth Jan 27, 1765.

Hannah Thomas md. Elias Keen Dec 24, 1747.

David Thomas md. Mary Walton May 31, 1750.

Margaret Thomas md. Matthias Keen Nov 23, 1752.

Martha Thomas md. Isaac Leech Jan 25, 1753.

Ann Thomas of Byberry md. Joseph Leech of Oxford Jun 11, 1755.

Sarah Thomas of Philadelphia Co. md. Jacob Kirkener of Philadelphia Co. Apr. 13, 1756.

Richard Thomas md. Margaret Leech Aug 28, 1759.

Elizabeth Towne md. Thomas Bartholomew Dec 7, 1750.

Samuel Waterman of Abington Twp md. Catharine Matthews of Abington Twp Apr. 25, 1754.

Thomas West md. Mary Combs aug 26, 1756.

Benjamin Walton md. Catharine Williamson md. Nov 23, 1756.

Sarah Walton of Philadelphia Co. md. William Francis of Philadelphia Co. Feb 2, 1754.

Mary Walton md. David Thomas May 31, 1750.

Richard Walton md. Abigail Comly, widow May 10, 1753.

Thomas White md. Hester Noble Mar 13, 1744.

Griffiths Williams md. Landina Naglem Mar 7, 1765.

Elizabeth Williamson md. Joseph Vandergrift May 2, 1759.

Mary Wright md. Andrew Hennis Apr. 2, 1765.

Elias Yerkes md. Rebecca Foster Mar 18, 1756.

Isaac Worrell of Chester Co. md. Mary Harris of Chester Co. Oct 16, 1752 N.S.

Isaiah Worrall of Oxford Twp. md. Elizabeth Harper of Oxford Twp. md. Apr. 17, 1753.

Thomas Worthington md. Hannah Duncan Aug 22, 1751.

PRESBYTERIAN CHURCH, ABINGTON - MARRIAGES

1744, Nov 6, Abernathy, Jane and Thomas Armstrong.
1797, Aug 2, Achuff, Jacob and Thomas Hannah.
1726, Jan 17, Ackly, Elizabeth and John Huntsman.
1793, Dec. 5, Adams, James and Rachel Finney.
1763, Jul, 28, Adams, Jane and George Nimmin.
1775, Nov 24, Adams, John and Elizabeth Walker.
1789, Oct 18, Adams, Margaret and Samuel Walker.
1733, Nov 22, Adams, William and Sarah Breden.
1754, Jan 29, Akin Andrew and Susannah Castner.
1793, Feb 8, Anderson, Sarah and Peter Jones.
1798, Oct 2, Armitage, Elizabeth and Samuel Wright.
1743, Jan 11, Armitage, Enoch and Barbara Baltes.
1766, Jan 20, Armstrong, Caleb and Mary Strecker.
1792, Apr 6, Armstrong, Joseph and Elizabeth Evans.
1744, Nov 6, Armstrong, Thomas and Jane Abernethy.
1797, Feb 29, Ashton, Jonathan and Martha Timbrel.
1721, May 5, Backer, Hannah and John Vandergrist.
1799, Dec. 5, Baker, John and Hannah Smith.
1720, Nov 29, Baker, Mary and William Evans.
1794, Apr 7, Baker, Polly and Lewis Horning.
1743, Jan 11, Baltes, Barbara and Enoch Armitage.
1789, Oct 13, Bannister, Nathaniel and Jane Kidd.
1745,Oct 8, Barclay, Hugh and Elizabeth Vandyke.
1747, Oct 29, Barkley, Adam and Martha Dickson.
1800, Mar, 13, Barnes, Abigail and John Edwards.
1777, May, 7, Barnie, John and Mary Major.
1735, May, 15, Barns, Elizabeth and James Morrey.
1787, Feb 20, Barns, Mary and Peter Lukens.
1777, Nov 6, Barns, Samuel and Priscilla Wilson.
1756, Mar 25, Bartle, Sebas and Elizabeth Cline.
1770, Mar 29, Bartleson, Phoebe and Joseph Breden.
1787, Aug 1, Baxter Andrew and Jane Harney.
1788, Oct 28, Bean, Joshua and Sarah Carney.
1770, June 7, Beatty, Mary and Rev. Enoch Green.
1767, Sep 1, Bedford, Gunning and Mary Stevens.
1732, Apr 8, Bell, Jane and George Logan.
1742, Nov 1, Bener, Jacob and Jane Crocket.
1772, Dec. 8, Bener, Mary and Charles Pennington.
1793, Mar 27, Benezet, Anthony and Peggy Mayer.
1791, Dec. 1, Bennet, Sarah and Christian Snyder.
1775, Mar 21,Bickley, Henry and Elizabeth Ryderpage.

1766, Dec. 25, Billieu, Ann and Thomas Mitchenor.
1767, Dec. 24, Billieu, Daniel, Sr. and Priscilla Wood.
1768, Jan 28, Billieu, Daniel and Rebecca Vansand.
1766, Apr 15, Billieu, Elizabeth and John Fallowel.
1772, Feb 13, Billieu, Jacob and Elizabeth Jones.
1773, Feb 4, Billieu, Rachel and John McSwiney.
1777, Aug 21, Billieu, Sarah and William Wilson.
1747, Oct 22, Billiou, Isaac and Rachel Brittin.
1767, Sep 24, Blair, Rev. Samuel and Susanna Shippen.
1796, Nov 17, Blake, Abraham and Margaret Ott.
1798, Oct 20, Blewet, Mary Ann and John Matthews.
1795, June 3, Boiliau, Nathaniel and Hetty Leech.
1798, Jan 19, Boiliau, Nathaniel Jr. and Mary Duncan.
1743, Jan 19, Boone, Joseph and Elizabeth Paxton.
1797, Feb 16, Boucher, Martha and Benjamin Colloun.
1792, Jan 10, Boullange, Frederick and Kitty Keiser.
1742, Nov 1, Bourn, Edward and Mary Green.
1736, Mar 12, Bowen, Margaret and John Trout.
1733, Jan 15, Bowen, Mary and Evan Jones.
1762, Sep 20, Boyce, Margaret and William Wood.
1722, June 6, Boyd, Frances and John Ruchi.
1744, Nov 22, Boyd, James and Mary Richey.
1794, June 14, Boyd, Mary and Timothy Lane.
1786, Mar 29, Bradey, Thomas and Elizabeth Hamilton.
1778, Aug 6, Bradford, Elizabeth and Thomas Houston.
1763, June 2, Brant, Simon and Hannah Morrey.
1737, Apr, 21, Breden, Frances and Robert Breden.
1770, Mar 29, Breden, Joseph and Phobe Bartleson.
1772, Oct 6, Breden, Margaret and James Fletcher.
1737, Apr 21, Breden, Robert and Frances Breden.
1749, Aug 10, Breden, Robert and Mary Campbell.
1733, Nov 22, Breden, Sarah and William Adams.
1777, Apr 22, Breden, Susanna and John McSwiney.
1724, Mar 28, Bredin, Judith and John Todd.
1723, Dec. 26, Bredin, Mary and Henry Mackenzie.
1742, Dec. 17, Breese, Henry and Margaret McKarte.
1738, May 4, Briggs, Hannah and Samuel Dyer.
1751, Jan 24, Brittin, John and Eve Dorland.
1789, Apr 9, Brittin, Martha and John Harper.
1742, Feb 4, Britton, Mary and Derick Van Pelt.
1740, Sep 17, Brock, Hannah and Nathaniel Davis.
1725, Mar 18, Bromle, Richard and Margaret Mees.
1789, Apr 30, Brooks, Fanny and Samuel Siddons.

1768, Sep 23, Bronse, Henry and Ann Craven.
1747, Jan 17, Brown, Elizabeth and John Huggins.
1775, Apr 10, Brown, Hannah and Cornelius Wynkoop.
1758, Apr 10, Brown, John and Mary McClaine.
1773, Feb 25, Brown, Margaret and Samuel Dunlap.
1746, Jan 30, Brown, Mary and Robert Fletcher.
1745, Mar 14, Brown, Samuel and Ann Moore.
1764, Nov 7, Brown, Sarah and John Mason.
1760, Apr 3, Brown, Stephen and Jane Dickson.
1739, Jan 16, Brown, William and Mary Low.
1775, Apr 4, Brown, William and Ann McSwiney.
1732, Aug 13, Bryan, Dennis and Sarah Midkaft.
1794, Nov 3, Bur, Margaret and Francis Kirkpatrick.
1754, Mar 24, Burke, John and Elizabeth Wood.
1775, Apr 10, Burton, Susannah and Levi Evans.
1718, June 27, Buskark, Joseph and Jacaminea Wincook.
1796, Oct 26, Buskirk, Rebecca and Amos Strickland.
1797, Jan 14, Butler, James and Sarah Hervey.
1755, Sep 10, Cadwalader, Alice and Benjamin Lukens.
1790, Dec. 30, Cadwallader, Rachel and Saxety Mckee.
1733, Jul 4, Cameron, David and Margaret Waters
1749, Aug 10, Campbel, Mary and Robert Breden.
1746, Nov 20, Campbell, Jane and John Foster.
1788, Oct 28, Carney, Sarah and Joshua Bean.
1754, Nov 26, Carr, Jane and George Kelsy.
1736, May 27, Carter, Christopher and Sarah Huste.
1794, Jan 2, Carter, Elizabeth and Charles Holt.
1742, Dec. 23, Carter, Hannah and Jacob Gilbert.
1787, Jan 18, Carver, Mary and John Kirk.
1800, May 29, Caskey, John and Rebecca Megargle.
1754, Jan 29, Castner, Susannah and Andrew Akin.
1750, June 14, Chambers, Martha and Michael Gould.
1771, June 11, Charlesworth, Ann and Archibald McClean, Jr.
1749, Dec. 19, Charlesworth, John and Mary Wood.
1762, Mar 4, Charlesworth, Rebecca and William McClean.
1763, Apr 14, Charlesworth, Sarah and Moses McClean.
1739, May 1, Charleton, Eleanor and Joseph Honey.
1787, Jul 5, Child Grace and Joseph Kirk.
1744, Mar 1, Clark, Mary and Richard Thomas.
1795, Jul 26, Clayton, Jonathan and Margaret Lunken.
1738, Jul 7, Clerk, James and Mary Deal.
1762, Dec. 9, Clift, Jonathan and Christinia Helviston.
1756, Mar 25, Clime, Elizabeth and Sebas Bartle.

1799, May 2, Collin, Phebe and Nathan Phillips.
1747, Dec. 17, Collins, Elizabeth and Timothy Thomas.
1797, Feb 16 , Collom, Benjamin and Martha Boucher.
1787, Dec. 13, Collom, Martha and Daniel Yerkes.
1791, Jul 21, Collum, Hannah and Joseph Dean.
1797, Sep 16, Coltman, Robert and Abigail Hathaway.
1721, Oct 24, Comely, Margaret and John Pares.
1789, May 7, Comely, Sarah and Isaac Wood.
1769, Nov 23, Comly, Benjamin and Elizabeth Dungan.
1768, Nov 3, Comly, Rebecca and James Vansandt.
1750, May 22, Commins, Robert and Mary Lindsey.
1788, Oct 28, Commons, Mary and Peter Turner.
1751, Dec. 24, Compton, Job and Susanna Potts.
1747, Feb 16, Conner, Edward and Ann Gallaugher.
1794, Dec. 2, Cooke, Mary, of Philadelphia and William Stewart.
1785, Dec. 22, Conrad, Jacob and Mary Glaws.
1726, Jan 25, Coste, Jacob and Ann Thomas.
1796, Feb 18, Coulston, Nathan and Jane Kennedy.
1735, Aug 6, Coursen, Cornelius and Ann Vanhorn.
1788, May 10, Cousty, Hugh and Nancy Jenkins.
1770, Nov 5, Cox, William and Sarah Wollard.
1789, May 19, Cravan, Giles and Anne McNair.
1768, Sep 23, Craven, Ann and Henry Brouse.
1775, Feb 16, Craven, James and Sarah Wynkoop.
1794, Mar 25, Craven, Thomas and Margaret Mann.
1793, Oct 3, Crawford, Anne and Joseph Fulton.
1721, Jan 6, Creed, John and Elizabeth White.
1741, Dec. 22, Crighton, Elizabeth and Collen McSwainey.
1742, Nov 11, Crocket, Jane and Jacob Bener.
1749, Aug 29, Crosley, John and Sarah Heaton.
1724, Nov 23, Cruisse, Nicholas and Mary Rowland.
1776, Jul 22, Cune, Michael and Christiana Kinneman.
1739, May 17, Curry, Mary and John Forster.
1752, June 15, Darby, John and Catherine Ross.
1791, Mar 3, Darrah, Archibald and Sarah Thompson.
1796, Aug 11, Darrough, Derick and Ann Mcdowell.
1794, May 23, Davidson, Robert and Hester Foster.
1786, Sep 19, Davies, Henry and Patty French.
1744, Dec. 6, Davies, Mary and Thomas Roney.
1785, Nov 23, Davies Rebecca and John Hamilton.
1787, Mar 28, Davies, William and Ann Landis.
1718, Oct 17, Davis, Edmund and Mary Folk.
1747, Apr 13, Davis, Elizabeth and Henry Vandyke.

1749, June 15, Davis, Hannah and Benjamin Vanhorn.
1761, Apr 21, Davis, John and Jane Smith.
1740, Sep 19, Davis, Nathaniel and Hannah Brock.
1747, June 11, Dary, Jane and David Morgan.
1738, Jul 7, Deal, Mary and James Clerk.
1791, Jul 21, Dean, Joseph and Hannah Collum.
1766, Jan 21, Dean, Sarah and John Slennoup.
1741, Dec. 2, DeCorsey, William and Hannah Jodon.
1767, Dec. 17, DeCorsey, Hannah and Jesse Jackson.
1718, Dec. 18, Deelbick, Isaac and Hoortsy Dunwik.
1743, Nov 3, Dewees, William and Rachel Huste.
1751, May 8, Dicke, John and Judah Saunders.
1799, Nov 14, Dickinson, Anna and Isaac Folwell.
1760, Apr 3, Dickson, Jane and Stephen Brown.
1747, Oct 29, Dickson, Martha and Adam Barkley.
1767, Jan 29, Dickson, Martha and Thomas Walker.
1759, Apr 3, Dicky, John and Mary Hessing.
1751, Jan 24, Dorland, Eve and John Brittin.
1753, Mar 8, Dorland, Isaac and Margaret Johnson.
1778, Sep 24, Dorland, Margaret and Casper Roch.
1735, Jan 1, Dorlandt, George and Catherine Whiteman.
1741, Oct 14, Dorlandt, Jacob and Ann Hewitt.
1753, May 16, Dubois, Elizabeth and Garret Newkirk.
1719, Apr 6, Ducket, George and Margaret Wallace.
1797, Aug 24, Dutfield, Elizabeth and Christopher Snyder.
1745, Aug 2, Dugdale, Mary and Alexander McGee.
1741, Dec. 3, Dunbar Andrew and Martha Kirton.
1770, Nov 13, Dunbar, Martha and Alexander Ramsey.
1798, Jan 19, Duncan, Mary and Nathaniel Boiliau, Jr.
1759, May 15, Dungan, Daniel and Sarah Hewit.
1769, Nov 23, Dungan, Elizabeth and Benjamin Comly.
1773, Feb 25, Dunlap, Samuel and Margaret Brown.
1763, Mar 31, Dunning, Elizabeth and Peter Storb.
1718, Dec. 18, Dunwik, Hoortsy and Isaac Deelbick.
1737, May 4, Dyer, Samuel and Hannah Briggs.
1791, Oct 22, Earl, Thomas and Parnel McVeagh, of Philadelphia.
1773, Mar 11, Eaton, Edward and Sarah Morgan.
1800, Mar 13, Edwards, John and Abigail Barnes.
1794, Dec. 18, Else, Jacob and Elizabeth Orr.
1743, May 28, Enoch, Gertrude and William Maxwell.
1758, Aug 26, Enoch, Jacamintie and Abraham Newkirk.
1747, Apr 16, Enoch, Joseph and Jemima Winkoop.
1747, Dec. 21, Enoch, Oliver and John Lawrence.

1770, Nov 15, Ervin, Samuel and Rebecca Leech.
1759, May 25, Erwin, Ann and John Gilky.
1754, May 1, Erwin, Margaret and John Vandyke.
1738, Nov 9, Evan, Judith and Herman Vansandt.
1747, June 9, Evan, Lewis and Margaret Humphreys.
1792, Apr 6. Evans, Elizabeth and Joseph Armstrong.
1753, May 15, Evans, Evans and Mary Watkin.
1799, June 3, Evans, Hannah and William Smith.
1775, Apr, 10, Evans, Levi and Susannah Burton.
1743, Aug 18, Evans, Mary and Benjamin Gilbert.
1744, Mar 29, Evans, Simon and Elizabeth Sloan.
1739, Sep 27, Evans, Thomas and Rebecca Harbour.
1720, Nov 29, Evans, William and Mary Baker.
1766, Apr 15, Fallowel, John and Elizabeth Billieu.
1767, Nov 3, Faries, Eleanor and William Ramsey.
1796, June 23, Fetters, George and Widow Hogland.
1776, Feb 1, Fetters, Mary and Andreas Vanbuskirk.
1744, Sep 26, Finley, Rev. Samuel and Sarah Hall.
1793, Dec. 5, Finney, Rachel and James Adams.
1793, Oct 14, Fisher, Elizabeth and Joseph Williams.
1750, Nov 29, Fisher, Sarah and Jacob Taylor.
1768, May 17, Flact, Robert and Mary Wier.
1770, Oct 4, Flack, Robert and Margaret Wilson.
1767, May 12, Fletcher, Elizabeth and Isaac Gardner.
1772, Oct 6, Fletcher, James and Margaret Breden.
1746, Jan 30, Fletcher, Robert and Mary Brown.
1796, Feb 25, Flintham, William and Elizabeth Oliphant.
1742, Dec. 21, Flore, Anne and George Sugden.
1718, Oct 17, Folk, Mary and Edmund Davis.
1794, Aug 11, Folkrod, Elizabeth and Henry Shock.
1799, Nov 14, Folwell, Isaac and Anna Dickinson.
1750, Dec. 4, Forbes, John and Elizabeth McCartel.
1739, May 17, Forster, John and Mary Curry.
1788, Nov 8, Forsyth, Jane and James Garvan.
1794, May 23, Foster, Hester and Robert Davidson.
1746 Nov 20, Foster, John and Jane Cambpell.
1798, Nov 29, Foster, Rebecca and Charles Johnson.
1800, May 27, Fowler, Sophia and Chillion Homer.
1786, Sep 19, ` French, Patty and Henry Davies.
1792, Nov 13, Fultimore, Jacob and Ann Wartenbey.
1762, Mar 30, Fulton, David, Sr. and Helena Wynkoop.
1768, Sep 8, Fulton, James and Sarah Vancourt.
1793, Oct 3, Fulton, Joseph and Anne Crawford.

1787, Jan 25, Fulton, Margaret and Cornelius Wynkoop.
1747, Feb 16, Gallaugher, Ann and Edward Conner.
1767, May 12, Garner, Isaac and Elizabeth Fletcher.
1788, Nov 8, Garvan, James and Jane Forsyth.
1744, Apr 17, Gibbs, Ann and Thomas Mule.
1756, Sep 9, Gibbs, Ann and John Mackey.
1743, Aug 18, Gilbert, Benjamin and Mary Evans.
1742, Dec. 23, Gilbert, Jacob and Hannah Carter.
1759, May 25, Gilky, John and Ann Erwin.
1722, Sep 2, Gillespy, Matthew and Lucy Pickin.
1759, Apr 28, Gissen, Tennant and Benjamin Paddin.
1750, May 15, Glaskow, Rachel and James Oglesby.
1785, Dec. 22, Glaws, Mary and Jacob Conrad.
1754, June 4, Glover, Mary and James Patterson.
1761, Mar 18, Gold, Margaret and William Miller.
1721, Jul 11, Gomery, Catherine and William Johnston.
1722, May 22, Gooldin, Samuel and Elizabeth Hilsewick.
1796 Jul 15, Gore, Elizabeth and John Royal.
1750, June 14, Gould, Michael and Martha Chambers.
1750, May 2, Grant, Mary and Cornelius Vandyke.
1765, Mar 11, Gray, Dorcas and James Huton.
1799, Dec. 16, Graydon, Alexander and Theodosia Pettit.
1770, June 7, Green, Rev. Enoch and Mary Beatty.
1742, Nov 1, Green, Mary and Edward Bown.
1768, Dec. 6, Grier, Martha and John Jamison.
1768, Apr 7, Grissy, Benjamin and Margaret Patterson.
1735, Aug 6, Gwin, Hannah and Joshua Jones.
1744, Sep 26, Hall, Sarah and Rev. Samuel Finley.
1785, Nov 23, Hambleton, John and Rebecca Davies.
1786, Mar 29, Hamilton, Elizabeth and Thomas Bradey.
1739, Sep 27, Harbour, Rebecca and Thomas Evans.
1760, Nov 4, Harden, Charles and Jane Stewart.
1777, Jan 23, Harmer, John and Rosanna Riderpage.
1739, Apr 9 Harper, John and Martha Brittin.
1739, Apr 3, Hart, Hannah and William Wilson.
1787, Aug 1, Harvey, Jane and Andrew Baxter.
1797, Jan 14, Harvey, Sarah and James Butler.
1797, Sep 18, Hathaway, Abigail and Robert Coltman.
1796, Jan 19, Hawkins, Issac and Polly Walton.
1747, May 26, Hayes, James and Mary Scott.
1799, Feb 11, Heath Andrew and Barbary Tyson.
1749, Aug 29, Heaton, Sarah and John Crosley.
1762, Dec. 9, Helveston, Christinia and Jonathan Clift.

1763, Mar 3, Helviston, Margaret and Nicholas Marrchar.
1761, Mar 13, Hervey, John and Jane Snodgrass.
1787, May 9, Hervey, Mary and Joseph Prichet.
1759, Apr 3, Hessing, Mary and John Dicky.
1759, May 15, Hewit, Sarah and Daniel Dungan.
1741, Oct 14, Hewitt, Ann and Jacob Dorlandt.
1787, Sep 17, Hill, Moses and Elizabeth Randall.
1722, May 22, Hilsewick, Elizabeth and Samuel Gooldin.
1753, Dec. 13, Hoey, Eleanor and Joshua Thomas.
1754, Jul 27, Hoey, John and Jane Morrison.
1767, Jul 3, Hogeland, George and Mary Wynkoop.
1787, Aug 2, Hogeland, Henry and Rebecca Wynkoop.
1796, June 23, Hogland, Widow and George Fetters.
1774, June 28, Hollis, Abraham and Martha Riche.
1787, Aug 21, Holmes, Charity and Neff Isaac.
1794, Jan 2, Holt, Charles and Elizabeth Carter.
1800, May 27, Homer, Chillion and Sophia Fowler.
1794, Apr 7, Horning, Lewis and Polly Baker.
1746, Mar 27, Honey, Abraham and Elizabeth Patten.
1789, May 1, Honey, Joseph and Eleanor Charleton.
1778, Aug 6, Houston, Thomas and Elizabeth Bradford.
1790, Jan 4, Howel, Dr. Ebenezer and Lydia Tukniss.
1773, Feb 25, Howey, Ann and John Stewart.
1794, Sep 4, Hubbs, Dorothy and Alexander McCalla.
1749, Oct 2, Hueston, William and Mary McDowel.
1737, Mar 17, Huste, Catharina and Joseph Laughlin.
1743, Nov 3, Huste, Rachel and William Dewees.
1736, May 27, Huste, Sarah and Christopher Carter.
1747, Jan 17, Huggins, John and Elizabeth Brown.
1798, Apr 5, Hughes, James and Jane McFadden.
1747, June 9, Humphreys, Margaret and Lewis Evan.
1793, Dec. 2, Hunter, Jane and John Stewart.
1726, Jan 17, Huntsman, John and Elizabeth Ackly.
1765, Mar 11, Hunton, James and Dorcas Gray.
1721, June 15, Incomb, James and Grace Jacoby.
1736, Mar 26, Inyard, Elizabeth and John Jackson.
1767, Dec. 17, Jackson, Isaac and Hannah DeCorsy.
1736, Mar 26, Jackson, John and Elizabeth Inyard.
1741, Nov 5, Jackson, Rebecca and Henry Kollum.
1798, Feb 1, Jacobs, Catharine and John McCrea.
1721, May 5, Jacoby, Grace and James Incomb.
1799, Jul 4, Jacoby, Wickard and Rachel Ottinger.
1796, Feb 8, James, John, of Philadelphia and Polly Ramsey.

1768, Dec. 6, Jamison, John and Martha Grier.
1795, Nov 19, Jenkins, Mary and John Ross.
1788, Jul 10, Jenkins, Nancy and Hugh Cousty.
1796, Sep 8, Jenkins, Priscilla and Isaac Kirk.
1752, Apr 7, Jennings, James and Catherine Quee.
1741, Dec. 2, Jodon, Hannah and William DeCorsey.
1767, Dec. 30, Johnson, Alexander and Mary Speir.
1770, Jan 11, Johnson, Catherine and John Watkins.
1798, Nov 29, Johnson, Charles and Rebecca Foster.
1721, Jul 17, Johnson, Jane and Clements Terry.
1741, Nov 12, Johnson, John and Elizabeth Jones.
1753, Mar 8, Johnson, Margaret and Isaac Dorland.
1720, Oct 25, Johnston, Grace and John Wosely.
1721, Jul 11, Johnston, William and Catherina Gomery.
1770, Jan 4, Jones, Eleazor and Rebecca Stirk.
1793, Apr 22, Jones, Eleazor and Sarah Shaw.
1741, Nov 12, Jones, Elizabeth and John Johnson.
1772, Feb 13, Jones, Elizabeth and Jacob Billieu.
1733, Jan 5, Jones, Evan and Mary Bowen.
1763, May 8, Jones, Jacob and Sarah Tomkins.
1735, Aug 6, Jones, Joshua and Hannah Gwin.
1756, Jul 8, Jones, Martha and Simon Thomas.
1761, Jan 20, Jones, Mary and James Middleton.
1793, Feb 8, Jones, Peter and Sarah Anderson.
1792, Jan 10, Keiser, Kitty and Frederick Boullange.
1766, May 19, Keiser, Rachel and William Long.
1772, Dec. 10, Kelly, Elizabeth and George Thomas.
1754, Nov 26, Kelsey, George and Jane Carr.
1762, Nov 18, Kenderdine, Rachel and William Lukens.
1760, Mar 31, Kennedy, Jane and William McIntyre.
1796, Feb 18, Kennedy, Jane and Nathan Coulston.
1740, Oct 7 Kennedy, Mary and John Mclaughlin.
1792, Oct 8, Kennedy, Robert and Jane Mcalla.
1793, Apr 4, Kerr, Elizabeth and James Major.
1761, Mar 31, Kerr, Margaret and Thomas McCune.
1752, Dec. 5, Kerson, Sarah and William Morrey.
1791, Dec. 8, Kidd, Hannah and Benjamin Mershon.
1789, Oct 13, Kidd, Jane and Nathaniel Bannister.
1773, Apr 6, Kinnard, Hester and John Purnel.
1776, Jul 22, Kinneman, Christiana and Michael Cune.
1796, Sep 8, Kirk, Isaac and Priscilla Jenkins.
1787, Jan 18, Kirk, John and Mary Carvar.
1787, Jul 5, Kirk, Joseph and Grace Child

1794, Nov 3, Kirkpatrick, Francis and Margaret Bur.
1741, Dec. 3, Kirton, Martha and Andrew Dunbar.
1796, Sep 4, Knox, Mary and David McNeely.
1800, Apr 6, Knox, Robert and Margaret McNeely.
1741, Nov 5, Kollum, Henry and Rebecca Jackson.
1793, Nov 23, Kroisen, John and Jane Vanartsalen.
1787, Mar 28, Landis, Ann and William Davis.
1794, June 14, Lane, Timothy and Mary Boyd.
1798, Mar 7, Lang, John and Anna Mann.
1769, Feb 16, Larue, Abraham and Elizabeth Praul.
1743, Oct 6, LaRue, Isaac and Rebecca Vansandt.
1738, Jan 17, Lattimer, Martha and Samuel Lockhart.
1737, Mar 17, Laughlin, Joseph and Catherine Huste.
1747, Dec. 21, Lawrence, John and Olive Enoch.
1758, June 6, Leadley, Mary and Thomas Miller.
1795, June 8, Leech, Hetty and Nathaniel Boiliau.
1777, Mar 11, Leech, Mary and Archibald McClean.
1770, Nov 15, Leech, Rebecca and Samuel Ervin.
1768, Feb 18, Leech, Samuel and Anne Stewart.
1724, Apr 30, Lewis, Thomas and Mary Waters.
1769, Mar 14, Lidiard, Thomas and Esther Scott.
1792, Oct 15, Likens, Hester and Daniel Yerkess.
1750, May 22, Lindsay, Mary and Robert Cummins.
1769, Nov 14, Lockart, Martha and William McKee.
1757, Aug 25, Lockert, Agnes and Collen McSwiney.
1757, Apr 12, Lockert, David and Mary Richard.
1767, Nov 12, Lockert, Mary and William Reyel.
1738, Jan 17, Lockhart, Samuel and Martha Lattimer.
1722, Apr 3, Logan, George and Jane Bell.
1766, May 19, Long, William and Rachel Billieu.
1742, Dec. 23, Loosborough, Margaret and David Rees.
1773, Apr 13, Lough, John and Elizabeth Speedy, (widow).
1768, Oct 20, Love, Benjamin and Eleanor McDowel.
1756, Apr 19, Lovsberry, Hannah and Nathan Spencer.
1739, Jan 16, Low, Mary and William Brown.
1795, Jul 26, Luken, Margaret and Jonathan Clayton.
1755, Sep 10, Lukens, Benjamin and Alice Cadwalader.
1787, Feb 20, Lukens, Peter and Mary Barns.
1762, Nov 18, Lukens, William and Rachel Kenderine.
1793, Dec. 7, Lusley, David and Margaret Morrar.
1771, May 14, Lykins, Jonathan and Susanna Watkins.
1746, Aug 19, Lyle, Daniel and Jane Roberts.
1794, Sep 4, McCalla, Alexander and Dorothy Hubbs.

1796, Jan 12, McCalla, Elizabeth and William Mann.
1792, Oct 8, McCalla, Jane and Robert Kennedy.
1761, Jan 8, McCalla, Robert and Ruth Morrey.
1750, Dec. 4, McCartel, Elizabeth and John Forbes.
1758, Apr 10, McClaine, Mary and John Brown.
1759, Mar 29, McClean, Archibald and Ann Trump.
1771, June 11, McClean, Archibald, Jr. and Ann Charlesworth.
1777, Mar 11, McClean, Archibald and Mary Leech.
1785, Dec. 13, McClean, Elizabeth and Jacob Styer.
1761, June 9, McClean, Joseph and Rachel Wood.
1763, Apr 14, McClean, Moses and Sarah Charlesworth.
1760, Mar 4, McClean, William and Rebecca Charlesworth.
1791, Aug 10, McClean, Joseph and Ann Thompson.
1748, Feb 2, McCrea, James and Ann Ross.
1798, Feb 1, McCrea, John and Catharine Jacobs.
1761, Mar 13, McCune, Thomas and Margaret Kerr.
1772, Jan 23, McDowel, Alexander and Ann Wyley.
1776, Nov 5, McDowel, Alexander and Margaret Major.
1768, Oct 20, McDowel, Eleanor and Benjamin Love.
1796, Aug 11, McDowel, Ann and Derrick Darrough.
1773, Dec. 23, McDowel, James and Mary Scoute.
1762, Apr 6, McDowel, Margaret and Isaac Wood.
1749, Oct 2, McDowel, Mary and William Hueston.
1748, Jan 5, McDowel, Robert and Elizabeth Scott.
1798, Apr 5, McFadden, Jane and James Hughes.
1792, Mar 6, McFarlane, Mary and David Todd.
1745, Aug 2, McGee, Alexander and Mary Dugdale.
1790, Dec. 30, McGee, Saxerty and Rachel Cadwallader.
1765, Dec. 31, McGlaughlin, Elizabeth and John Mann.
1740, Oct 7, McGlaughlin, John and Mary Kennedy.
1760, Mar 31, McIntire, William and Jane Kennedy.
1742, Dec. 17, McKarte, Margaret and Henry Breese.
1758, Aug 10, McKee, Agnes and John Thompson.
1752, Jan 16, McKee, Susannah and William Settlington.
1769, Nov 14, McKee, William and Martha Lockart.
1738, May 9, McKelvie, John and Mary Wilson.
1789, May 19, McNair, Anne and Giles, Cravan.
1796, Sep 4, McNeely, David and Mary Knox.
1800 Apr 6, McNeely, Margaret and Robert Knox.
1789, Mar 17, McPharland, Margaret and Stephen Porter.
1741, Dec. 22, McSwainey, Colle and Elizabeth Crighton.
1775, Apr 4, McSwiney, Ann and William Brown.
1757, Aug 25, McSwiney, Collin and Agnes Lockert.

1777, Jan 7, McSwiney, Elizabeth and William Wood.
1773, Feb 4, McSwiney, John and Rachel Billieu.
1777, Apr 22, McSwiney, John and Susanna Breden.
1776, Apr 4, McSwiney, Margaret and James Mathers.
1791, Oct 22, McVeagh, Parnel of Philadephia and Thomas Earl.
1723, Dec. 26, Mackenzie, Henry and Mary Bredin.
1768, Apr 28, Mackey Andrew and Mary Murray.
1756, Sep 9, Mackey, John and Ann Gibbs.
1793, Apr 29, Macklewain, James and Agnes White.
1794, Mar 12, Madary, George and Nancy Millar.
1789, Apr 12, Major, Ebenezer and Mary Shirley.
1793, Apr 4, Major, James and Elizabeth Kerr.
1791, Aug 25, Major, Jane and Samuel White.
1776, Nov 5, Major, Margaret and Alexander McDowel.
1777, May 7, Major, Mary and John Barnie.
1798, Mar 7, Mann, Anna and John Lang.
1765, Dec. 31, Mann, John and Elizabeth McGlaughlin.
1794, Mar 25, Mann, Margaret and Thomas Craven.
1796, Jan 12, Mann, William and Elizabeth McCalla.
1763, Mar 3, Marschar, Nicholas and Margaret Helviston.
1726, Aug 15, Marshall, Moris and Sarah Valentin.
1764, Nov 7, Mason, John and Sarah Brown.
1776, Apr 4, Mathers, James and Margaret McSwiney.
1795, Apr 18, Matthews, Catherine and Daniel Winsley.
1798, Oct 20, Matthews, John and Mary Ann Blewt.
1743, May 28, Maxwell, William and Gertrude Enoch.
1793, Mar 27, Mayer, Peggy and Anthony Benezet.
1725, Mar 18, Meese, Margaret and Richard Brontel.
1800, May 29, Megargle, Rebecca and John Caskey.
1789, Jan 21, Mershan, Stephen and Martha Nixon.
1791, Dec. 8, Mershon, Benjamin and Hannah Kidd.
1798, Nov 22, Middleton, Hannah and Samuel Thatcher.
1761, Jan 20, Middleton, James and Mary Jones.
1732, Aug 13, Midkast, Sarah and Dennis Bryan.
1742, Apr 19, Midlack, Jerimiah and Elizabeth White.
1751, Feb 14, Miles, Ann and Samuel Thomas.
1794, Mar 12, Miller, Nancy and George Madary.
1795, Aug 20, Miller, Elizabeth and Abiatha Walton.
1758, June 6, Miller, Thomas and Mary Leadley.
1761, Mar 18, Miller, William and Margaret Gold.
1736, Mar 4, Milner, Joist Arian and Christiana Vandergrist.
1756, Feb 3, Mitchel, Elizabeth and Charles Weer.
1766, Dec. 25, Mitchenor, Thomas and Ann Billieu.

1745, Mar 14, Moore, Ann and Samuel Brown.
1791, Dec. 29, Morford, Mary and William Morgan.
1773, Mar 11, Morgan, Sarah and Edward Eaton.
1791, Dec. 29, Morgan, William and Mary Morford.
1747, June 11, Morgan, David and Jane Davy.
1793, Dec. 7, Morrar, Margaret and David Lusley.
1762, June 2, Morrey, Hannah and Simon Brant.
1735, May 15, Morrey, James and Elizabeth Barns.
1761, Jan 8, Morrey, Ruth and Robert McCalla.
1752, Dec. 5, Morrey, William and Sarah Kerson.
1754, Jul 27, Morrison, Jane and John Hoey.
1768, Nov 29, Mucklehouse, Samuel and Hannah Watkins.
1744, Apr 17, Mule, Thomas and Ann Gibbs.
1768, Apr 28, Murray, Mary and Andrew Mackey.
1773, Nov 11 , Murray, Samuel and Barbara Woolman.
1787, Aug 21, Neff, Isaac and Charity Holmes.
1764, Jan 17, Nesmith, John and Margaret Yerkus.
1758,Aug 26, Newkirk, Abram and Jacamintie Enoch.
1753, May 16, Newkirk, Garret and Elizabeth Dubois.
1763, Jul 28, Nimmin, George and Jane Adams.
1789, Jan 21, Nixon, Martha and Stephen Mershan.
1750, May 15 , Ogleby, James and Rachel Glaskow.
1796, Feb 25, Oliphant, Elizabeth and William Flintham.
1791, Jan 25, Orham, Jonathan and Laetitia Whartenby.
1794, Dec. 18, Orr, Elizabeth and Jacob Else.
1796, Nov 17, Ott, Margaret and Abraham Blake.
1799, Jul 4, Ottinger, Rachel and Wickard Jacoby.
1749, Apr 4 Owens, Hannah and David Todd.
1759, Apr 8, Paddin, Benjamin and Tennant Gissen.
1721, Oct 24, Pare, John and Margaret Comely.
1748, May Parker, Benjamin and Mary Brittin.
1780,Mar 16, Parker, Robert and Elizabeth Porter.
1748, May 26, Parker, William and Elizabeth Todd.
1776, Mar 28, Patrick, George and Elizabeth Rush.
1746, Mar 27, Patten, Elizabeth and Abraham Honey.
1754, June 4, Patterson, James and Mary Glover.
1760, Apr 28, Patterson., John and Sarah Wilson.
1800, Feb 8, Patterson, John and Martha Stewart.
1768, Apr 7, Patterson, Margaret and Benjamin Grissey.
1743, Jan 19, Paxton, Elizabeth and Joseph Boone.
1772, Dec. 8, Pennington, Charles and Mary Bener.
1724, Jan 2, Perick, Elizabeth and Robert Pock.
1776, May 5, Pekey, Mary and Archibald Wilson.

1799, Dec. 16, Pettit, Theodosia and Alexander Graydon.
1750, June 19, Phillips, Ephraim and Elizabeth Titus.
1799, May 2, Phillips, Nathan and Phebe Coffin.
1722, Sep 2, Pickin, Lucy and Matthew Gillespy.
1791, Oct 22, Pinkerton, John and Jane Thompson, of Philadelphia.
1724, Jan 2, Pock, Robert and Elizabeth Perick.
1789, Mar 16, Porter, Elizabeth and Robert Parker.
1791, Mar 28, Porter, Polly and Robert Porter.
1791, Mar 28, Porter, Robert and Polly Porter.
1789, Mar 17, Porter, Stephen and Margaret McPharland.
1751, Dec. 24, Potts, Susannah and Job Compton.
1733, Apr 3, Pratt, Jeremiah and Mary Watkins.
1769, Feb 16, Praul, Elizabeth and Abraham Larue.
1760, Nov 6, Praul, John and Mary Ridge.
1750, Nov 14, Praul, Mary and John Vandergrist.
1737, Apr 21, Praul, Peter and Elizabeth Vanhorn.
1741, Nov 11, Price, Mary and David Summerel.
1787, May 9, Pritchet, Joseph and Mary Hervey.
1793, Nov 21, Purdy, Mary and Joseph Yerkes.
1773, Apr 6, Purnel, John and Hester Kinnard.
1752, Apr 7, Quee, Catherine and James Jennings.
1770, Nov 13, Ramsey, Alexander and Martha Dunbar.
1796, Feb 8, Ramsey, Polly and John James, of Philadelphia.
1767, Nov 3, Ramsey, William and Eleanor Faries.
1789, Sep 17, Randell, Elizabeth and Moses Hill.
1722, Nov -- , Rear, Jane and Christopher Vanlaer.
1742, Dec. 23, Rees, David and Margaret Boosborough.
1767, Nov 12, Reyel,William and Mary Lockert.
1797, Sep 1, Reynold, Joseph and Hannah Toland.
1757, Apr 12, Richard, Mary and David Lockert.
1799, Mar 28, Richards, George and Sarah Roberts.
1774, June 28, Riche, Martha and Abraham Hollis.
1744, Nov 22, Richey, Mary and James Boyd.
1777, Jan 23, Riderpage, Rosanna and John Harmer.
1760, Nov 6, Ridge, Mary and John Praul.
1746, Aug 19, Roberts, Jane and Daniel Lyle.
1736, Oct 28, Roberts, Jonathan and Sarah Titus.
1799, Mar 28, Roberts, Sarah and George Richards.
1761, Dec. 19, Robertson, Robert and Margaret Sowders.
1799, June 13, Robinson, James and Eliza. Wild, of Philadelphia.
1778, Sep 24, Roch, Casper and Margaret Dorland.
1754, June 20, Rogers, Eleanor and Alexander Trimble.
1774, Dec. 6, Roney, Thomas and Mary Davies.

1748,Feb 2, Ross, Ann and James McCrea.

1752, June 25, Ross, Catherine, and John Darby.

1795, Nov 19, Ross, John and Mary Jenkins.

1721, Nov 28, Rowland, Mary and Nicholas Cruisse.

1796, Jul 15, Royal, John and Elizabeth Gore.

1722, June 6, Ruchi, John and Frances Boyd.

1735, Jan 9, Rue, Richard and Jane Vandyke.

1776, Mar 28, Rush, Elizabeth and George Patrick.

1775, Mar 21, Ryderpage, Elizabeth and Henry Bickley.

1751, May 8, Saunders, Judith and John Dicke.

1748, Jan 5, Scott, Elizabeth and Robert McDowel.

1769, Mar 14, Scott, Esther and Thomas Lidiard.

1775, Nov 12, Scott, Margaret and Herman Yerkes.

1747, May 26, Scott, Mary and James Hayes.

1773, Dec. 23, Scoute, Mary and James McDowel.

1752, Jan 16, Settlington, William and Margaret McKee.

1766, Feb 19, Severns, Joseph and Olive Titus.

1768, May 17, Severns, Mary and William Titus.

1793, Apr 22, Shaw, Sarah and Eleazer Jones.

1767, Sep 24, Shippen, Susanna and Rev. Samuel Blair.

1789, Apr 12, Shirley, Mary and Ebenezer Major.

1794, Aug 11, Shock, Henry and Elizabeth Folkrod.

1786, Nov 3, Shoemaker, Peter and Elizabeth Spencer.

1788, Apr 22, Siddons, Deborah and William Tyson.

1789, Apr 30, Siddons, Samuel and Fanny Brooks.

1760, Oct 8, Simons, Andrew and Anna West.

1743, June 2, Slaght, Catherine and George Van Pelt.

1766, Jan 21, Slennoup, John and Sarah Dean.

1744, Mar 29, Sloan, Elizabeth and Simon Evans.

1770, Apr 10, Smith, Catherine and Thomas Wilson.

1795, May 9, Smith, Eliza and James Spencer, Jr.

1799, Dec. 5, Smith, Hannah and John Baker.

1761, Apr 21, Smith, Jane and John Davis

1799, June 3, Smith, William and Hannah Evans.

1759, Nov 12, Snodgrass, James and Ann Wilson.

1761, Mar 13, Snodgrass, Jane and John Hervey.

1791, Dec. 1. Snyder, Christian and Sarah Bennet.

1797, Aug 24, Snyder, Christopher and Elizabeth Duffield.

1761, Dec. 19, Sowders, Margaret and Robert Robertson.

1773, Apr 13, Speedy, Elizabeth and John Lough.

1767, Dec. 30, Speir, Mary and Alexander Johnson.

1786, Nov 3, Spencer, Elizabeth and Peter Shoemaker.

1795, May 9, Spencer, James and Eliza. Smith.

1756, Apr 19, Spencer, Nathan and Hannah Lovsberry.

1743, Jan 11, [Spiner,] Barbara Baltes and Enoch Armitage.

1794, Jan 16, Stephenson, Nancy and Hugh Terrance.

1767, Sep 1, Stevens, Mary and Gunning Bedford.

1768, Feb 18, Stewart, Anne and Samuel Leech.

1760, Nov 4, Stewart, Jane and Charles Harden.

1773, Feb 25, Stewart, John and Anne Howey.

1793, Dec. 2, Stewart, John and Jane Hunter.

1800, Feb 8, Stewart, Martha and John Patterson.

1794, Dec. 2, Stewart, William and Mary Cooke, of Philadelphia.

1770, Jan 4, Stirk, Rebecca and Eleazer Jones.

1722, Oct 24, Stoll, Mary and Henry Van Leuvenig.

1763, Mar 31, Storb, Peter and Margaret Dunning.

1766, Jan 20, Strecker, Mary and Caleb Armstrong.

1796, Oct 26, Strickland, Amos and Rebecca Baskirk.

1785, Dec. 13, Styer, Jacob and Elizabeth McClean.

1742, Dec. 21, Sugden, George and Anne Florey.

1741, Nov 11, Summerel, David and Mary Price.

1750, Nov 29, Taylor, Jacob and Sarah Fisher.

1797, Feb 23, Taylor, Malachi and Sally Worrell.

1794, Jan 16, Terrance, Hugh and Nancy Stephenson.

1721, Jul 17, Terry, Clement and Jane Johnson.

1798, Nov 22, Thatcher, Samuel and Hannah Middleton.

1726, Jan 25, Thomas, Ann and Jacob Coste.

1787, Nov 1, Thomas, Elizabeth and David Yerkess.

1772, Dec. 10, Thomas, George and Elizabeth Kelly.

1797, Aug 2, Thomas, Hannah and Jacob Achuff.

1753 Dec. 13, Thomas, Joshua and Eleanor Hoey.

1744, Mar 1, Thomas, Richard and Mary Clark.

1751, Feb 14, Thomas, Samuel and Ann Miles.

1756, Jul 3, Thomas, Simon and Martha Jones.

1747, Dec. 13, Thomas, Timothy and Elizabeth Collins.

1791, Aug 10, Thompson, Ann and Joseph McClelan.

1791, Oct 22, Thompson, Jane, of Philadelphia and John Pinkerton.

1791, Mar 3, Thompson, Sarah and Archibald Darrah.

1758, Aug 10, Thomson, John and Agnes McKee.

1797, Feb 29, Timbrel, Martha and Jonathan Ashton.

1750, June 19, Titus, Elizabeth and Ephraim Phillips.

1764, Jan 26, Titus, Francis and Margaret Wynekoope.

1767, Feb 19, Titus, Olive and Joseph Severns.

1736, Oct 28, Titus, Sarah and Jonathan Roberts.

1768, May 17, Titus, William and Mary Severns.

1749, Apr 4, Todd, David and Hannah Owens.

1792, Mar 6, Todd, David and Mary McFarlane.

1748, May 26, Todd, Elizabeth and William Parker.

1724, Mar 28, Todd, John and Judith Bredin.

1796, Sep 1, Toland, Hannah and Joseph Reynold.

1763, May 3, Tomkins, Sarah and Jacob Jones.

1716, Oct 23, Touley, Choyes and Jacob Vandegret.

1742, May 3, Towers, Mary and George Watson.

1754, June 20, Trimble, Alexander and Eleanor Rogers.

1736, Mar 12, Trout, John and Margaret Bowen.

1759, Mar 29, Trump , Ann and Archibald McClean.

1790, Jan 4, Tukniss, Lydia and Dr. Ebenezer Howel.

1788, Oct 28, Turner, Peter and Mary Commons.

1799, Feb 11, Tyson, Barbary and Andrew Heath.

1798, Dec. 20, Tyson, Widow Mary and Robert Wilson.

1788, Apr 22, Tyson, William and Deborah Siddons.

1716, Oct 17, Un---------, Maria and Abraham Vandigrist.

1726, Aug 15, Valentine, Sarah and Morris Marshall.

1793, Nov 23, Vanartsalen, Jane and John Kroisen.

1776, Feb 1, Vanbuskirk Andreas and Mary Fetters.

1768, Sep 8, Vancount, Sarah and James Fulton.

1800, Jul 23, Vancount, Sarah and John Webster.

1716, Oct 23, Vandegret, Jacob and Choyes Touley.

1716, Oct 17, Vandigrist, Abraham and Maria Un-----.

1736, Mar 4, Vandegrist, Christiana and Joist Arian Milner.

1721, May 5, Vandegrist, John and Hannah Backer.

1750, Nov 14, Vandegrist, John and Mary Praul.

1719, May 6, Vandegrist, Valheit and Elizabeth Vansand.

1750, May 2, Vandyke, Cornelius and Mary Grant.

1745, Oct 3, Vandyke, Elizabeth and Hugh Barclay.

1747, Apr 13, Vandyke, Henry and Elizabeth Davis.

1735, Jan 9, Vandyke, Jane and Richard Rue.

1754, May 1, Vandyke, John and Margaret Erwin.

1735, Aug 6, Vanhorn, Ann and Cornelius Coursen.

1749, June 15, Vanhorn, Benjamin and Hannah Davis.

1737, Apr 21, Vanhorn, Elizabeth and Peter Praul.

1793, Mar 28, Vanhorn, Nancy and Garret Wynkoop.

1768, Apr 14, Vanhorn, Peter and Pricilla Von Buskark.

1791, Jan 20, Vanhorne, Catharine and Philip Wynkoop.

1722, Nov Vanlaer, Christopher and Jane Rear.

1722, Oct 24, Van Lenvenig, Henry and Mary Stoll.

1742, Feb 4, Van Pelt, Derick and Mary Britton.

1743, June 2, Van Pelt, George and Catharine Slaught.

1719, May 6, Vansand, Elizabeth and Valheit Vandegrist.

1744, May 18, Vansand, Nicholas and Mary Brittin.
1768, Jan 28, Vansand, Rebecca and Daniel Billieu.
1738, Nov 9, Vansandt, Harman and Judith Evan.
1768, Nov 3, Vansandt, James and Rebecca Comly.
1743, Oct 6, Vansandt, Rebecca and Isaac LaRue.
1761, Jan 22, Von Buskark Andrew and Rebecca Wynkoop.
1768, Apr 14, Von Buskark, Priscilla and Peter Vanhorn.
1775, Nov 24, Walker, Elizabeth and John Adams.
1789 Oct 23, Walker, Samuel and Margret, Adams.
1767, Jan 29, Walker, Thomas and Martha Dickson.
1719, Apr 6, Wallace, Margaret and George Ducket.
1795, Aug 26, Walton, Abiathar and Elizabeth Miller.
1796, Jan 19, Walton, Polly and Isaac Hawkins.
1792, Nov 13, Wartenbey, Ann and Jacob Fultimore.
1733, Jul 4, Waters, Margaret and David Cameron.
1724, Apr 30, Waters, mary and Thomas Lewis.
1733, Apr 3, Watkin, Mary and Jeremiah Pratt.
1753, May 15, Watkin, Mary and Evan Evans.
1768, Nov 29, Watkins, Hannah and Samuel Mucklehouse.
1770, Jan 11, Watkins, John and Catherine Johnson.
1771, May 14, Watkins, Susanna and Jonathan Lykins.
1788, Jul 27, Watson, Charles and Mary Wetherill.
1742, May 3, Watson, George and Mary Towers.
1737, June 9, Watts, Ann and Lewis Williams.
1800, Jul 23, Webster, John and Sarah Vancourt.
1756, Feb 3, Weer, Charles and Elizabeth Mitchel.
1760, Aug 22, Wells, Ann and Nathaniel Wilson.
1760, Oct 8, West, Anna and Andrew Simson.
1788, Jul 27, Wetherill, Mary and Charles Watson.
1791, Jan 25, Whartenby, Laetitia and Jonathan Orham.
1793, Apr 29, White, Agnes and James Macklewain.
1742, Apr 19, White, Elizabeth and Jeremiah Midlack.
1721, Jan 6, White, Elizabeth and John Creed.
1791, Aug 25, White, Samuel and Jane Major.
1735, Jan 1, Whiteman, Catherine and George Dorlandt.
1768, May 17, Wier, Mary and Robert Flact.
1799, June 13, Wild, Eliza., of Philadelphia and James Robinson.
1793, Oct 14, Williams, Joseph and Elizabeth Fisher.
1737, June 9, Williams, Lewis and Ann Watts.
1759, Nov 12, Wilson, Ann and James Snodgrass.
1776, May 5, Wilson, Archibald and Mary Pekey.
1770, Oct 4, Wilson, Margaret and Robert Flack.
1738, May 9, Wilson, Mary and John McKell.

1760, Aug 22, Wilson, Nathaniel and Ann Wells.
1777, Nov 6, Wilson, Priscilla and Samuel Barns.
1798, Dec. 20, Wilson, Robert and widow, Mary Tyson.
1760, Apr 28, Wilson, Sarah and John Patterson.
1770, Apr 10 Wilson, Thomas and Catherine Smith.
1739, Apr 3, Wilson, William and Hannah Hart.
1777, Aug 21, Wilson, William and Sarah Billieu.
1718, June 27, Winecook, Jacaminca and Joseph Buskark.
1747, Apr 16, Winkook, Jemema and Joseph Enoch.
1795, Apr, 18, Winsly, Daniel and Catherine Matthews.
1754, Mar 21, Wood, Elizabeth and John Burk.
1762, Apr 6, Wood, Isaac and Margaret McDowel.
1789, May 7, Wood, Isaac and Sarah Comely.
1749, Dec. 19, Wood, Mary and John Charlesworth.
1767, Dec. 24, Wood, Priscilla and Daniel Billieu, Sr.
1761, June 9, Wood, Rachel and Joseph Wood.
1762, Sep 20, Wood, William and Margaret Beyce.
1777, Jan 7, Wood, William and Elizabeth McSwiney.
1773, Nov 11, Woolman, Barbara and Samuel Murray.
1798, Apr 10, Worrell, Dennis and Alice Yerkes.
1797, Feb 23, Worrell, Sally and Malachi Taylor.
1720, Oct 25, Wosely, John and Grace Johnston.
1798, Oct 2, Wright, Samuel and Elizabeth Armitage.
1772, Jan 23, Wyley, Ann and Alexander McDowel.
1764, Jan 26, Wynekoope, Margaret and Francis Titus.
1775, Apr 10, Wynkoop, Cornelius and Hannah Brown.
1787, Jan 25, Wynkoop, Cornelius and Margaret Fulton.
1793, Mar 28, Wynkoop, Garret and Nancy Vanhorn.
1762, Mar 30, Wynkoop, Helena and David Fulton, Sr.
1767, Jul 3, Wynkoop, Mary and George Hogeland.
1791, Jan 20, Wynkoop, Philip and Cathaerine Vanhorne.
1761, Jan 22, Wynkoop, Rebecca and Andrew Von Buskark.
1787, Aug 2, Wynkoop, Rebecca and Henry Hogeland.
1775, Feb 16, Wynkoop, Sarah and James Craven.
1798, Apr 10, Yerkes, Alice and Dennis Worrell.
1775, Nov 12, Yekes, Herman and Margaret Scott.
1793, Nov 24, Yerkes, Joseph and Mary Purdy.
1787, Dec. 13, Yerkess, Daniel and Martha Collom.
1792, Oct 15, Yerkes, Daniel and Hester Likens.
1787, Nov 1, Yerkess, Daniel and Elizabeth Thomas.
1764, Jan 17, Yerkus, Margaret and John Nesmith.

AUGUSTUS EV. LUTHERAN CHURCH, TRAPPE

Marriages (Rev. Johann Caspar Stoever)

Raush, Daniel and Opdografsin, Elisabeth md. March 18, 1730.

Sebastia, Andreas and Krausin, Elisabeth md. April 27, 1730.

Bergheimer, Johan Caspar and Hauserin, Elisabeth Catharina md. October 20, 1730.

Müller, Johan Jacob and Hartmannin, Anna Maria Appolonia md. February 12, 1731.

Geelwichs, Friedrich Heinrich and Bulerin, Anna Dorothea md. April 10, 1733.

Beyer, Andreas and Bergheimerin, Susanna Catharina, md. July 1, ?.

Kohl, Johan Georg and Beerin, Barbara md. January 8, 1734.

Amborn, Christoph and Klauerin, Susanna md. May 21, 1734

Corper, Nicolaus and Marstellerin, Anna Margretha, md. December 3, 1734.

Wertz, Jacob and Hofin, (?) Anna Barbara md. December 29, 1734.

Bien, David and Tabernien, Elisabetha, md. January 10, 1735.

Crösmann, John George and Schrakken, Eva Barbara, eldest dau. of Hans Jacob and Euphrosina Schrakken, md. October 9, 1735. [Rev. Falk or Eneberg]

Kun, Johan Adam Simon and Schrackin, Anna Maria Sarina, youngest dau. of Hans Jacob and Euphrosina Schrackin md. December 11, 1740. [Probably by Dylander.]

Unterkofner, Johan Jacob and Schmiedin, Maria Eva, from Goshoppen living in Friederich Township, md. 1744.

Leber, Philipp, Lutheran and Müllerin, Anna Margretha, Reformed, living on the Schippach md. March 12, 1745. [Pastor Brunholtz.]

Marriages by Rev. Muhlenberg

Schoimer, Conrad, widower and Nussin, Anna Margretha, widow, md. February, 1745.

Heilman, Jürg Adam and Dufrene, Elisabeth from beyond the Schuylkill md. March 1745.

Appele, George and Manzerin, Maria Juliana md. March, 1745 in Philadelphia.

Stambach, Johann Philip and Kuhezin, Maria Christina md. 1745 in the Oley Mountains.

Kuhez, Johan Bernhard and Eberhardin, Catharina Elisabeth md. 1745 in the Oley Mountains.

Reiter, Johannes, widower and Carlin, Anna Maria md. December 31, 1745.

Gaugler, Johannes Kilian and Bittelin, Ann Margretha md. November 19, 1745.

Campbell, John and Ball, Anna md. in Philadelphia Co, by license dated April 4,1744.

Israel, Michael and Lamplugh, Mary by license dated md. February 22, 1745-6.

Merckel, Abraham and Ickesin, Anna Barbara, md. September, 1745.

Götthy(?)Beatus and Jürgerin, Catharina Elisabeth md. March 6,1746.

Wagner, Johannes and Dürrin, Anna Barbara, md. 1746.

Bächle, Christian and Friedrichsen, Catharina, md. 1746 (?)

Nagel, Conrad and Peterman, Margretha, widow, on the Schippach, md. April 17, 1746.

Preiss, Daniel and Weychardin, Johanna, md. May 22, 1746.

Scheibele, Johan Jacob and Schäfer, Anna Catharina, widow of Ludewig Schäfer, md. July 6, 1746.

Denk, (?) Johan Simon, widower and Schulzin, Catharina Dorothea, md. July 8, 1746.

Nunemacher, Johannes and Müllerin, Maria, living in Indian Field, md. July 20, 1746.

Ernst, Johan Wendel, widower and Davidsin, Maria, widow, beyond the Schuylkill md. August 5, 1746.

Meissenheimer, Johan Jacob and Reiterin, Anna Margretha, md. November 16, 1746.

Wagner, Jürg Adam, son of Hanes Jurg and Schmiedin, Anna Catharina, dau of Hans Jürg, md. at Goshehoppen, January 8, 1747.

Müller, Andreas and Ehewaldin, Anna Maria, dau of Ludewig, md. publicly February 5, 1747.

Schiring, Johann Nicol and Molzin, the virgin dau of schoolmaster, Molzen, md. March 12, 1747, at Matecha.

Kittelman, Johann Peter, widower and Hitzbergerin, Anna Juliana, md. May 10, 1747, beyond the Schuylkill.

Lindeman, Johan Heinrich, son of Justus and Uhlin, Anna Margretha, md. May 26, 1747, both Reformed religion.

Heiser, Valentin and Howin, Anna, md. May 4, 1747.

Moritz, Wilhelm and Heiselin, Anna Maria, md. July 21, 1747.

Wambold, Adam, widower and Dannhauserin, Ottilia, md. August 16, 1747.

Pab, Johann Conrad, widower and Lehrin, Margretha, md. August 16, 1747.

Vogle, Johan Jurg and Sämin, Maria Catharina, md. September 22, 1747, at Goshoppen.

Müntz, Benedict, widower and Reilin, Schön: Elisabeth, widow, md. September 30, 1747, in Colebrookdale twp.

Vetter Michael, from Elsass and Schmiedin, Maria Catharina, step- dau of Simon Pelzen, md. November 24, 1747.

Koch, Heinrich, son of Johannes and Beierin, Anna Maria, dau of Jacob, md. December 15, 1747, live in New Hanover twp.

Gmelin, Christian and Heiserin, Christina, md. December 29, 1747, at Matetcha.

Linck, Adam and Müllerin, Elisabeth, md. January 31, 1748

Gerber, Johann Adam and Schleucherin, Anna Maria, md. February 15, 1748, in Limbourg twp.

Jüger, Johannes and Schneiderin, Eva Elisabeth, md. April 12, 1748, in New Hanover twp.

Rambow, Peter, and Peters, Mary, dau of Peter, md. April 13, 1748, in Providence twp.

Wolffer, Simon and Baumanin, Maria Margretha, md. April 14, 1748, in the Swedes church Philadelphia.

Weichel, Johan Christoph and Hillin, Catharina, md. April 26, 1748, at New Hanover.

Matthes, Mathias and Davis, Mary, md. May 31, 1748.

Loos, Christoph, widower and Heinrichin, Dorothea, widow, md. June 15, 1748.

Streil, Leonhard and Reimerin, ---, widow, md. July 31, 1748, by License at Raritan, NJ.

Früh, Jacob, widower and Roserin, Maria Dorothea, md. August 17, 1748.

Griffith, Abraham, widower and Harris, Sarah, md. August 31, 1748, living in Chester Co.

Wentz, Valentin and Jenneweinin, Anna Barbara, md. September 11, 1748.

Theus, John Henry and Johnson, Anna Mary, widow, md. September 11, 1748.

Hippel, Johannes and Hassin, Maria Catharina, md. September 20, 1748.

Hatten, John and Evans, Esther, md. November 14, 1748, at Comerytown.

Stepelton, Robert and Richardtin, Catharina, widow, md. November 20, 1748.

Bostert, Samuel and Engelin, Catharina, md. November 20, 1748, at Oley.

Angel, Philip and Schmiedin, Anna Maria, md. November 24, 1748, at New Hanover.

Schuler, Lamburtus, widower and Larichin, Maria Ursula, md. December 11, 1748.

MaCochly, Cornelius and Parker, Johanna, widow of Stephen Müller, md. January 16, 1749.

Renn, Bernhard, widower and Riegelin, Sibitta, widow, md. January 19, 1749.

Brachen, Caspar, widower and Lauterin, Sophia Margretha, widow, Philip, md. February 14, 1749.

Hopkin, William and Mory, Christina, widow, md. April 2, 1749.

Fried, Philip and Benerin, Regina, md. April 13,1749, at New Hanover township by license dated April 10.

Megrawh, Francis and Cavenahnoh, Susannah, widow, md. May 1, 1749.

Wambold, Adam, widower and Petzin, Eva Catharina, md. June 18, 1749.

Johns, Daniel and Morgan, widow of James, md. July 3, 1749, in Lancaster county.

Gutman, Christoph and Rügnerin, Catharina, md. July 24, 1749, in Upper Milford.

Huber, Michael and Lahrin, Barbara, md. August 22, 1749, at New Goshoppen.

Becker, Johan Dieterich, widower and Muthhardtin, Anna Barbara, widow, md. September 5, 1749.

Jürger, Veit and Rennin, Sybilla, widow, md. November 20, 1749.

Schmied, Peter and Krausin, Maria, md. November 28, 1749.

Simon, John and Scot, Elisabeth, md. December 25, 1749, in Providence township.

MacRay, William and Edmondson, Margreth, md. December 25, 1749, in Providence township.

Liebegut, John Adam and Gansertin, Christina, md. January 4, 1750, in New Hanover township.

Fetter, Johan Philip and Schumannin, Anna Margretha, md. February 19, 1750, in Vincent township, Chester county.

Zing, Michael and Ryel, Mary, md. February 20, 1750, in Coventry township, Chester county.

Hoven, Jacob and Buckerin, Margretha, md. March 28, 1750.

Hörner, Christian and Krebsin, Barbara, md. March 22,1750.

Schrack, Johan Jacob and Mühlhanin, Elisabeth, md. March 22, 1750.

Protzman, Jürg Adam and Sählerin, Anna Martha, md. March 22, 1750.

Loag, Samuel and Handly, Mary, md. April 2, 1750, both of Chester county.

Sauer, Friedrich and Schmiedin, Anna Margretha, md. April 3, 1750, live at Schippach.

Gatter, Martin and Schäferin, Maria Catharina, md. April 8, 1750, live in Philadelphia.

Blair, John and Johns, Elisabeth, widow of John, md. May 28, 1750, in Worchester township.

Wolfgang, Johan Nicolaus, widower, and Weberin, Catharina, widow, md. June 1, 1750.

Cooper, James and Simmons, Mary, of Providence township, md. June 16, 1750.

Hofman, Joh: Michael, widower, and Schedlerin, Engel, md. July 2, 1750, in New Hanover township.

Schmell, Adam and Rielin, Catharina Barbara, md. July 31, 1750.

Reinhard, John Peter and Sieden, Maria Clara, servant maid of Val. Steinmetz, md. August 7, 1750.

Schädler, Johan Jürg, widower and Bechtelin, Anna Maria, widow, Jürg, md. August 7, 1750.

Schmied, Walter, widower and Scheidin, Anna Maria, widow, md. August 12, 1750, in Coventry township.

Schmied, Adam, from New Hanover township and Behnerin. Gertraut, md. October 9, 1750, by license.

Müller, Heinrich and Kleinin, Susannah Margretha, md. October 16, 1750, in Providence.

Schnauber, Johann Heinrich from Menissing, [sic] N J. and Hillbartin, Anna Maria, dau of Jürg Adam, md. October 29, 1750.

König, Michael, widower and Kachlerin, Eva, md. December 2, 1750, m. across the Schuylkill, in Muhlenberg's name by Pastor Johan Philip Leidich.

Croesman, Friedrich and Stagerin, Susannah, md. December 6, 1750.

Mäurer, Johan Jacob, widower and Weitzelin, Margretha, md. January 2, 1751, over the Schuylkill.

Wirth, Johan Martin and Grabilerin, Anna Maria, md. January 21, 1751, at New Hanover.

Schnell, Johann Jacob, schoolmaster at Schippach, and Schlottin, Anna Margretha, widow, md. January 31, 1751.

Hausler, Andreas, widower and Zinckin, Maria, md. February 5, 1751, live in Whitpain township, on the Schippach.

Jaxtheimer, Johann Philip and Adams, Catharine, md. February 24, 1751, Carl Rayer's servants with consent of the master for necessity.

Schooling, Francis and Powel, Elisabeth, md. March 21, 1751, in Providence township.

Schäfer, Philip Jacob and Jungin, Anna Margretha, md. March 31, 1751, live across the Schuylkil.

Sahler, Johann Michael, son of Peter and Engelin, Elisabeth, md. April 11, 1751, in Providence.

Heilman, Heinrich, widower, and Bersons, Anna Maria, dau of Heinrich, md. April 22, 1751.

Rehkopf, Friedrich and Schambachin, Elisabeth, md. April 25, 1751.

Bahrt, Johan Peter and Linckin, Catharina, dau of Jacob (dec'd), md. April 25, 1751.

Croesman, Balthasar, widower and Fuchsin, Anna Maria, md. April 28, 1751, at Molatton.

Schwenck, George and Merckelin, Veronica, dau of Jacob, md. April 30, 1751.

Corker, Robert and Farrel, Helena, md. November 17, 1751.

Meisheimer, Casimir, Lutheran and Brandtin, Margretha, Reformed, md. November 19, 1751.

Beck, Christian Heinrich, servant and Fröhlichin, ---, md. December 10, 1751, with consent of John Potts.

Osterman, Bartholomaeus and Jagerin, Dorothea, md. January 5, 1752, beyond the Schuylkill. [This was the first marriage by Rev. Pastor Friedrich Schultz.]

Schlanacker, Michael, widower and Wustin, Eva Filicitas, widow Caspar, md. January 19, 1752, in New Hanover.

Schilling, Johannes and Glimmin, Anna Maria, md. February 2, 1752, former servants of Rev. H. M. Muhlenberg.

Hawk, John and Johnson, Mary, md. February -- 1752, former servants of Mr. Rochard Nord in Providence township.

Scheumer, Friedrich and Bachin, Magdalena, md. February 7, 1752, live beyond the Schuylkill.

Haag, Jacob, widower and Eberhardtin, Catharina, servant girl to Rev. Muhlenberg, md. February 16, 1752.

Silber, Jürg and Schmiedin, Margretha, widow, md. February 18, 1752.

Schnerr, Wendel and Lohrin, Eva, former servants of Theobald Endt, now live in Pikestown,Chester county md. February 23, 1752.

Eble, Johan Adam, step-son of Jürg Beck, and Gmelin, Maria Sophia, dau of Matthias, md. March 31, 1752.

Rothermel, Leonhard and Joakims, Mary, dau of Jonas, md. March 31, 1752.

Zoll, Johann Heinrich and Runckelin, Margretha, md. March 31, 1752, at Schippach.

Jans, Philip and Detweilerin, ----, live at Schippach, md. April 28, 1752.

Wohlfarth, Adam and Wiegelin, Anna Maria, md. April 28, 1752, live at the Iron Works beyond the Schuykill, Chester county.

Williams, John and Rose, Nanny md. August 2, 1752, in the church of Providence; they live over the Schuylkill, Chester county.

Schweinhard, Jürg, from New Hanover and Schmiedin, Anna Maria, Ackers step-dau from Limerick township md. Providence church. No date.

Here Commences the New Stylus.

Beyer, Philip and Gratzin, Elizabeth, widow, md. October 24, 1752, in Providence church, both were former servants, but now free.

Busch, Johan Nicol, widower, and Fuchsin, Anna Maria, md. November 23, 1752, formerly servants in Chester county, but now free according to Indenture.

Heim, Valentin and Rees, Jane, md. November 23, 1752, both born at Pikestown, Chester county.

Moser, Christian and Graberin, Magdalena, md. December 21, 1752 both from Schippach.

Schmid, Heinrich and Franzin, Anna Maria, md. January 2, 1753, beyond the Schuylkill.

Schleyter, Friederich and Giessin, Catharina, dau of Nicolaus, md. January 2, 1753, beyond the Schuylkill.

Bauer, Adam and Kollerin, Dorothea, Mr. Marstellar's former servant, md. January 25, 1753.

Ray, Robert, an Irishman, and Pfeisterin, Catharina, md. February 18, 1753.

Jung, Johan Peter, son of David and Fahdin, Anna Magdalena, dau of Jacob, md. February 20, 1753.

Davis, John, from Wales and Langin, Anna, md. February 22, 1753.

Unstatt, Herman, widower and Adams, Abigail, single, md. March 6, 1753.

Magens, Heinrich, widower, and Weydin, Catharina, md. June 11, 1753.

Priess, Heinrich and Burchardtin, Margretha, step-dau of Theobald Lange, md. June 11, 1753.

Walter, Robert and Chambers, Elisabeth, md. June 19, 1753, living in Vincent township, Chester county.

Staud, Friedrich and Gerberin, Christina, June 25, 1753.

Stostlet, Johan Michel and Engelin, Elesabeth, md. July 1, 1753, at New Hanover.

Bradford, Hugh and Schrack, Catharina, dau of the widow, Eva Rosina, md. June 20, 1753.

Rauss, Lucas, Reverend pastor, and Gemlingin, Anna Sophia youngest, dau of Emrici, md. August 7, 1753.

Spannagle, Johan Ludwig and Ludewig, Anna Maria, dau of Johann Philip, md. September 2, 1753, living in Chester county.

Ickes, Johann and Müllerin, Christina, dau of Johannes from New Hanover, md. September 4, 1753.

Simon, Anthon, widower and Waldin, Euphronica, widow Caspar, md. September 20, 1753, at Schippach.

Klinger, Johannes, son of Odewald and Fussin, Christina, dau of Johan Nicolaus, md. October 25, 1753, at New Hanover.

Rau, Johannes, son of Friedrich and Heldin, Catharina, dau of Hans Peter, md. October 25, 1753, at New Hanover.

Held, Johan Ludewig, son of Hans Peter and Rauin, Maria Magdalena, dau of Friedrich, md. October 25, 1753, at New Hanover.

Vogler, Andreas and Barthin, Catharina, md. November 11, 1753.

Bechtold, Philip Jacob and Mackelin, Anna Maria, dau of Christoph, md. November 20, 1753.

Du-frene, Peter and Schewerin Eva, md. November 20, 1753.

Croesmann, Johan Nicolaus, son of Hans Jürg and Langenäckerin, Elisabeth, md. November 27, 1753, by license dated November 20, 1753.

Langler, Jacob and Köhlerin, Catharina, dau of Heinrich, md. October 16, 1753, at New Hanover.

Henkenius, Bernhard, widower and Eirichs, Margretha, widow md. December 2, 1753, at New Hanover.

Heible, Christoph and Schuppin, Sophia Catharina, md. December 9, 1753, m. in Augustus church.

Marstellar, Heinrich, son of Friedrich and Vossin, Barbara, dau of Adam md. December 13, 1753.

Fröhlich, Nicolaus, son of Johannes and Wartmiannin, Christina, dau of Adam md. December 18, 1753, at New Hanover.

Burk, William and How, Anna, widow of Valentin Heiser. md. December 20, 1753, by license dated Dec. 18.

Stoner, Frideric and Op de Graf, Debora. Servants of Mr. Brooks in New Hanover, who had previously transgressed the 6th Commandment. Md. in presence of Mr. George Jürger, Andreas Kebner, Jürg Beck, Heinrich Krebs and Mr. Brooks.

Evans, Benjamin, son of Justice Evans and Rees, Hanna, md. January 10, 1754, before evidences in church.

Pears, Lewis and Hammer, Mary, md. January 17, 1754, after publication in Providence township.

Robison, Thomas and Simons, Jane, md. January 20, 1754, in Providence township.

Von Campe, Frantz Carl,widower and Hopperheimierin, Margretha, widow, md. January 29, 1754, at New Hanover.

Davis, Simon and Reuterin, Margretha, widow, md. January 31, 1754, after publication.

Petz, William, stepson of John Frölich and Butler, Mary, dau of Richard, md. February 4, 1754, in Chester county after publication.

Hummel, Johan Heinrich, widower and Marstellerin, Ursula, dau of Peter, md. February 5, 1754, in church.

Pietermann, Heinrich, Reformed and Essigin, Maria Anna, md. February 7, 1754, proxy for Pastor Leydig.

Hofman, Adam and Vetterin, Anna Christina, md. February 19, 1754, at Schippach.

Gross, Jacob as widower and Schuberin, Maria Magdalena widow, md. February 19, 1754, at Schippach.

Jürger, Johannes and Kleinin, Sybilla, dau of Isaac, md. March 7, 1754.

Lightcape, Solomon and How, Mary, dau of Thomas, md. April, 1754.

Hörner, John Michael and Krebsin, Anna Maria, dau of Simon, md. March 12, 1754.

Diel, Christian and Krebsin, Regina, dau of Henrich, md. May 6, 1754, publicly in New Hanover.

Schultz, Friederich (wohl Ehrurdiger Herr Pfarrer) and Lochmanin, Maria Catharina, md. May 8, 1754, properly in Lutheran Trappe church.

Wolfenger, Peter and Wagnerin, Sophia, md. May 14, 1754, in Parsonage, both from Chester county.

Carl, Johannes, widower and McEntire, Catharine, md. May 31, 1754, in publicly, both living in Pikestown.

Raup, Michael, son of Peter and Meyerin, Maria Elisabeth, step-dau of Christoph Buttebinder, md. June 11, 1754, from Williams township.

Matthies, Christian and Conradin, Maria Magdalena, md. August 3, 1754, by another pastor after bans were read three times, both from Matetscha.

Gassänger, Johan Georg and Brunner, ---, widow Paul, md. August 3, 1754, by Justice Rowland Evans after banns were called three times.

Beck, Andreas and Bucherin, Catharina md. July 30, 1754, by Pastor Heinzelman.

Setzler, Friedrich, son of Philip and Borgerin, Elisabeth, dau of Christian, md. August 5, 1754, in Augustus church.

Behringer, Heinrich, son of Jacob and Rupin, Anna Maria, dau of Martin, md. August 19, 1754, in the church.

Krieger, Caspar, formerly Mbg's servant and Von Burg, Catharina, widow, md. October 1, 1754.

Ziegler, Christian, widower and Stanch, Rosina, Joh. Schrack's servant girl, md. October 22, 1754, m. in Chester county.

Vogler, Jürg, widower and Ise, Dorothea Elisabeth, widow Caspar, md. October 24, 1754, in Providence.

Breysach, Michael and Fischerin, Barbara, dau of Peter, md. November 10, 1754.

Oberdorf, Johan Adam, widower and Schlauferin, Anna Maria, md. November 11, 1754, in New Hanover.

Zehrfass, Friedrich and Fadin, Margretha md. December 17, 1754, at Matetcha.

Müller, Andreas and Kieferin, Elisabeth, md. February 13, 1755, at Schippach.

Rehkoff, John Nicolaus, widower and Manhardt, Margretha Gertraut, widow, md. March 2, 1755, in the church.

Leonhard, Hans Michael, Roman Catholic and Numerichin, Elisabeth Catharina, md. April 8, 1755, in Jürg Weichardt's house.

König, Johannes and Schmiedin, Margretha, dau of Jost, md. April 10, 1755, in the church.

Jung??, Christoph, son of Wendel and Matherin, Eva, Robert White's servant girl, md. April 10, 1755.

Kirchner, Friedrich and Arendsen, Anna Barbara, dau of Peter, md. April 13, 1755.

Wiesler, Johan Michael, widower and Schreierin, Eleonora, widow Jürg, md. April 13, 1755.

Tappe, Jost Heinrich, widower and Schneiderwin, Anna Maria living in New Hanover, md. April 22, 1755.

Zimmerman, Peter and Mackesin, Anna Maria, Peter Schrack's former servant, md. May 1, 1755.

Heil, Jacob and Müllerin, Anna, both servants of Michael Rodabach, with his consent at the "cricked Bille" Crooked Billet, md. May 11, 1755.

Stumpf, Johan Peter, widower and Pflantzin, Anna Catharina, widow, md. May 27, 1755 in New Hanover.

Strobel, Johan Michael and Mutschler, Anna Barbara, widow Johannes, md. June 29, 1755, at New Hanover.

Krug, Joh. Jacob and Nollin, Clara, dau of Michael, md. August 17, 1755.

Frohäuser, Johan Kraft, widower and Weltin, Christina, widow, md. September 7, 1755, in New Hanover.

Gotesman, Hans Jürg, widower and Hermanin, Eleonora, widow, md. September 9, 1755.

Collaghan, John and Russel Mary, md. September 16, 1755, after three times publishing in Providence township.

Acker, Anthon and Schmiedin, Anna Maria, md. October 9, 1755, properly in Providence church, live in Vincent township, Chester county.

Schüttler, Johan Ludewig and Kalbin, Maria Barbara, dau of Martin, md. October 28, 1755, properly in Providence church.

Fuchs, Johannes and Schilligin, Catharina, dau of Philip, md. October 28, 1755, in the church.

Hartman, Johan Jürg, widower and Edelmannin, Maria Barbara, md. November 30, 1755, at Colebrookdale.

Cullagan, Thomas and Horstin, Anna Catherina, md. December 2, 1755, in Providence in presence of witness, formerly servants to William Butt.

Stauch, Nicolaus and Allemannin, Elisabeth md. December 21, 1755, from Tomenson township.

Gilbert, Jürg and Marolsin, Margretha, md. December,3o, 1755, at New Hanover.

Joachim, Jacob and Mülhaus, Maria Christina, dau of Peter, dec'd Dec 30, 1755 at Providence.

Goeler, Johan Michael and Müllerin, Anna Margretha, dau of Nicolaus, md. February 29, 1756.

Richardson, William and Robison, Elizabeth, md. March 3, 1756, in Providence township.

Schneider, Nicolaus and Heinrichs, Magdalena, w. Johan, md. March 4, 1756.

Campbel, George and Mercil, Grace, widow of Dennis Bryan, md. March 5, 1756, after three times publishing.

Schlätzer, Johan Jacob and Spring, Susannah, widow Caspar, md. March 7, 1756, live in Limbrick [sic] township.

Davis, Isaac and North, Sophia, md. March 11, 1756.

Jones, Mounce and Jocum, Margreth, dau of Jonas, md. March 25, 1756, in Douglas township.

Kautz, Joh, Jürg, Thomas Belfield's servant and --- -- [his Wench], md. March 25, 1756, from Necessity.

Schmied, Johan David and Rollerin, Jacobina, dau of Jacob, md. April 8, 1756, at New Hanover.

Zoller, Peter, widower and Hertlein, ---, widow, md. May 12, 1756, at Schippach.

Gebhard, Jacob, widower and Althausin, Anna Maria, md. June 8, 1756 beyond the Schuylkill.

Boulton, Thomas and Robison, Mary, md. June 15, 1756, in Providence, after three times publishing.

Städle, Jacob and Hufin, Catharina, md. June 24, 1756, in the church, live in Matetcha.

Dressler, Jürg and Klemmin, Catharina, md. July 4, 1756, in Augustus church.

Bredo, Martin and Rothin, Maria Dorothea, widow, md. July 5, 1756, after three Sunday Proclamations.

Griesle, Jürg, widower and Jagesin, Catherina, widow, md. August 8, 1756, in New Hanover. not paid

Kop, Jacob and Behrens, Catharina, md. August 15, 1756, from New Hanover.

Schuler, Christian and Zauterin, Juliana, md. August 23, 1756, in Molotton church.

Kohler, Henrich and Heldin, Anna Margretha, md. September 5, 1756, in New

Hanover.

Stein, Johannes, son of Adam and Wollertin, Elisabeth, md. September 13, 1756, in Chester county.

Dannefaltzer, Jacob and Heinrichs, Anna Barbara, dau of Wendel, md. September 13, 1756, both from Pikestown.

Schleuter, Peter and Heilmannin, Magdalena, dau of Johannes, md. September 13, 1756, at Pikestown.

Ward, Joseph and Reece, Elisabeth, md. October 5, 1756, by authority of license dated md. October 2, both from Philadelphia county.

Weichard, Georg and Reinarin, Maria Magdalena, dau of Lorentz, md. October 7, 1756, in Augustus church.

Reece, Abel and Davies, Catharine, md. October 7, 1756, by virtue of license dated Sept. 25, both of Providence township.

Essig, Johan Georg, son of Michael and Jungin, Anna Maria, md. October 21, 1756, in Augustus church.

Hirster, Andreas and Marstellerin, Anna Maria, dau of Peter md. December 16, 1756, at John Koplin's house.

Evans, Enoch and Evans, Mary, md. January 2, 1757, by virtue of license dated January 2, both single, from Limerick township.

Wuchter, Sebastian and Penterin, Elisabeth, md. January 4, 1757, in Richard North's house after due proclamation.

Giess, Johan Nicol and Schlagelin, ---, md. January 12, 1757, in New Hanover.

Kop, Ludewig, from Schippaeh and Eschbachin, Maria, md. February 1, 1757.

Koppelberger, Christian and Sanftlebin, Anna Elisabeth, md. February 8, 1757, at New Hanover.

Anderson, William and MacDaniel, Hanna, md. February 8, 1757, in Charlestown, Chester County after due proclamation.

Stichter, Valentin and Schweinhardtin, Eva Barbara, md. February 15, 1757, at New Hanover.

Schott, Johan Georg and Lauin, Anna Barbara, md. March 10, 1757, at Matetcha.

Heilman, Conrad and Carlin, Elisabeth, dau of Johannes, md. March 25, 1757, at Vincent beyond the Schuylkill.

Schlätzer, Jacob, widower and Keplerin, Philippina, widow, md. April 13, 1757, in Conrad Jost's house.

Haunshield, Johan Caspar and Messerschmiedin, Christina, md. April 2, 1757, from Westtown township, Chester county.

Baker, John and Treebe, Mary, md. April 14, 1757, after three times publishing, living in Vincent township, Chester county.

Jager, Valentin and Dockenwadlerin, Maria Magdalena, the deserted wife, md. April 17, 1757 of Hans Jürg Ramsberger.

Gilbert, Johan Conrad and Stöltzin, Elisabeth, dau of Christian, md. April 19, 1757, at New Hanover.

Wells, Isaac and Frey, Hanna, dau of John, md. May 19, 1757, at Indianfield after due proclamation.

Emrich, Johan Georg and Haasin, Anna Elisabeth, md. May 26, 1757, in Vincent township by Pastor Hartwich.

Hülsebeck, Friedrich and Pärsin, Catharina, md. May 30, 1757, in Augustus church.

Ernst, Johan Jacob and Spannagelin, Anna Maria, md. June 14, 1757, at White Horse, Chester county by Pastor Kurtz.

King, Sebastian and Been, Rebecca, md. June 14, 1757, at Providence.

Köhler, Johan Jacob and Fisher, Catharina, md. June 22, 1757, from Towamensing township.

Bean, Thomas and Evans, Sarah, widow, md. June 30, 1757, after three times publishing.

Schleuer, Henrich and Dirlin, Magdalena, dau of Christian, md. June 23, 1757, in Charlestown, Chester county.

Brenneman, Christian and Merkelin, Catharina, dau of Jacob, md. June 23, 1757.

Kalb, Johannes and Müllerin, Maria Elisabeth md. July 18, 1757, at Limerick, in presence of Johannes Ickes and Herman Neuman.

Bedman, John and Owens, Annamd. August 2, 1757, at East Nantmeal township, Chester county, in presence of Abraham Hammer [Providence] and James Allison.

Acker, Johan Jürg and Klotzin, Susanna, md. August 8, 1757, at New Hanover, in Mr. Campbel's house.

Hofman, Philip, Randal Malin's servant and Spahaver, Hannah, md. August 14 1757, at the church at White Horse sign [St. Peter's Great Valley] after thrice publication, and by written consent of Randal Malin.

Spring, Jacob, widower from Modde Creek and Schmied, Anna Maria, widow Johannis, md. August 15, 1757, at parsonage after thrice publishing and waiting six weeks.

Bunn, Johannes and Conrad, Euphronica, dau of Peter, md. August 18, 1757, in Augustus church.

Kenney, Peter and Schipman, Elisabeth, dau of Jacob, md. September 22, 1757, at Raritan, NJ by license.

Schwartz, Friedrich and Schleicherin, ---, md. September 29, 1757, at Raritan, NJ.

Gründler, Paulus and Baschin, Catharina Elisabeth, md. October 15, 1757, at Providence, both from Goshen township, Chester county.

Lancker, (Lumker?) Joh. Michael and Jäcklerin, Catharina, md. September 11, 1757, at Providence by Rev. Kurtz, Jr., after public notice, both from Chester county.

Albrecht, Adam and Friedlin, Eva Barbara, md. October 16, 1757, at New Hanover.

Emmert, Jürg and Weicselin, Elisabeth, dau of Michael, md. October 16, 1757, at New Hanover.

Biegel, Jacob and Müllerin, Anna Maria, dau of Mattias, md. November 5, 1757, in New Hanover township.

Robison, David and Hinton, Eleanora, widow, md. November 14, 1757.

Bieler, Christoph Friedrich and Lupoldin, Maria Agnes, md. November 28, 1757, at New Hanover, both live with John Potts, Esq., in Douglass township.

Ernst, Adam, from Bedman township and Hillebartin, Eva Catharina, dau of Adam md. December 6, 1757.

Schäfer, Philip Jacob, widower and Heinrichin, Anna Catharina md. December 8, 1757, beyond the Schuylkill.

Scot, Josua and Jones, Rachel, dau of David md. December 22, 1757, in the township of Providence and New Hanover.

Kebler, Simon and Bullingerin, Elisabeth, md. January 8, 1758, at New Hanover.

Wagner, Mattheus, widower and Baumannin, Eva, widow Martin, md. January 15, 1758, in Douglas township.

Rupert, Valentin and Degen, Catharina, widow of late Henrich, md. January 22, 1758, at New Hanover, by Rev. Kurtz.

Schmied, Jacob from Lemerick and Münnichinger, Anna Margretha, dau of Andreas, md. January 29, 1758.

Böhm, Adam and Stein, Elisabeth, dau of Adam, md. February 5, 1758, at Pikestown.

Müller, Jacob and Ludewig, Sybilla, md. February 26, 1758, at Pikestown Schoolhouse.

Würtenberger, Hans Jürg and Benedict, Anna Maria, md. February 26, 1758, at Pikestown Schoolhouse.

Breder, Wendel and Ducken, Elisabeth, dau of Philip, md. January 10, 1758, in Augustus church.

Peck, John, son of Jeremiah Mecklin, and Anna Margretha, dau of Christoph, md. March 7, 1758, in Chester county.

Lange, Daniel and Bussmannin, Maria Catharina, md. March 19, 1758, at New Hanover both from Hanover, Germany .

Bleyer, John Adam and Schrabin, Anna Margretha, dau of Johan, md. March 28, 1758, in Providence.

Schweinhard, Johan Jürg and Schmiedin, Anna Maria, dau of widow Schmied, md. April 4, 1758, at New Hanover.

Gerstemeier, Johan Jürg and Müllerin, Margretha, dau of Christoph, md. April 4, 1758, at Schippach.

Leimbach, Friedrich and Ritter, Catharine, md. April 9, 1758, in Colebrookdale township, by license dated, md. April 1.

Murry, Garret, widower and Morris, Elisabeth, md. April 13, 1758, after three times publishing.

Schneider, Jacob and Heilman, Christian, dau of Heinrich, md. May 16, 1758, in Providence church both from Schippach

Frey, Jacob and Wells, Jemima, md. May 23, 1758, at Indianfield after thrice publication.

Bartle, Peter and Jacobs, Catharine, dau of Peter, md. June --, 1758.

Bahrt, Michael, widower and Sprögel, Susanna, dau of late Johan Heinrich Spogel, md. August 1, 1758.

Sachse, Johan Georg and Kuntzman, Elisabeth, dau of Heinrich, md. August 1, 1758.

Conningham, Robert and Setzler, Hannah, dau of Philip, md. September 12, 1758, in Augustus church.

Krumrein, Stephan and Roth, Catharina, dau of Conrad, md. October 3, 1758, live in New Hanover.

Mayberry, Sylvanus, widower and Hall, Rosina, widow, md. October 9, 1758, after three times publishing.

Luther, George and Dean, Mary, widow of William, md. October 10, 1758, in Charlestown, Chester county.

Frey, Samuel and Wells, Diana, md. October 12, 1758, at Indianfield, after three times publishing.

Spahard, Johannes and Schneiderin, Catharina, md. October 15, 1758, in Pikestown Schoolhouse.

Keller, Fredrich and Jung, Catharina, dau of Wendel, md. October 19, 1758.

Fenchel, Simon and Sulier, Apollonia, md. October 22, 1758, by consent of his Master, Wm. Conerly, after due proclamation.

Frieman, Abraham, widower and Trietschin, Maria Margretha, md. October 22, 1758, in Vincent township, Chester county.

Wieseler, John Wolfgang and Jungblut, Maria Martha, step-dau of Christian Rehkopf, md. October 24, 1758.

Fuchs, Heinrich, single and Schäferin, Elisabeth, spinster, md. November 7, 1758, by order of Justice Keplin in presence of the Constables.

Gerber, Benedict and Loreth, Dorothea, md. November 12, 1758, in presence of Johannes Loreth and Philip Sperr.

Scherstig, Caspar and Heilmanin, Magdalena, widow of Peter Schleuter, md. December 14, 1758.

Bracher, Johann Georg and Wuchterin, Catharina md. December 19, 1758, living in Charlestown township, Chester county.

Staunch, Gottfried and Kesslerin, Anna Charlotta md. December 26, 1758, at Vincent, Chester county.

Boltner, Philip and Halbin, Anna Catharina, md. January 2, 1759, at New Hanover.

Oxlein, Jürg and Krausin, Maria Catharina, md. January 2, 1759, at New Hanover.

Heinkel, Johan Christoph and Sieger, Maria Eva, dau of Caspar, md. January 23, 1759, at New Hanover.

Rutter, Thomas and Potts, Martha, (Ms), md. February 20, 1759, by authority of license at Pott's Grove.

Frey, Johan George and Hechlerin, Elisabeth, md. February 23, 1759, at Pikestown school house, with consent of their master.

Fuchs, Matthias, widower and Meir, Anna Maria, dau of Johannis, md. March 6, 1759, at New Hanover, by Pastor Schaum.

Blocher, Matthias and Schwabin, Barbara, md. May 6, 1759, in the church, both from Vincent township.

Bostick, William and Lum, Mary, md. April 2, 1759, at New Hanover, by Pastor Schaum.

Graaf, William and Heiserin, Barbara, md. May 8, 1759.

Fuchs, Jürg, son of Jacob and Schieligin, Catharine Elisabeth, dau of Philip, md. April 10, 1759.

Frack, Jacob and Krebs, Christina, dau of Henrich, md. May 22, 1759.

Davis, Elisha and North, Sarah, dau of Rochar, md. October 11, 1759 by authority of license.

Scheidel, Martin and Kreulin, Christina, md. October 11, 1759, by authority of license.

Schweinhard, Johannes and Reichard, Johanna, dau of Caspar, md. February 17, 1760, at New Hanover.

Lloyd, William and Jordan, Rachel, md. March 5, 1760, by authority of license. Both from Limerick township.

Priest, Absalom and Hare, Catharine, md. March 21 1760, after thrice publishing, both from Upper Merion township. Witness: Henry Priest and Jeremia Rambow.

Theus, Matthias, son of Cornelius and Heilman, Catharina, dau of Johannis, md. March 20, 1760, in Worcester township.

Schlanecker, Georg, son of Michael and Burchard, Anna Catha: Elisabeth md. July 6, 1760.

Penter, Ludewig and Seiberin, Eva Catharina, md. September 2, 1760.

Benson, John and Valfesson, Anna, md. September 23, 1760, upon certificate of Rev. Provost de Wrangel, that they were published three several Sundays in the church at Wicacoa, witness: Daniel Reif and Vandensluise.

Vogeler, Jürg, widower and Rennin, Catharina, widow, md. September 30, 1760.

Friess, Michael and Nied, Catharina, dau of late Jürg, md. October 28, 1760, at New Hanover.

Heilman, Anthon, son of Johannes and Thomas, Sarah, md. November 27, 1760.

Kuntzman, Martin and Ebelin, Margretha, md. December 14, 1760.

Klein, John Peter and Eulin, Anna Margretha md. December 17, 1760, at New

Hanover.

Barlow, John and Savage, Hannah md. December 31, 1760, in Limerick by license.

Sander, Peter and Gerhardin, Sara, dau of Leonhard, md. December 31, 1760, at Norrington, before Mr. Casselberger, Leonhard, Gerhard, etc.

--- [a German miller] and Kolben, ---, dau of Ludewig, md. January 6, 1761, in Christoph Raben's house after proper proclamation by Rev. Bryzelius in Whitemarsh township.

Trump, Johannes and Jürg, Margretha, dau of Wendel, md. February 10, 1761, in Augustus church.

Weisel, Ludewig, widower, and Schmiedin, Anna Maria, *nee* Heiser, widow, md. February 12, 1761, in Providence.

Haas, Johannes and Christmannin, Elisabeth, dau of Daniel, md. March 12, 1761, in Vincent township.

Kepner, Bernhard and Zieber, Rebecca, dau of the late Johannis, md. March 3, 1761, in the church.

Fuss, Nicolaus and Stein, Anna Maria, dau of the late Adam, md. March 25, 1761, in Vincent township.

Custer, Johannes and Hauser, Elisabeth, md. March 31, 1761, at Barren Hill, proper proclamation having been made in the Swedish church at Wicacoa.

Bisbing, Henrich, from Goschehoppen, and Kugler, Elisabeth, dau of Michael, md. April 12, 1761, in New Hanover.

Barthman, Johan Adam and Kurtz, Anna Barbara, dau of Michael, md. April 12, 1761, in New Hanover.

Müller, Peter and Pugh, Margreth, md. April 16, 1761, in Vincent township, Chester county.

Becker, Johannis, son of Frantz and Lahr, Maria, md. April 19, 1761, at Providence, *ex necessitate.*

Müller, Martin, son of Matthias and Wambold, Anna Maria, dau of Adam, md. April 21, 1761, in New Hanover.

Meyer, Michael and Müller, Eva, dau of Matthias, md. April 21, 1761, in New Hanover.

Maurer, Balthaser, widower and Rupertin, Eva, md. April 27, 1761, at Providence.

Hausile, Johan Friederich and Hechlerin, Barbara, md. May 5, 1761, beyond the Schuylkill, by Rev. B(oskerck) .

Stock, Johan Adam and Diem, Susanna, dau of Thomas, md. May 5, 1761.

May, Thomas and Holland, Sarah, md. May 7, 1761 by authority of license.

Berger, Johan Jost and Woltz, Anna Margretha, dau of widow Woltzin, md. June 14, 1761.

Schlerr, Johan Jacob and Schmid, Elisabeth, widow Johannis, md. June 15, 1761, in Vincent township.

Schlätzer, Georg and Beck, Catharina, widow, md. May 10, 1761. Marsteller,

Johan Georg and Küster, Elisabeth, dau of Nicolaus, md. June 25, 1761, in Augustus church.

Haas, N --- from Oley and Müller, ---, dau of Isaac, md. July 7, 1761, in Limerick.

Kercher, Johan Nicol and Hardmannin, Maria Elisabeth, md. August 9, 1761, from dire necessity, in Pike township, Chester county.

Hannes, Wendel and Fiedlerin, Philippina, md. August 20, 1761, in Providence, both from Pike township.

Schädler, Henrich, widower and Hofman, Michael, md. August 23, 1761.

Bauer, Michael and Lübin, Catharina, md. September 20, 1761, in Augustus church after proclamation.

Dörolf, Andreas and Fertig, Catharina, dau of late Peter, md. October 18, 1761, in Augustus church.

Ickes, Johannes, son of Nicolai from Limerick township and Frey, Margretha, dau of late Jacob, md. November 1, 1761, in Providence.

Krug, Mattheus and Hartlein, Susanna, dau of Michael, md. November 8, 1761.

Schick, Ludewig and Friedrich, Anna Maria, dau of Jürg Michael, md. May 9, 1762, in New Hanover.

Shelves, John and Davies, Margreth, md. June 7, 1762, by Mr. B[runholtz] after thrice proclamation.

Wealthy, Jacob and Lehrin, Anna Maria, md. August 15, 1762, at New Hanover, after proclamation.

Fertig, Johann Adam and Bauer, Elisabeth, md. August 15, 1762, at New Hanover, after proclamation.

Sell, Anthon and Kurtz, Elisabeth, dau of Michael, September 12, 1762, at New Hanover.

Fertig, Johannes and Diemin, Elisabeth, md. October 24, 1762, at New Hanover, by Mr. B[oskerk].

Wageman, Martin and Schwabin, Maria Margretha, widow, md. November 1, 1762, beyond the Schuylkill, by Mr. B[oskerk].

Kelchner, Matthias and Krohnin, Maria, md. November 30, 1762, in Augustus church, by Mr. B[oskerk].

Keyser, Johannis and Marstellerin, Elisabeth, dau of Peter, md. January 27, 1763, in Limerick.

Ickes, Michael and Keplin, Alice, md. April 10, 1763, at New Hanover, by license dated March 30.

Hebbenheimer, Georg and Kargin, Catharina, md. March 22, 1763, at New Hanover, after due publication.

Bender, Christian, widower, and Hermannin, Anna Maria, md. April 10, 1763, at New Hanover, after due publication.

Pfliman, Johann and König, Maria Elisabeth, dau of Michael, md. April 18, 1763, beyond the Schuylkill, after due proclamation.

Maurer, Conrad, son of Baltzer and Lendin, Margreth, md. April 24, 1763, at

New Hanover, after due proclamation.

Weidner, Adam and Walker, Mary, md. August 9, 1764, at New Hanover, by license dated August 1.

Brand, Georges, son of Philipp and Reinert, Susanna, dau of Philipp, md. May 19, 1765, after due proclamation.

Lesch, Henrich, son of late Martin and Bliczli, Catharina, dau of Martin, md. January 26, 1766, after due proclamation.

Marsteller, Valentin and Hennrichin, Magdalena, md. May 22, 1766, in Augustus church after due proclamation.

Minz, Jacob and Schumannin, Maria Margretha, md. June 10, 1766.

Kebner, Benedict and Reierin, Maria Elisabeth, md. January 27, 1767.

Schumann, Peter and Schönholzen, Elishel, md. February 10, 1767.

Hartmann, Philipp and Maureren, Anna Elisabeth, md. March 8, 1767.

Essig, Rudolph and Bergeren, Maria, md. March 10, 1767.

Gerber, Philipp and Marxen, Margretha, md. April 19, 1767.

Weber, Wilhelm and Bornen, Agnesa, md. October 3, 1767.

Hausan, Anton and Beckeren, Elisabeth, md. October 29, 1767.

Haas, Hennrich and Pannebeckern, Elisabeth, md. November 29, 1767.

Küster, Nicolaus and Schracken, Catharina, md. December 1, 1761.

Martini, Friedrich and Miller, Mary, md. January 10, 1768, by license dated September 29, 1767.

Schrack, Hennrich, and Beckerin, Maria Magdalena, Jan 10, 1768.

Moore, Tobias and Pannebeckern, Elisabeth, md. March 6, 1768.

Pannebecker, Samuel, and Gilberten, Hanna, md. May 15, 1768.

Ritter, Matthias and Heillemann, Anna Maria, md. October 30, 1768.

Rettenbach, Hennrich and Osterlein, Margretha, md. October 30, 1768.

Bolich, Johan Valentin and Fewinger, Maria Elisabeth, md. May 23, 1773.

Conner, Barnabas and Fischern, Elisabeth, md. July 4, 1773.

Rieser, Michael and Pannebeekern, Hanna, md. May 29, 1774.

Fuchs, Baltzer and Fenchel, Mary, md. May 29, 1774, by license dated md. December 20.

BURIALS.

May 20, 1745 Keim, Hans Michael, bur. July 31, 1678, at Oberroth, Hohenlohe. Came here 16 years ago. d. May 19, on his plantation. Leaves a widow and two daus.

August 26, 1745 Köster, Samuel, son of Nicolaus, bap. a few months ago.

August 29, 1745 Reiter, Johannis, wife and child, bur. in one grave in Mennonite ground. She was Reformed.

September 26, 1745 Heilman, Maria Salome, wife of Anthon, age 73 years.

September 29, 1745 Heilman, ---, son of Heinrich, age 3 years, -- months.

October 2, 1745 Heiser, Rebecca, dau of Johannis, aged 6 years.

October 17, 1745 Toppelius, Johan Jacob age 83 years. An old Reformed neighbour.

July --, 1745 Wagner, ---, dau of Bastian.

1745 Wagner, ---, dau of Bastian. Reformed, both bur. beyond the Schuylkill.

November 30, 1745 Berg, Caspar, single age 30 years.

July 6, 1746 Dürrbehr, Peter, age 72 years. An old Reformed man who lived with Hieronymus Haas.

May 31, 1746 Spyker, Johann Peter, son of Peter, at Schippach, age 1 year, - - weeks; drowned in a spring.

July 17, 1746 Wishan, Johannes, son of Johannes, age 3 years, 10 months, 14 days.

July 25, 1746 Croesman, Esther, dau of Johannes, of Indianfield, age 1 year, - weeks.

August 6, 1746 Wintermuthin, widow Elisabeth.

October 7, 1746 Haag, Maria Barbara Magdalena, *nee* Krurnreinin, wife Michael, age 31 years.

January 7, 1748 Weichard, Anna Margretha, dau of Hans Jürg.

February 7, 1748 Heinrich, Jürg, bur. beyond the Schuylkill.

March 1, 1748 Heinrich, Bernhard, son of Johann.

March 7, 1748 Dromb, Philip Tobias.

October 11, 1748 Heilman, Johannes, bur. beyond the Schuylkill.

February 6, 1749 Heiser Johannes, bur. in Mennonite ground.

April 29, 1749 Renn Bernhard.

January 16, 1750 Gansert, Jürg, in New Hanover.

February 9, 1750 Held, Dietherich, age 48 years.

May 27, 1750 Dissman,---, son of Daniel.

June 3, 1750 Dissman, Daniel himself .

January 27, 1751 Gehringer, Anna Margretha, *nee* Meytzinger, wife of Thomas.

January 30, 1751 Haass, Johan Heinrich.

February 8, 1751 Dober, Regina, wife of Thomas, age 82 years.

November --, 1751 Vander Sluis, Anthon.

December 5, 1751 Dismann,---, widow of Daniel.

December 8, 1751 Sühler, Peter.

February 1, 1752 Dober, Thomas.

October 30, 1752 Müller, Anna Maria, wife of Jacob.

November, 1752 Custer,---, dau of Nicolaus, age 9 days.

December 22, 1752 Haas,---, wife of Hieronymus.

January 3, 1753 Bauerin, Magdalena, single, age 45 years.

January 5, 1753 Setzler,---, wife of Philip.

January 8, 1753 Reif, ---, mother of Jacob, an old widow, age 90 years, 8 months, bur. in Mennonite ground.

January 23, 1753 Protzmann, Johannes, son of Adam, age 3 months.

March 26, 1753 Koch,---, wife of Jacob.

April 1, 1753 How, Thomas, our neighbour, age 72 years less 14 days.

August 17, 1753 Amborn Christopher, a former member of the Congregation.

October 17, 1753 Marstellar, Friedrich Ludewig, who died in the night 14-15 October. Pastor BrunhWtz had German Sermon and I. Mülhlenberg preached in English.

November 27, 1753 Kressen,---, wife of Jacob, Reformed at Schippach.

August 7, 1753 Heiser Valentine, bur. in Mennonite ground at Schippach.

January 4, 1754 Spring, Andreas, age 34 years,-- months.

February 9, 1754 Muhlan, Johan Peter, age 63 years.

October, 12, 1754 Haas, Conrad, age 71 years, bur. beyond the Schuylkill.

October 27, 1754 Rühl, Maria Elisabeth, dau of Michael, age 17 years.

November 9, 1754 Croesman, Catharina w. Hans Jürg, age 56 years, d. November 7.

November 16, 1754 Klem, Johan Conrad, age 76 years, a native of Ottlingen.

February 14, 1755 Bussmann, Heinrich, a native of Hanover.

April 13, 1755 Heinrich, Johan, age 50 years, Reformed.

April 25, 1755 Sily, Sarah, dau of Samuel, age 13 months.

May 16, 1755 Weichard, Jürg, over 70 years old.

September 1, 1755 Rinselsdorfer, Johannes, bur. New Hanover.

October 25, 1755 Hörnerin, widow Catherina, who died with apoplexy.

October 26, 1755 Sauer,---, dau of Friedrich, age 1 ½ years.

October 30, 1755 Roth, John Ludewig, age 53 years.

November 4, 1755 Leber,--- of child of Erasmus, age 1 year, 6 months.

November 26, 1755 Müller, Johan Jacob, from Heuchelheim, b. January 10, 1706, d. November 24, 1755.

December 10, 1755 Peters, Peter, Jr. who fled from Virginia to escape the Indians.

December 23, 1755 Comens,---, wife of John, formerly widow of John Simons, bur. on Manor Land in Providence.

1756

March 18, 1756 Reichard, Maria, widow Johan Friedrich, age 71 years, who proved herself a true widow, bur. in New Hanover.

April 12, 1756 Bolton, Henry, an English churchman, bur. in James Brooks' grave-yard.

June 1, 1756 Bradfort, Hugh, brother-in-law to John Schrack bur. in Augustus ground.

June 22, 1756 Heilman, ---, dau of Heinrich, age 4 months, bur. in Mennonite ground.

August 24, 1756 Neuhaus, Anthon, age 96 years, bur. in Augustus ground.

October 21, 1756 Schrack, Euphrosina, widow Johan Jacob, age 68 years, 6 months, born in Ulm, married 31 years, and a widow 14 years.

December 10, 1756 Bukel, Christoph, father of Ludewig, bur. Massebach, November 27, 1682. Married 1715, came to Pennsylvania 1732 with 5 children, who were baptized there by Pastor Koenig.

November 24, 1756 Petz, Agatha, widow, bur. at New Hanover. By the schoolmaster, a pious soul.

December 13, 1756 Seidel, Maria Barbara, dau of Johan Nicolai, age 3 years, 3 weeks.

December 14, 1756 Hollebach, widow Maria Catharina, age 72 years, 1 month, from Wurtemberg, was 20 years a widow and 39 years in Penna.

December 22, 1756 Schaller, ---, only dau of Jürg, age 1 year, 6 months.

December 23, 1756 de Haven, Mary, dau of Abraham, age 3 years.

1757

January 10, 1757 Fleischer, Eleonora, dau of Johannis, schoolmaster of the congregation, age 5 years.

February 8, 1757 Sühler, Peter, age 78 years, from Barsillai.

January 26, 1757 Bühl, ---, wife of Peter.

February 14, 1757 Jochum, John, age 41 years, bur. Molotton.

February 28, 1757 Henrichs, ---, dau of late Johan, step-dau of Johann Nicol Schneider, age 19 months, 9 days.

April 4, 1757 Hulen, Marcus, a Swede, age 70 years, at Molotton, was converted at Jochum's funeral, *vide subra.*

April 5, 1757 Straub, --- deserted wife of Heinrich, age between 50 and 60 years, bur. at New Hanover, she made her home with Michael Weichel and received the sacrament half an hour before her death.

July 2, 1757 Randel, Joseph, thrown out of a wagon and died.

July 7, 1757 Brunnholtz, d. in Philadelphia, July 5, 4 a.m., bur. July 7.

July 15, 1757 Disman, Daniel single.

July 31, 1757 Becker,- youngest son Jost, bur. in Disman's graveyard

September 30, 1757 Klein, Anna Helena, widow of Christian, bur. New Germantown in Jersey.

November 3, 1757 Staut, Christina *nee* Gerber, wife of Friedrich, bur. at Schippach.

March 20, 1758 Neuhauss, Catharina, age 22 years, bur. in Providence.

---, 1758 Barth, ---, wife of Michael.

January 23, 1759 Schunck, Magdalena, wife of Simon, age 36 years.

January 23, 1759 Schunk, --- son of Simon, 3 hours.

January --, 1759 Reifschneider. Dorothea, widow John, bur. New Hanover.

February 8, 1759 Hartlein, Eva Catharina, dau of Michael, age 21 years.

March 15, 1759 Nährmarin, Elisabeth, an old spinster from Hanover.

July 16, 1759 Heilman, Anthon, church warden of this Congregation, age 88 years.

August 21, 1759 Schmidt, Elisabeth, wife of Wilhelm, age 66 years.

October 11, 1759 Bastian, ---, son of Jürg Michel, age 8 weeks.

October 11, 1759 Pannebecker, wife of Adolph.

August --, 1759 Essig, Michael, bur. Providence, by pastor Schaum.

January 31, 1760 Essig,---, wife of Jürg Jürg, Sr., age 70 years, b. a Roman
Catholic, received in the Evangelic church, 2 years ago, a pious soul.
January 31, 1760 Rayer, Jürg Adam, son of Carl, bur. April 16, 1745. Killed
January 29 by falling under a loaded wagon on a trip to Philadelphia.
March 2, 1760 Campbel, Mr. John, bur. New Hanover.
February 24, 1760 Protzmann, Elisabeth, dau of Adam.
February 19, 1760 Protzmann, William, son of Adam.
January 20, 1760 Diems,---, son of Andreas, age 21 years.
March 22, 1760 Jost, Conrad. Remarkable in life, blessed in death.
July 15, 1760 Weiser, Conrad, my father-in-law, bur. Heidelberg by Pastor
Kurtz.
November 12, 1760 Schweinhard, George Michael, Church Warden at New
Hanover. Born Jungholtzhausen, district Hohenlohe. 28 years in Penn. and a
true Member of the Congregation, d. November 10, age 64 years.
November 24, 1760 Mey,---, mother Jürg, age 79 years, 5 months, bur.
Providence.
November 25, 1760 Mühlenberg, Johan Carl, son of Rev. Heinrich Melchoir
and Anna Maria, age 5 ½ days.
December 22, 1760 Hoppin, Anna Elisabeth *nee* Sprögel, age 75 years.
December 3, 1760 Dreher, Helena Maria, wife of Jürg, dau of Johannis
Schimmel, age 20 years, bur. New Hanover.
January 23, 1761 Schrack, Nicolaus, son of Jacob, age 3 years, 3 months.
February 14, 1761 Franckenberger, Conrad, age 46 years.
September 18, 1761 Steinhauer, William, age 70 years.
September 18, 1761 Vail der Sluis ---, widow, age 61 years, 3 months.
October 25, 1761 Schädlerin, Anna Margretha, widow age 63 years, bur. New
Hanover.
June 27, 1762 Teussen, Catharina, dau of Matthias, age 1 year, 8 months. bur.
Mennonite ground at Schippach, by Mr. B[uskerk].
July 21, 1762 Haassenmeyer, --- wife of Hartman, d. from a deadly wound.
September 11, 1762 Marstellar, Henrich, son of Henrich, age 1 year, 5 months,
1 week. Accidentally scalded.
September 28, 1762 Koplin, ---, dau of Esq., b. Nov. 16, 1742, buried Augustus
ground.
October 5, 1762 Moserin, ---, widow, b. Eckersweiler in Rothenburgischen,
1685, a pious and true widow, buried New Hanover, by Mr. Buskerck.
December 31, 1762 Dures, ---, wife of Andreas.
January 6, 1763 Becker, Peter, son of Georg.
April 11, 1763 Westlis, Maria Elisabeth, wife of Solomon, bur. Molotton.
January 21, 1766 Löber, Barbara, dau of Erasmus and Catharina.
February 22, 1766 Löber, Catharina, dau of Philip and Anna Margretha, age 6
years, 2 weeks.
March 22, 1766 Marstaller, Elisabeth, dau of Heinrich and Barbara, age 2 years,

5 months, 1 week, 3 days.

May 29, 1766 Setzler, Elisabeth, dau of Friedrich and Elisabeth, age 5 years, 11 months, 3 days.

September 23, 1766 Schrack, Maria, wife of Philip, age 51 years.

January 21, 1773 Guth, Adam, son of George and Margrethia, age 1 year, 5 months, 6 days.

February 11, 1773 Bayer, Valentine, son of Conrad and Elisabeth, age 12 days, b. on family ground.

February 17, 1773 Hessler, Jacob, son of Friedrich and Catharina, age 6 months, 2 weeks, 4 days.

February 18, 1773 Aschenfeldern, Maria Catharina, 23 years, 10 months.

February 20, 1773 Gerber, Joseph, son of Benedict and Dorothea, age 11 months, 3 weeks, 3 days.

February 24, 1773 Bender, Samuel, son of Ludewig and Eva, age 1 year, 1 month, 1 week, 3 days.

March 20, 1773 Kebner, Catharina, dau of John and Maria Magdalena, age 2 years, 9 months, 3 weeks.

March 30, 1773 Adam, son of John and Maria Magdalena, age 1 year, 1 month, 3 weeks, 1 day.

April 1, 1773 Roos, Elisabeth, dau of Heinrich and Catharina, age 1 year, 8 months, 3 weeks, 3 days.

August 10, 1773 Mercklin, Isaac, age 26 years, 9 months, 2 weeks, 4 days.

November 20, 1774 Haas, Elisabeth, dau of Heinrich and Elisabeth, age 3 years, 6 months, 1 week, 5 days.

December 27, 1775 Reyer, Anna Maria, dau of Johannes and Catharina, age 2 years, 2 months, 4 days.

March 7, 1776 Schrack, Susanna, dau of Johannes and Gertraut, age 1 year, 8 months, 7 days.

May 26, 1777 Jung, Wendel, age 72 years.

June 8, 1777 Haas, Hartmann, son of Hartman and Maria Barbara, age 11 years, 4 months, 2 weeks, 2 days.

November 9, 1777 Marstellar, Anna Maria, wife of Peter, age 70 years, 2 weeks.

NEW GOSHENHOPPEN REFORMED CONGREGATION
Transcribed by Rev. William John Hinke, Ph.D., D.D.

Marriages by Rev. George Michael Weiss, at Goshenhoppen, beginning in 1747
John Neiss and Catharina Hahn.
George Neiss and Anna Dotter.
Jacob Arend and Anna Elizabeth Geiger.
Abraham Arend and Catharina Ried.
J. George Leidich and Catharina Arend.

John Schicher and Catharina N---.
John Gressman and widow Hank.
John Gressman's son and ---.
John Gressman's two daughters and ---.
Jacob Ried and Magdalena Leidich.
J. Zirkel and N---.
Benedict Schwob and Susanna Welcker.
Dietrich Welcker and Sara de Haven.
Philip Wentz and dau. of Ulrich Hartman of Schipbach.
Stoffel Wagner and second dau. of Bastian Schmid of Schipach.
J. Breneman and N---.
Benjamin Sommer and Anna Maria Scholl.
J. Denig and Elizabeth Eichel.
Jacob Riedi and Susanna Gucker.
Andreas Ohl and Eva Gucker.
Peter Beissel and Maria Schwenk.
N. Ohl and Elisa Barbara Gucker.
Michel Welcker and Anna Maria Ried.
Theobald Wink and Cretha Ried.
J. Adam N. and Maria Magdalena Beissel.
Michel Ried and Anna Maria Mauer.
Michel Schell and Catharina Lauer.
John Schell and Veronica Mauer.
David Haag and Elisa Catharina Wagenseil.
Melchior Schultz and Catharina Kalhbach.
Adam Hillikas and Catharina Bitting.
Peter Hillikas and Barbara Hornberger.
Philip Huth and Eva Weiss.
John Huth and Barbara Zimmerman.
J. Arendt Weiss and Susanna Huth.
Georg Schley and Catharina N---.
Caspar Berend and Elisa Lena Wannenmacher.
Hennerich Berendt and Anna Maria Luer.
Harmon Luer and Katharina Kieffer.
J. Luer and Barbara Weber.
Jacob Fischer and Hannah Dankler.
Roland Jung and Catharina Fischer.
Henrich Haas and N. Jung.
J. Huebner and Anna Dotter.
Jacob Zimmerman and Sophia Wigand.
Abraham Segler and Barbara Moll.
Henrich, a blacksmith, and Elizabeth Moll.
Daniel Hamm and Maria Segler.

Wendel Lemli and Scharl. M. Wigand.
Jacob Weidknecht and Creth [Margaret] Boehm.
Antoni Hamser and Anna Marg. Raudenbusch.
Benedict Strohm and Maria N---.
Andreas Mauerer and Maria Barbara Steinman.
Paulus Rothaermel and Maria Cretha Mauer.
J. Schmidt and Gentrude N---.
Leonhardt Griesemer and N. Leveber.
Georg Lauer and Maria Barbara N---.
Michel Roeder and Catharina Erb.
Henrich Lobach and Margaretha Roeder.
Michel Stab and Catharina N---.
Mathys Reicherdt and Creth Hillikas.
Nicolaus Jeger and Anna Hillikas.
J. Kiefer and Barbara Hillikas.
Wilhelm Gedman and Susanna Jekel.
Andres Greber and Anna Maria Bitting.
Ulrich Greber and Creth Labar.
Peter Laub and Creth Muss.
Carl Doerr and Christina Muss.
John Dankel and N---.
Hennerich Mueller and Gertrudt Diefendoerffer.
Nicolaus Ohl and Anna Marg. Diefendoerffer.
Gabriel Klein and Elisabetha Dorothea Bitting.
Alexander Diefendoerffer and Gertrude N. [Leidig].
Fridrich Lang and N. Scholl.
Christian Mueller and Elisabeth Wetzler.
Jacob N--- and Veronica Wetzler.
J. Haag and Anna Marg. Wetzler.
Peter Wetzel and Creth Eberhard.
J. Mecklin and Creth Kehler.
N. Weitzel and Barbara Kehler.
Andreas Muehlschlagel and Anna Maria Emet.
Henrich Kumpf and Catharina Emet.
Michel Eberhardt and Catharina Bleyler.
Peter Bleyler and Hannah N---.
Philip Vackenthal and Elisabeth Bleyler.
Ulrich Hornecker and Barbara Eberhard.
Ulrich Hornecker and Creth Eberhard.
Valentin Keiser and Barbara Huber.
H. Heger and Eva Huber.
N--- and Creth Huber.
Nicolaus Mombauer and Magdalena N---.

J. Adam N--- and Creth Hitz.
Jacob Huber and Elisabetha Samsel.
Henrich Huber and Barbara N---.
Philip Schmidt and Creth Doerr.
J. Goetz and Catharina N---.
N. Zimmermann and Jacob Hoffman's dau.
N. Zimmermann and Jacob Hoffman's dau.
Of the Henerichs in Schipbach several have intermarried.
J. Oftengraff (Op ten Graf) and N. Offengraf.
Abraham, a tailor, and N. Hamman.
Henrich Bartholome and Elisa Barbara Erb.
J.Reiswick and Creth Erb.
N. Dickenschitt and N---.
Henrich Frey and N---.
J. Schmidt and N---.
Conrad Moll and Elisa Barbara Hill.
Georg Weidner and Catharina Moll.
N--- and Anna Marg. Moll.
Diel Neiss and N. Hahn.
Salomon Rockenstuhl and widow of Grossjockel.
J. Adam Schneider and N. Levan
J. Brobst and Jacob Levan's oldest dau.
Ludwig Workman and Catharina Braun.
Richardt Klein and Elisabeth Horneck.
Georg Hertzel and Catharina Neiss.
Andreas Workman and Catharina Frey.
Mathys Brickerdt and Maria Elisabetha N---.
Andres Niet and Catharina N---.
Georg Edelman and N---.
J. Mueller and N---.
Marcus Wannenmacher and N---.
J. Schmidt and Anna Margaretha N---.
Lorentz Bamberger and Scharlotta N---.
J. Kugeler and Catharina Bamberger.
Jacob Hildenbeitel and Anna Maria ---.
J. Button and N.Klein.
Widow Fried and her servant.
Simon Hirsch and Maria Elisabth Lawar.
Philip Boehm and Elisabeth Cath. Mombauer.
Philip Jans and Barbara Detweiler.
Jost Keller and Hannah N---.
Johannes Schneider and Catharina Dieringer.
Johannes Jost and Creth Schneider.

J. Koster and John Johnson's dau.
N--- and Bastian Schmidt's dau of Schipbach.
N--- and Brennaman's dau. of Schipbach.
Georg Meyer and Weiderman's oldest dau.
Philip Henrich's second son and N. Johnson.
J. Georg Linckheimer and N---.
Jacob Schaefer and Catharina, widow of Henrich Bitting.
Abraham Schriener and Anna Maria Schmid.
Samuel Somani and N. Greff.
N. Henrichs and N. Gottschalk.
N--- and a dau. of the young Gottschalk.
N--- and a dau. of the young Gottschalk.
Son of Leonhardt Hennerichs and dau. of Paul Hennerichs.
Son of Leonhardt Hennerichs and dau. of Paul Hennerichs.
Son of Leonhardt Hennerichs and N---.
Son of Paul Hennerichs and dau. of John Frey.
N--- and dau. of Christian Weber of Madetschi.
Son of Kaiser of Madetschi and N---.
N--- and dau. of Jost Becker.
Son of John Frey and daugther of Paul Hennerichs.
Son of Felix Lee and N---.
Servant of Uly Stauffer and his maid servant.
N--- and dau. of W. Keiber.
N--- and oldest dau. of Mathys Ochs.
N. Obenbeck of Cockscreek and N---.
J. Weitzel and dau. of John Gressman.
John, son of Philip Zimmer and dau. of Kilian Zimmerman.
Son of Lorentz Hennerichs and N. Gottschalk.
Third son of Lorentz Hennerichs and N--- of Madetchi.
W. Weitzel and N--- of Dinikum.
Henrich Gremmeling and Catharine, stepdau. of Georg Heilig.
N--- and Catharina, dau. of Philip Zimmer.
N--- and dau. of Killian Zimmerman.
J. Weiss and N----.
Jacob N. And Anna Weiss.
N--- and N. Weiss.
Henrich N--- and Anna Maria Gemehli.
Henrich Huber and Christina N---.
Casper Huber and Anna N---.
N. Weiss and N---, widow living at Hosensack.
J. Schlosser and N---.
Thomas Koch and N---.
Abraham Lucken and Margreth Frey.

J. Hoffman and Catharina Zimmerman.
Casper Hoffman and Dorothea Leiser.
Henrich Schmidt and Rachel Denny.
J. Seller and Nany Johnson.
Baltasar Rabanus and Elisabetha Kremer.
Christian Buhler and Sarah Huntzberger.
Melchoir Schultz and Catharina Kohlbeck.
Jan. 7, 1758 J. Adam Eckmin and Christina N---.
Jan. 26, 1758 Balthasar Stiel and Christina Wickerd.
Jan. 26, 1758 Johann Jacob Mueller and Margaretha Eckerd.
Feb. 7, 1758 Johann Schwenck and Anna Cath. Christ.Huber.
Mar. 6, 1758 J. Martin Mueller and Catharina Gruen.
Mar. 30, 1758 Matthys Rittenhausen and Catharina Von Vasen.
Mar. 28, 1758 Georg Schill and Eva Merg. Kraessler.
Mar. 4, 1758 Philip Heiss and Susana Schmid.
Mar. --, 1758 J. Jacob Huber and Anna Cath. Kehler.
Mar. 26, 1758 Wilhelm Mueller and Catharina Schultz.
Apr 20, 1758 Joseph Schmidt and Catharina Frey.
Apr. 18, 1758 Johan Adam Willauer and Anna Maria Linn.
Apr. 11, 1758 Johan Peter Seib and Anna Maria Erb.
May 2, 1758 Georg Reinheimer and Maria Cath. Suessholtz.
May 30, 1758 David Brunner and Maria Landess.
Jun. 6, 1758 Paul Schwanger and Barbara Bieker.
Jun. 27, 1758 David Schultz and Elisabeth Lar.
Jul. 15, 1758 Henrich Fritz and Maria Anders (?).
Sept 26, 1758 Mathys Kern and Veronica Weidman.
Oct 19, 1758 Georg Gangwehr and Maria Melchior.
Nov. 14, 1758 Andres Beyer and Philippina Wigand.
Jan 4, 1759 Wendel Reiniger and Anna Marg. Mey.
Jan. 9, 1759 Joh Christ. Kahlbach and Anna Cath. Fabian.
Jan. 18, 1759 Jacob Griesemer and Catharina Hahlmann.
Jan. 27, 1759 Valladin [Valentin] Schillig and Maria Elis. Moll.
Apr. 3, 1759 Joseph Eberhardt and Catharina Siegel.
Apr. 5, 1759 Henrich Huber and Ann Cath. Huber.
Apr. 17, 1759 Jacob Beyer and Anna Maria Worth.
Apr. 15, 1759 J. Zeller and Anna Barbara Jeckels.
Apr. 20, 1759 Sylvanus Mabury and Le Miatta de Blema.
Jun. 26, 1759 Andreas Haag and Christina Hinderleiter.
Aug. --, 1759 Peter Sell and N--- Allwein.
Sept 27, 1759 Peter Mauerer and C. Berst.
Oct. 9, 1759 Peter Kumpf and Eva Elisabetha Kiefer.
Oct. 8, 1759 Johan Fischer and Catharina Gabel.
Oct. 26, 1759 Jacob Wetzel and Anna Maria Hag.

Oct. 23, 1759 Peter Weber and Anna Marg. Kayser.

Nov. 13, 1759 Johannes Wiehn and Appolonia Moll.

Nov. 18, 1759 Daniel Gicheidt and Barbara Mosser (?).

Nov. 20, 1759 Peter Samsel and Maria Catharina Sem.

Dec. 18, 1759 Henrich Jacob Rauch and Magdalena Kierner.

Jan. 8, 1760 Ludwig Bieder (?) And Margaretha Fischer.

Feb. 5, 1760 Johannes Meyer and Esther Contir.

Feb. 26, 1760 Michael Roeder and Barbara Meyer.

Feb.28, 1760 Wilhelm Rittenhaus and Margaretha Umstett.

Mar 25, 1760 Hartman Leibenguth and Anna Barbara Hornberger.

Apr 15, 1760 Johann Michel Seib and Anna Barbara Eidel.

Apr. 17, 1760 Jacob Kuester and Elisabeth von Vossen.

---, 1760 J. Georg Lahr and Catharina Fink.

Oct. 28, 1760 J. Christian Scheitt and Maria Elis. May.

Nov. 25, 1760 Philip Lahr and Elisabeth Mack.

Nov. 25, 1760 J. Henrich Stedler and Anna Catharina Mack.

Nov 26, 1760 Johann Fridich Reiss, Lutheran minister at New Goshenhoppen, and N---.

Jun. 17, 1760 Johann Jacob Dankel and Elisabeth Roeder.

Jun. 19, 1760 Simon Conrad Grineus and Anna Marg. Rab.

Oct 14, 1760 Casper Bucher and Catharina Wannenmacher.

Dec. 14, 1760 Johann Michael Hettenbach and Anna Maria Dahl.

Nov. 25, 1760 Johannes Maurer and Anna Marg. Ohl.

May 12,1761 Johann Philip Dosch and Veronica Eberhard.

May 12, 1761 Georg Fischer and Anna Barbara Eberhard.

May 19,1761 Johannes Wetzel and Eva Meyer.

May 13, 1761 Philip Hahn a nd Anna Marg. Hiester.

Jun. 16, 1761 Johannes Eberhardt and Cath. Elisabetha Ried.

Burial Records of New Goshenhoppen

Persons buried by John Th. Faber:

1766, Oct. 21. Abraham Segler's little dau. was buried.

1766, Dec. 8. Andreas Graber's little dau. was buried.

1766, Dec. 26. Jacob Meyer was buried.

1767, Jan. 3. Bernd Lent's little dau. was buried.

1767, Feb. 20. The old Mr. Layendecker was buried.

1767, Jun. 4. A little son of Peter Hellieas was buried named Johannes, aged 1 year less 14 das.

1767, Jun. 23. A son of Georg Reinheimer was buried, named Johannes, aged 2 yrs, 2 mos, 4 das, of New Goshenhoppen.

1767, Jul. 20. A dau. of Johannes Staut was buried named Anna Maria, aged 1 year, 3 mos, less several das.

1767, Aug. 17. A dau. of Michael Raeder was buried, aged 2 yrs, 8 mos, 4 weeks.

1767, Nov. 24. Peter Mack, brother of Peter Mayer's wife of New Goshenhoppen, was buried; born 1707, aged 55 years.

1767, Nov. 14. The wife of Mathias Walder was buried, named Anna Maria, born 1714, Nov. 4; aged 53 yrs, less several das.

1768, Jun. 7. A dau. of Peter Hellicas was buried, named Eva, born 1768, Mar. 20; aged 11 weeks and 1 day.

1768. An old woman was buried, born in the year (I don't know), aged about 6o years.

1769, Mar. 7. A dau. of Mr. Lauer was buried, named Sara, born 1769, Jan 23; aged 6 weeks and 3 das.

1769, Mar 18. A dau. of Henrich Barleman was buried, named Anna Margaretha, born 1766, Jun. 4; aged 4 yrs, 9 months and 5 das.

1769 May 28. David Mayn was buried; born in 1738; aged 38 yrs, 8 months and 15 das.

1770, Feb. 14. A son of --- was buried, named John Erhart, born 1769, May 15; aged 8 mos, 3 weeks, 4 das.

1770, Jan. 21. Anna Margareta Faabin was buried; born 1749, Oct 9; aged 20 yrs, 4 mos, 9 das.

1770, Feb. 14. Michael Moll was buried; born 1700; aged 70 years.

1770 Apr. 10. Michael Huper's son was buried named Johannes, born 1769, Dec. 16; aged 17 weeks and several das.

1770, Apr. 23. A son of John Jacob Danckel was buried, named Henrich, born 1761, Mar. 21; aged 9 yrs, 1 month.

1770 Dec. 14. A dau. of Peter Panebecker was buried, named Anna Maria, born 1770 Dec. 4; aged 9 das and 1 night.

1771 Mar. 25, Elisabeth Panebecker was buried; born 1750, Jun. 8; aged 20 yrs, 9 mos, 3 weeks.

1771, Apr. 18. Anna Margaretha Danckel was buried; born 1696, Feb. 10; aged 75 yrs, 2 Mos, 5 das.

1771, Jul. 27. Margaretha Getto Morin (a negress), dau. of Getto Mor, was buried; born 1756; aged 15 years.

1771, Aug. 27. Robert Bel was buried; born 1735; aged 36 yrs, 20 weeks and several das.

1772, Feb. 7. The old Mr. Conrad was buried; born 1699; aged a little above 73 years.

1772, Apr. 1. Conrad Wannemnacher was buried; born 1701; aged 70 yrs, 3 months and 20 das.

1772, May 30 Magdalena Schuler was buried; born 1715, Jun. 17; aged 57 years less 16 das.

1772 Jun. 3. Catharina Gucker was buried; born 1696; aged about 76 years.

1771 Aug. 4. Georg Reinheirner's son was buried, named Joh. Philippus, born

1771, Sept. 8; aged i year less 5 weeks.

1772, Sept. 6. Michael Raeder's dau. was buried, named Elisabetha, born 1772, Feb 18; aged half a year less 4 weeks.

1771, Nov. 21. Peter Gesell was buried; born 1726, Sept 7; aged 46 yrs, 2 mos, 1 week and 5 das.

1773 Jan 24. Sarah Laur was buried; born 1731, Oct 20 aged 35 yrs, 3 months.

1773, Jan. 29. Michael Raeder's child was buried; born 1772, Jan 16; 1 year, 2 weeks.

1773, Feb. 12. Michael Raeder's child was buried; born 1770, Apr. 11; aged 3 years less 8 weeks and 3 das.

1773, Feb. 21. A child of Michael Raeder; born 1762, Mar. 5; aged 11 years less 2 weeks.

1773, Apr. 8. A negro child of John Adam Hellicas; born about 1771; aged about 2 years and several months.

1773, Apr. 10. A dau. of Wilh. Geiger was buried; born 1756, Nov. 29; aged 16 yrs, 4 mos, 10 das.

1773, Mar. 17. The wife of young Mr. Mack was buried; born 1743, Apr. 3; aged 27 yrs, 11 mos, 13 das.

1773, May 18. A son of Andreas Jung was buried; born 1770, Mar. 12; aged 3 yrs, 2 mos, 5 das.

7773, Jun. 3. Joh. Valentin Grisemer was buried; born 1688, Jan 4; aged 85 yrs, 5 months less 4 das.

1773, Jun. 22. A dau. of Rudolph Dresch was buried; born 1772, Aug. 7; aged 1 year less 8 weeks.

1773, Aug. 13. Peter Lauer's dau. was buried; born 1770, Jan. 24; aged 3 yrs, 5 mos, 13 weeks and several das.

1773, Oct 11. A dau. of Michael Schell was buried; born 1758, Mar. 10; aged 14 yrs, 7 months.

1773, Nov. 12. A dau. of Leonhart Kriesemer was buried; born 1773, Jan 14; aged 10 mos, 4 das.

1774 Jan 5. A son of Henr. Rauch was buried; born 17773, Dec 24; aged 11 das.

1774, Fehr. 23. Anna Maria Gillwein (a negress) was buried; born 1750; aged 23 years and about 6 months.

1774, Feb 2. Joh. Engel was buried; born 1706; aged 68 years.

1774, Mar. 25. Adain Bossert was buried; born 1714; aged 62 years.

1774 Jun 3. A son of Conrad Helligas was buried; born 1774, Jan 13; aged 4 mos, 2 weeks, 5 das.

1774, Jun. 13. Michael Lieser was buried; born 1720; aged about 54 years.

1774, Sept. 18. A dau. of John. Georg Kolb was buried; born 1773, May 16; aged 1 year, 4 months.

1774 Dec 15. A dau. of Abr. Gerhart was buried; born 1771, Jan 2; aged 3 yrs, 11 mos, 12 das.

1775 Jan 15. A dau. of Philip Leidecker was buried; born 1774, Jun. 1; aged 7 mos, 13 das.

1775, Feb. 14. A dau. of Conrad Nuss was buried; born 1773, Nov. 4, aged 1 year, 3 mos, 1 week.

1775, Jan. 17. A dau. of the late Michael Lieser was buried; born 1774, Dec. 9; aged 1 year, 5 mos, several das.

1775, Apr. 19. The old Mrs. Steinmann was buried; born 1709, Mar. 18; aged 68 yrs, 6 weeks, 1 day.

1775, Apr. 19. A dau. of Joseph Kolb was buried; born 1775, Jan 25; aged 11 weeks, 3 das.

1775, Apr. 11. A son of Justus Eckhart was buried; born 1773, Sept. 18; aged 1 year, 6 mos, 3 weeks.

1775, Mar. 6. A son of Georg Schutz was buried; born 1768, Mar. 25; aged 7 years less 3 weeks.

1775, Mar. 8. A son of Henr. Schneider was buried; born 1775, Jan 24; aged 6 weeks, 5 das.

1775, Mar. 14. A son of Jacob Kugler was buried; born 1774, Sept, 7; aged 6 mos, 6 das.

1775 Apr. 27 Jacob Frack was buried; born 1690, Aug. 16; aged 84 yrs, 8 months.

1775, Apr. 27. A son of Conrad Gillam was buried; born 1774, Jan. 19; aged 1 yrs, 3 mos, 6 das.

1775, May 23. Anna Maria Reninger was buried; born 1745, May 6; aged 30 years.

1775, Aug, 15. Elis. Barbara Staut was buried; born 1748, Jul. 24; aged 27 yrs, 21 das.

1775, Aug. 9. A son of Peter Heisst was buried; born 1773, Jul. 22; aged 2 yrs, 18 das.

1775, Aug. 17. A son of Jacob Lang was buried; born 1774, Feb. 7; aged 3 years 6 mos, 8 das.

1775, Aug. 23. A dau. of Peter Maurer was buried; born 1762, Jun. 28, aged 13 yrs, 7 weeks, 6 das.

1775 Sept. 13. A dau. of Joh. Cunius was buried; born 1772, Nov 6; aged 2 yrs, 10 mos, 6 das.

1775 Dec 20. A son of Henr. Bachmann was buried; born 1773, Feb. 2; aged 2 yrs, 11 mos, 14 das.

1775 Dec. 23. A dau. of Daniel Lambrecht was buried; born 1774, Aug. 9; aged 1 year, 4 mos, 3 weeks, 3 das.

1775 Dec. 26. A dau. of Daniel Lambrecht was buried; born 1773, Mar 4; aged 2 yrs, 9 mos, 20 das.

1775, Dec. 27. Ludwig Bitting was buried; born 1703; aged about 73 years.

1776 Jan. 6. A dau. of Joh. Schell was buried; born 1773, Jul 29; aged 2 yrs, 5 mos, 8 das.

1776 Jan 22. A dau. of Jacob Holzhausen was buried; born 1774, Mar. 25; aged

1 yr, 9 mos, 26 das.

1776 Feb 22. The wife of Phil. Wischang was buried; born 1702; about 74 years of age.

1776, Apr. 25. John George Hering was buried; born 1755, Nov. 13; aged 22 yrs, 6 months.

1776, May 1. A dau. of Henr. Mueller was buried; born 1770, Nov. 13; aged 5 yrs, 5 mos, 13 das.

1776, May 17. Catharine Weber was buried; born 1709, Apr. 6; aged 67 yrs, 1 month, 9 das.

1776, Jul. 5. Anna Maria Gertruta Reiter was buried; born 1709, Apr. 26; aged 67 yrs, 2 mos, 7 das.

1776, Sept. 24. Rudolph Segler was buried; born 1747, May 4; aged 29 yrs, 4 Mos, 3 weeks, several das.

1776, Nov. 24. Margaretha Raudebusch was buried; born 1702; aged 74 years and 8 weeks.

1776, Des 26. A son of Wendel Wiant was buried; born 1776, Aug. 4; aged 20 weeks and some das.

1777, Jan. 7. A son of Caspar Bastian was buried; born 1777, Jan. 18; aged 2 weeks and 4 das.

1777, Jan. 7. A son of Joseph Leopold was buried; born 1775, Mar. 26; aged 1 year, 10 mos, 1 week.

1777, Feb. 5. A son of Jacob Wetknecht was buried; born 1757, Mar. 11; aged 19 yrs, 10 mos, 12 das.

1776, Oct. 20. A son was born ? to Fried. Schell named Magdalena. Witnesses Georg Kolb and wife.[This may be a birth mistakely placed with deaths.]

1777, Jan. 5. The old Mrs. Segler was buried; born 1709, Dec 25; aged 68 years 8 das.

1777, Mar. 3. Michael Huper was buried; born 1715, Jul. 29; aged 61 yrs, 7 months.

1777, Mar. 14, Johannes Gillam was buried; born 1761 Nov. 22; aged 15 Yrs, 3 mos, 3 weeks.

1777, Mar. 19. Anna Maria Berret was buried; born 1699; about 78 years old.

1777, Apr. 12. Anna Maria Holshaus was buried; born 1740, Mar. 19; aged 37 yrs, 12 das.

1777, Apr. 14. Peter Maurer's wife was buried; born 1740, Feb. 15; aged 36 yrs, 2 mos, less a few das.

1777, Apr. 18. Benedict Moll was buried; born 1742, about Nov.; aged about 35 Years.

1777, May 4. Joh. Schell was buried; born 1729, Jan. 22; aged 48 years and 3 months.

1777, May 6. A dau. of Adam Hilligas was buried; aged 9 das.

1777, May 25. A child of Peter Loch was buried; aged 12 das.

1777, May 23. A son of Fried. Muller was buried; aged 12 yrs, 2 mos, 6 das.

1777, Aug. 12. Three children of Andreas Weiller were buried, namely, two dau.s and one son; the oldest dau. was born 1758, Apr. 16; aged 19 yrs, 4 mos, less some das; the second dau. was born 1759, Aug. 25; she was 18 years less a week and some das; the son was born 1766, Jun. 9; aged 11 yrs, 2 mos, 2 das.

1777 Aug 7. A dau. of Peter Maurer was buried; born 1773, Feb. 7; aged 4 years and 6 months.

1777, Aug. 4. A son of Hermin Fischer was buried; born 1774, Jan. 5; aged 3 yrs, 7 months.

1777, Aug. 25. A son of Andreas Weiller was buried; born 1763, Oct. 6; aged 14 yrs, 1 month, 5 das. Eight das later another son was buried.

1777, Aug. 26. The old Mrs. Haas was buried; born 1702; aged 75 years.

1777 Aug. Joh. Staut was buried; born in, Jul. 27; aged 1 year, 3 weeks.

1771 Aug. 30. A child of Jacob Espenschiedt was buried; born 1775, Jan. 18; aged 2 yrs, 7 mos, 8 das.

1777, Sept. 21. A child of Benedict Horne was buried; born 1771, Apr. 5; aged 6 yrs, 5 mos, 14 das.

1777, Sept 30. A child of Peter Timich was buried; born 1776, Dec. 3; aged 10 months less 4 or 5 das.

1777, Oct. 22. A son of Jacob Mueller was buried; born 1766, Jan. 7; aged 11 yrs, 9 mos, 2 weeks.

1777, Dec. 1. The wife of the Schoolmaster Schubart was buried; born ---; aged 68 yrs, less 3 months and 4 das.

1777, Nov. 20. Margaretha Geiger was buried; born 1762, Aug. 4; aged 15 yrs, 3 mos, 12 das.

1778, May 1. A child of Martin Eisenhauer was buried; born Jan 5; aged 4 months less 4 das.

1778, May 17. A dau. of Eberh. Christoffel Schart was buried; born 1762, Dec 20; aged 15 yrs, 22 weeks and 3 das.

1778, May 21. A child of Lorens Schmidt was buried; born 1776, Sept. 2; aged 1 year, 9 mos, 17 das.

1778, Dec. 10. Georg Reinheimer was buried; born 1727, Feb. 21; aged 51 yrs, 10 mos, several weeks.

1779, Jan. 2. A dau. of Peter Gucker was buried; born 1771, Jul 5; aged 7 yrs, 6 mos, less 5 das.

1779, Jan. 12. A dau. of Peter Gucker was buried; born 1773, Oct. 23; aged 5 yrs, 3 mos, less 9 das.

1779, Mar. 13. The old Adam Hilligas was buried; born 1717, Jan. 5; aged 62 yrs, 3 mos, 8 das.

1779, May 2. A child of Joh. Sanger was buried; born 1775, May 31; aged 4 yrs, 2 monts.

1779, Jun. 7. A son of Henry Schlieger was buried; born 1777, Oct 17; aged 1 year, 7 mos, 3 weeks.

1779 Jun. 15. A child of Conrad Nus was buried; born 1778, Aug. 17; aged 10 mos, less 3 das.

1779, Jun. 18. A child of Georg Hilligas was buried; born 1778, Oct 5; aged 1 year, 9 mos, 12 das.

1779, Aug. 5. A dau. of the late Michael Moll was buried; born 1739, about Mar.; aged about 40 years.

Persons buried during the Ministry of Friedrich Delliker, in the congregation of New Goshenhoppen:

1783, Jan. 5. Abraham, 1 year, 1 Month, 14 das old; parents are Benedict Horning and his wife Elisabeth.

1783, Jan. 11. Joh. Adam, 8 das, hours old; parents are Andreas Rid and wife Maria.

1783, May 23. Johannes Steinmann, his age 39 yrs, 4 months.

1783, Jun. 25. Maria, 1 year, 8 mos, 11 das old; parents Georg Steineman and Catharine, his wife.

1783, Jun. 30. Samuel Kolb, his age 29 yrs, several das.

1783, Aug. 12. Georg Raudenbusch, his age 84 years.

1783, Sept. 5. Joh. Philip Rid, born 1698, Jan. 26; his age 85 yrs, 7 mos, 8 das.

1783, Oct. 15. Johannes Mack, his age 32 yrs, 9 Mos, 4 das. He died by an accidental fall from a wagon within 17 das.

1783, Dec. 4. Elisabeth, 14 yrs, 7 mos, 6 das old; parents Daniel Ekbrett and Elisabeth his wife.

1783, Dec.5. Abraham Segler, his age 54 yrs, 2 months. He fell from his horse near his house and was found dead in the water.

1784, Feb 8. Catharine, 14 das, 6 hours old; parents Andreas Rid and his wife, Maria.

1784, Mar. 11. David Levi, his age not quite 56 years.

Buried during the ministry of Fried. Wilh. Von der Sloot:

1784, Apr. 25 Peter May, his age 70 yrs, 2 mos, a Lutheran.

1784, Jun. 12. Maria Nuss, nee Reder, aged 27 years.

1784, Oct. 16. Anna Margaretha, her father, Georg Fischer; her age 19 yrs, 8 months.

Persons buried by Joh. Theob. Faber:

In the year 1786 with their date of birth.

1785, May 4. Sus. Cath. Nus, aged 1 year, several weeks.

1783, May 24, Petrus Huper, aged 3 years less 5 weeks.

1786, Apr. 27, Johannes Huper, aged 1 month, 2 weeks.

1786, May 4, child of young Grisermer, aged 4 mos, 2 das. 1786, 1786, Jul. 27, child of Val. Brobst, aged 11 das.

1786, Jul. 18, child of Peter Hilligas, aged 7 weeks, 2 das. 1751, Jos. Leobold, aged 35 years.

1786, Sept. 27, child of Georg Dorr, aged 13 das.

1720, old Mrs. Benkes, aged 66 years.

1718, Nov. 6, Adam Geri, aged 68 years.

1786, Nov. 27, child of Jacob Geri, aged 2 yrs, 3 weeks.

1716, Oct. 16, Conrad Zimmerman, aged 70 yrs, 1 month, 3 weeks. 1761, Dec. 19, Peter Zimmerman, aged 25 years.

In the year 1787 with their date of birth.

1764, Mar. 13, Henr. Herger, aged 22 yrs, 11 mos, 11 das.

1775, Aug. 18, Peter Rautebusch, aged 11 yrs, 8 mos, less 10 das.

1784, Sept. 29, Johannes Heisst, aged 2 yrs, 6 mos, 2 weeks. 1786, Oct. 5, Johannes Trumb, aged 6 mos, 11 weeks.

1730, Jacob Holshauser, aged 57 years.

1767, Mar. 25 dau. of Phil. Jacob Schmid, aged 20 yrs, 2 months.

1709, Jul. 14, old Mr. Wendel Wiant, aged 78 years.

1787 Feb. 23 a child of Mr. Dimig, aged 3 mos, 12 das.

1787, Aug 10, child of Andr. Ried, aged 8 das.

1781 Nov. 22 child of Georg Fischer, aged 3 yrs, 10 mos, 11 das.

1784, Mar. 25. child of Joh. Bidling, aged 3 yrs, 6 mos, 17 das.

1735 Apr. 3, Joh. Fischer, aged 52 yrs, 6 mos, 10 das.

1784, Feb. 6. child of Joh. Muller, aged 3 yrs, 9 months.

1787 Oct 9, child of Peter Trumb, aged 2 yrs, 1 month, 3 das.

1785 Aug. 13, child of Adam Roeder, aged 2 yrs, 3 months.

1783 Aug. 18 child of Adam Roeder, aged 4 yrs, 3 months.

1787, Oct 12, child of Joh. Fischer, aged 7 mos, 18 das. 1717, old Mrs. Jung, aged 71 years.

1713, old Win. Grisemer, aged 75 yrs, several months.

In the year 1788 with their date of birth.

1794, Feb. 1, child of Jacob Stahl, aged 4 years less a month. 1787, Apr. 27, child of young Adam Schneider, aged 8 mos, 14 das.

1786, Feb. 8, child of Georg Lang, aged 1 year, 11 mnths, 11 das.

1787, Aug. --, child of Mr. Schwartz.

1786, Nov. 29, child of Joh. Lambrecht, aged 13 mos, 21 das. 1786, May 12, child of Zach. Wagner, aged 1 year, 8 mos, 12 das.

1726, Cath. Schlieger, aged 62 years.

1783, Jan. 27, Maria Cath. Hillegas, aged 5 yrs, 1 week, 4 das.

1782, Jul. 28, son of Ludwig Bitting, aged 5 yrs, 7 months.

1784, Mar. 5, child of Georg Dorr, aged 4 years less 4 das.

1784, Oct. 26, child of Henr. Panebecker, aged 3 yrs, 4 mos, 5 das.

1788, Sept. 19, Joh. Georg, aged 1 year, 6 months.

1746, Henrich Maurer, aged 42 years.

1781, Feb. 9, Catharina, aged 7 yrs, 6 mos, 4 weeks.

Members NeW Goshenhoppen who died and were buried by N. Pomp in 1789 with their date of birth.
1768, Dec. 6, Jacob Rieth, aged 20 years 11 mos, 28 das.
1718, Dec. 25, Peter Miller, aged 70 yrs, 11 mos, 19 das.
Buried Feb 16, 1789. George Michael Kolb, aged 81 yrs, 25 das.
Buried Feb. 16, 1789. Anna Maria Stroh, aged 59 yrs, 7 mos, 2 das.
Buried Mar, 25, 1789. Dorothea Hollebusch, aged 68 years.
Buried Jun. 16, 1789. Elisabeth Gehry, aged 25 yrs, 10 mos, 21 das.

Those persons who were buried by Joh. Theob. Faber, Jr. 1791 with their date of birth.
1787, Jun. 3, child of Peter Hilligas, aged 4 years 6 mos, 8 das.
Those persons who were buried by Joh. Theob. Faber, Jr. 1792 with their date of birth.
1790, Jul. 24, Susan, child of George Wigner, aged 1 year, 8 months.
1707, Sept 29, Maria Kemp, widow, aged 82 yrs, 6 mos, 2 weeks.
1716, Jul. 27, Fried. Miller, aged 75 yrs, 8 mos, 3 weeks, 2 das.
--- child of Joseph Kolb, aged 12 yrs, 2 mos, 13 day.
--- Andr. Weiler, aged 68 yrs, 5 mos, 3 weeks, 4 das.
--- wife of Stev. Shoner.
--- wife of Georg Horlacher, aged 33 yrs, 2 montht 3 week 2 das.
May 6, Georg Orffer (?).
May 12 (buried), Wife of Heinr. Miller, aged 56 yrs, 1 month, 1 day.
Mar. 1, Elisabeth.

Those persons who were buried by Joh. Theob. Faber, Jr. 1795 with their date of birth.
1746, Jul. 31, Anna Marg. Borleman, aged 48 yrs, 5 mos, 2 weeks, 4 das.
1717, Dec., Weyand Panebecker, aged 79 yrs, 2 mos, 2 das.
1785, Dec 25, Susana, child of Godf. Wissler, aged 9 years 2 mos.
1785, Apr. 16, Jacob, child of Adam Hittel, aged 9 yrs less 3 das.
1794, Apr. 25, Maria Cath., dau of Henry Geiger, aged 11 mos, 4 days.

Marriages
1767, Mar 3, Johannes Hellicas, son of Adam Hellicas, of New Goshenhoppen, and Anna Maria Geri, dau of Jacob Geri, also of New Goshehoppen.
1767, May 26, Wendel Fischer, son of the late Herman Fischer, of Upper Hanover, and Juliana Schneider, dau of Adam Schneider, of Douglas twp.
1767, May 26, Michael Moll, son of Michael Moll, of Upper Hanover, and Margaretha Schmeck, dau. of the late Johannes Schmeck, of·Elsass twp.
1767, Jun. 16, Johannes Steinmann, son of the late Georg Steinmann, of Herford

twp., and Anna Catharina Maurer, dau. of the late Jacob Maurer, of New Goshenhoppen.

1767, Jun. 23, Christoph Schliger, son of the late Johannes Otto Schlinger, of New Goshenhoppen, and Margaretha Mack, dau. of Johannes Mack, of New Goshenhoppen.

1767, Jun. 23, Friedrich Maurer, son of the old Friedrich Maurer, of New Goshenhoppen, and Catharina Beyer, dau. of the late Henrich Beyer, of Herford twp.

1767, Nov. 10, Michael Hellicas, son of Adam Hellicas, of New Goshenhoppen, and Catharina Geri, dau. of Jacob Geri, of New Goshenhoppen.

1768, Feb.4, Andreas Riedt, son of Philip Riedt, of New Goshenhoppen, and Anna Maria Leidi, dau. of Jacob Leidi, of Franconia twp.

1768, Jun. 28, Jacob Segler, son of the late Joh. Segler, of New Goshenhoppen, and Christina Filcher, dau. of the late Herman Filcher, of Upper Hanover Twp.

1768, Sept. 6, Jacob Frack's son, Daniel Frack, of New Goshenhoppen, and Catharine, dau. of the late Jost Wiant, of New Goshenhoppen.

1768, Nov. 22, Jacob Kammerer, son of Friedrich Kammerer, of Upper Milford, and Andreas Maurer's dau., Elisabetha Maria, of New Goshenhoppen.

1769, Jan. 10, Jacob, son of the late Joh. Taub, of New Goshenhoppen, and Anna Margaretha, dau. of Conrad Zimmerman, of New Goshenhoppen.

1769, Apr. 25, George Michael, son of George Michael Kolb, of New Goshenhoppen, and Eva Maria, dau. of Friedr. Stellwagen, of Marion Twp.

1769, Aug. 22, Conrad, son of the late Jacob Nus, of Upper Hanover Twp, and Maria Margaretha Roeder, dau. of Michael Roeder, of Upper Hanover Twp.

1769, Aug. 15, Lorentz, son of David Schmid, of Plumstet Twp, and Susanna Kolb, dau. of George Michael Kolb, of Hanover Twp.

1769, Oct. 12, Jacob, son of Jacob Schlosser, of Old Goshenhoppen, and Anna Cath. Schwartz, dau. of Weiland Schwartz, of Old Goshenhoppen.

1769, Oct. 17, Jacob, son of the late Jacob Lutz, of Maxatawny, and Anna Christina Bossert, dau. of Ada Bossert, of New Goshenhoppen.

1770, Apr. 17, Jacobus, son of the late Jost Wiant, of New Goshenhoppen, and Catharine Schlichter, dau. of John Schlichter, of New Goshenhoppen.

1770, Sept. 30, Joh. Georg, son of Adam Hellicas, of New Goshenhoppen, and Elisabeth Jung, dau. of Joh. Nicolaus Jung, of New Goshenhoppen.

1770, Oct. 2, Melchior Kolb, widower, of New Goshenhoppen, and Anna Maria Stettler, widow, of Falkner Swamp.

1771, Jan. 4, Jost, son of Wendel Wiant, of Upper Hanover Twp, and Anna Barbara Roder, dau. of Michael Roder, of Upper Hanover.

1772, Jan. 14, Valentin, son of Joh. Nicolas Finck, of Herford Twp, and Elisabetha, dau. of Melchoir Sussholz, of New Goshenhoppen.

1772, May 5, Johannes, son of Joh. Krisemer, of Leter (!) Creek, and dau. of Joh. Adam Hellicas, of New Goshenhoppen.

1772, Oct. 13, Marty, son of Marty Hiller, of Limerick Twp, and Anna Roeder, dau. of Michael Raeder, of New Goshenhoppen.

1772, Oct. 13, Jacob, son of the late Jacob Hohl, of New Goshenhoppen, and Magdalena, dau. of Jacob Datismon, of New Goshenhoppen.

1773, Sept. 23, Christian, son of Joh. Henr. Schmid, of Upper Milford Twp, and Maria Geri, dau. of Thomas Geri, of Rockhill Twp.

1773, Nov. 2, Peter, son of Engle Binkes, of New Goshenhoppen, and Barbara, dau. of the late Henrich Stettler, of New Goshenhoppen.

1773, Oct. 25, Adam, son of Zach. Haller, of Lynn Twp, and Catharine, dau. of Wilh. Geier, of New Goshenhoppen.

1773, Dec. 7, Andreas, son of Andreas Weiller, of New Goshenhoppen and Anna Maria, dau. of Joh. Mack, of New Goshenhoppen.

1774, Jun. 14, Albertus Spring, son of the late Andreas Spring, of New Goshenhoppen, and Barbara, dau. of Peter Gettel, of New Goshenhoppen.

1774, Aug. 14, Carl Schelleberger, son of Joh. Schelleberger of Hatfield Twp, and Margaret Hellicas, dau. of Adam Hellicas, of New Goshenhoppen.

1774, Nov. 20, Friedrich Panebecker, son of the late Weiant Panebecker, of New Goshenhoppen, and Elis. Neukomer, dau. of Joh. Neukomer, of Lower Saucon.

1774, Dec.27, Joh. Taudt, of New Goshenhoppen, and Susanna Benvil, dau. of the late Thomas Benvil, of Berks County.

1775, Mar. 21, Joh. Klein, son of Joh. Klein, of Nentmil [Nantmill] Twp, and Cath. Bitting, dau. of Ludwig Bitting, of Great Swamp.

1775, Jul. 4, Wendel Wiant, widower, of New Goshenhoppen, and Magdalena Datismann, wife of the late Mr. Datismann, but now widow, of New Goshenhoppen.

1775, Jul. 2, Jost Wiant, son of Jost Wiant, of Upper Milford Twp, and Margaretha Long, dau. of Peter Long, of Upper Milford Twp.

1775, Aug. 15, Jacob Bossert, son of the late Adam Bossert, of Lower Salford, and Eva Schlieger, dau. of Just Schlieger, of New Goshenhoppen.

1775, Dec. 12, Henr. Schlieger, son of Jost Schlieger, of New Goshenhoppen, and Christina Weiller, dau. of Andreas Weiller, also of New Goshenhoppen.

1776, Feb. 20, Joh. Mack, son of Joh. Mack, of New Goshenhoppen, and Anna Maria Schell, dau. of Joh. Schell, also of New Goshenhoppen.

1776, May 7, Joh. Roeder, son of Michael Roeder, of New Goshenhoppen, and Maria Cath. Wiegner, of New Goshenhoppen.

1776, May 5, Valentin Schneider, son of the late Georg Schneider, of New Goshenhoppen, and Maria Wagner, dau. of Michael Wagner, of Old Goshenhoppen.

1776, Jun. 11, Henr. Panebecker, son of Weyant Panebecker, of New Goshenhoppen, and Susana Huper, dau. of Michael Huper, of Douglas Twp.

1776, Jun. 11, Joh. Adam Geri, son of Jacob Geri, of New Goshenhoppen, and Barbara Weiller, dau. of Andreas Weiller, of New Goshenhoppen.

1776, Jun., 9, Philip Vorschong, of New Goshenhoppen, and Anna Benges, of New Goshenhoppen.

1776, Jul. 2, Adam Helligas, son of Joh. Adam Helligas, of New Goshenhoppen, and Anna Schultz, dau. of Melchior Schultz, of New Goshenhoppen.

1777, Sept. 30, Michael Diel, son of the late Jacob Diel, of Upper Milford Twp, and Barbara Sussholtz, dau. of Melchior Sussholtz, of New Goshenhoppen.

1777, Dec. 2, Georg Faust, son of Georg Faust, of Tulpehocken, and Christina Maurer, dau. of Andreas Maurer, of New Goshenhoppen.

1778, Jan. 13, Jacob Dorr, son of Joh. Dorr, of Great Swamp, and Margaretha Muller, dau. of Henr. Muller, of New Goshenhoppen.

1778, Dec. 22, Dietrich Reiher, son of Martin Reiher, of Malbrick [Marlborough] Twp, and Elisabeth Graeber, dau. of Andreas Graeber, of New Goshenhoppen.

1779, Feb. 23, Jacob Nus, son of the late Jacob Nus, of New Goshenhoppen, and Anna Maria Roeder, dau. of Michael Roeder, of New Goshenhoppen.

1779, Mar. 9, Andreas Graeber, son of Andreas Graeber, of New Goshenhoppen, and Anna Weiss, dau. of Georg Weiss, of Upper Milford Twp.

1779, Mar. 16, Joh. Petrus Helligas, son of Georg Petrus Helligas, of New Goshenhoppen, and Anna Maria Maurer, dau. of Andreas Maurer, of New Goshenhoppen.

1779, Jun. 22, Jacob Brendel, son of the late Andreas Brendel, of Colebrookdale Twp, and Elis. Ritschert, dau. of James Ritschert, of Daumensich [Toamensing] Twp.

1779, Sept.17, Georg Long, son of the late Elis. Long, of New Goshenhoppen, and Anna Maria Graeber, dau. of Ulrich Graeber, of New Goshenhoppen.

1779, Jul. 21, Ludwig Graeber, son of Andreas Graeber, of New Goshenhoppen, and Elis. Joter, dau. of Jacob Joter, of Rocklin [Rockland] Twp.

1779, Sept. 30, Peter Lauer, son of Peter Lauer, of New Goshenhoppen, and Margaretha Filcher, dau. of Joh. Filcher, of New Goshenhoppen.

These were joined in marriage by Friedrich Delliker.

1782, Mar. 24, Georg Zerby and Maria Klein.

1782, Jun. 25, Georg Grob, son of Jacob Grob, of New Hanover Twp, and Margaretha Lar, dau. of Philip Lar.

1782, Sept. 3, David Sussholtz, widower, of New Hanover Twp, and Elisabeth Muller, dau. of Peter Muller, of Rockhill Twp.

1783, May 20, Samuel Kolb, son of Melchior Kolb, and Anna Maurer, dau. of Peter Maurer.

1784, Feb. 3, Heinrich Segler, son of Abraham Segler, and Elisabeth Gugger, dau. of Peter Gugger, of Upper Hanover Twp.

1784, Feb. 15, Philip Pauly and Elisabeth Mosch, of Eastown.

These were joined in marriage by Fridrich Wilhelm Von der Sloot
1784, Mar. 16, Hans Nioclas Mud, Jacob Mud's son and Anna Margaret Greber,
   dau. of Andreas Greber, both of this congregation.
1784, May 11, Johannes Keri [Geri], son of Jacob Keri, of New Goshenhoppen,
   and Susanna Wigner, dau. of the late George Wigner.
1784, May 25, Peter Jost, son of Johannes Jost, of Frederick Twp, and Eva
   Hillegas, dau. of Conrad Hillegas, of New Goshenhoppen.
1784, Jun. 27, Johannes Bergman, of Germany, and Anna Stromann.
1784, Jun. 29, Rev. Daliker married me, Friedrich Wilhelm Von der Sloot, only
   son of Friedrich Henrik Von der Sloot, late minister in Anhalt-Zerbst,
   Germany, to Anna Margaretha Ried, oldest dau. of Jacob Ried, of Hatfield
   Twp, Philadelphia County.
1784, Jul. 13, Conrad Wolf, son of Conrad Wolf, of Upper Milford Twp, and
   Catharine Jakels, dau. of Jeremias Jakel of Upper Milford Twp.
1784, Sept. 28, Peter Trump, son of Adam Trump, of Milford Twp, and Eva
   Rheder, dau. of Michael Reder, of Upper Hanover Twp.

These were joined in marriage by John Theobald Faber.
1786, Aug. 6, Joh. Stephan Linck, of Malburi [Marlborough] Twp, and
   Margaret Maurer, of New Hanover.
1786, Dec.19, Math. Hinerleiter, of Maxatawny, and Catharine Gerhard, of
   Douglas Twp.
1787, Mar. 6, Jacob Maurer, of New Goshenhoppen, and Eva Hornecker, of the
   same place.
1787, Mar. 13, Henr. Graeber and Christina Haas, both of Lower Saucon.
1787, Mar. 13, Martin Wetkecht, of New Goshenhoppen, and Maria Pertroin, of
   Old Goshenhoppen.
1787, Apr. 22, Petrus Stehler, of Upper Milford, and Christina Graeber, of New
   Goshenhoppen.
1787, Apr. 24, Jeremias Schiefer, of Upper Milford, and Catharine Schlieger,
   New Goshenhoppen.
1787, Apr. 24, Jacob Bierman and Christina Filcher, both of Berks County.
1787, May 3, ----- Weitner, of ----, and ---- Wagner.
1787, May 15, Wendel Wiant, of New Goshenhoppen, and Margaretha Sell, of
   New Goshenhoppen.
1787, Jun. 12, Johannes Finck, of New Goshenhoppen, and Elisabetha Neudorf,
   in New Goshenhoppen.
1787, Jun. 24, Peter Lang and Cath. Hageberg, both of Upper Milford Twp.
1787, Jun. 26, Joh. Faust, of Frederick Twp, and Susanna Walber, of the same
   Twp.
1787, Jul. 7, Georg Reinheimer, of New Goshenhoppen, and Margareth Cogg.
1787, Oct. 23, Georg Frey, of Limerick Twp, and Margaretha Griesemer, of
   New Goshenhoppen.

1787, Dec 18, Peter Willauer, of New Goshenhoppen, and Rebecka Geri, also of New Goshenhoppen.

1788, Jan. 8, Joh. Martin Schmidt, of Malbork [Marlborough] Twp, and Barbara Wetknecht, of the same Twp.

1788, Apr. 22, Georgus Maurer and Catharine Schultz, both of New Goshenhoppen.

1788, May 6, Johannes Wittner, of Oly, and Anna Margaretha Cunius, of New Goshenhoppen.

1788, May 13, Fried. Hering and Anna Levi, both of New Goshenhoppen.

N. Pomp, minister of the three united congregations, has duly married the following persons, beginning with Dec. 1, 1789.

1789, Dec. 22, Philip Schmayer, of Macungie, and Catharina Miller, dau. of Peter Miller, of New Goshenhoppen.

1789, Dec. 26, Philip Hubner, of Frederick Twp, Montgomery County, and Elisabeth Neiss, of Old Goshenhoppen.

1790, Jan.17, Henrich Raudenbusch and Catharine Schneider, both of New Goshenhoppen.

1790, Mar. 23, Johannes Dorr and Gertraut Schliecher.

1790, Mar. 30, Johannes Raudenbusch and Salome Hildebeutel.

1790, Jun. 1, Christophel Schlicher and Gertraut Schneider, married at Upper Milford.

1790, Apr. 10, Michael Dotter and Maria Margareth Hillegas.

Those persons who were duly united in marriage by John Faber, in New Goshenhoppen.

1793, Andreas Graeber and Sibilla Wolzelter.

1793, Samuel Brode and Barbara Berckstroser.

1793, Jacob Geri and Elisabeth Dreisler.

1793, Joseph Filcher and Barbara Miller.

1793, Jan. 22, John Christman and Catharine Wiant, both of New Goshenhoppen.

1793, Feb.26, Michael Moll and Elizabetha Sell.

1793, Apr. 2, Henrik Rhoeder and Margaretha Kowern.

1793, May 7, Michael Diederle and Barbara Borlemann.

1793, Jun. 2, John Hauswirth and Elisabeth Miller.

1793, Aug. 20, Jacob Roth, of Lower Saucon, and Margaretha Barkstroser.

1793, Michael Brauchler, of Berks County, and Elisabetha Kittlemann.

1794, Apr. 15, John Maurer and Maria Stahl, both of New Goshenhoppen.

1794 Apr. 15, Abraham Joder and Elisabeth Maurer, both of New Goshenhoppen.

1794, May 11, Abraham Levi and Eva Hillegas, dau. of Peter Hillegas.

1794, Nov. John Kuhler, son of John Kuhler, and Eva Sussholtz, dau. of Lorenz

Sussholtz.

1795, Jan. 4, Johannes Loch and Caty Neudig.

1795, Apr. 7, Daniel Zimmerman and Catharine Weiss.

1795, May 10, Henrich Boyer and Madlena Wissler.

1795, May 31, Jacob Ache and Maricha Hillegas.

1795 Jun. 7, William Lick and Catharine Wiand.

1795 Jun. 7, John George Hillegas and Maria Hillegas.

1795, Jun. 25, Peter Gerhard and Elisabetha Himmels.

1795, Jun. 28, Johannes Young and Barbara English.

1795, Aug. Johannes Haulages and Catharine Haulages.

1795, Dec., Henrich Sell and Margaretta Schmitt.

1796, Nov., George Staud and Hanna Sell.

1797, Apr., Michael Rhaudenbusch and Maria Sell.

1797, May. George Renninger and Mary Hein.

1797, Jun. 1, David Zerby and Maria Magdalena Jung.

OLD GOSHENHOPPEN CONGREGATION

The persons who were buried by J. T. Faber, in the years 1766 - 1778.

1766, Dec. 26, was buried Jacob Mayer, of Old Goshenhoppen.

1767, Jan 3, Bernd Eitel's little dau., living at Old Goshenhoppen, was buried.

1767, Jan. 7, Johannes, son of Antoni Lichti, was buried, of the congregation of Rittswell.

1767, Apr. 6, Henrich Bamberger was buried, of the congregation of Old Goshenhoppen.

1767, May 8, Johannes, son of Johannes Maurer, was buried, of New Goshenhoppen.

1767, May 20, Andreas, son of Hermann Gerlach was buried, of Old Goshenhoppen.

1767, May 29, Albertina, dau. of Andreas Ohl, was buried; aged 2 yrs, 9 months and several weeks, of Old Goshenhoppen.

1767, Mar. 6, Anna Maria, dau. of Johann Merden [Martin] Wer, was buried; aged half a year, several weeks, of Old Goshnehoppen.

1767, Sept. 8, a son of Jacob Wentz was buried, named ---; aged 2 yrs, 9 mos, 5 das.

1767, Sept 8, Johannes Alsentz, son of Johann Georg Alsentz, was buried; aged 4 year, 5 mos, less 2 das, of Germantown.

1768, Jan 31, Alleda, dau. of Sem Schuler, was buried; aged 19 yrs, 3 weeks less 2 das.

1768, Apr. 14, Peter Hollenbusch was buried; aged 59 years.

1769, Feb. 27, a woman, named Regula, of Old Goshenhoppen was buried; aged 70 years.

1769, Jul. 10, Margaretha, wife of Jost Keller, of Old Goshenhoppen was buried; aged about 40 years.

1769, Aug. 24, Margaretha, dau. of Georgus Kuchler, of Old Goshenhoppen, buried; aged 2 years and several months.

1769 Aug. 26, Elisabetha, dau. of Joh. Mainer of Old Goshenhoppen, was buried; aged 2 years and several months.

1769, Oct. 16, Elisabetha, dau. of Adam Schmidt, was buried, of Old Goshenhoppen, aged 1 year and 1 day.

1769, Nov. 8, Johannes, son of Wilhelm Bayer, of Old Goshenhoppen was buried; aged 1 year, 7 months and about 8 das.

1770, Mar. 6, Johann Petrus, son of George Mayer, of Old Goshenhoppen, was buried; aged 3 yrs, 4 months and 20 das.

1770, Apr. 19, Anna Catharina Eckert, of Old Goshenhoppen, was buried; born in the year 1740, about Apr., aged 30 yrs, 4 months and several das.

1770, Jun. 30, the old Mr. Panebecker, of Old Goshenhoppen, was buried; aged 59 yrs, 4 months and 8 das; he was born Mar. 10, 1710.

1771, Jan 4, a widow, named Barbara, of Old Goshenhoppen, was buried; aged 61 years less 9 weeks.

1771, Feb. 12, Ulrich Herzel, of Old Goshenhoppen, was buried; born 1705 Aug. 20, aged 65 and a half years less 9 das.

1771, Feb. 12, Johann Marx Hertzel, of Old Goshenhoppen, was buried. He was born 1746, date unknown, aged 24 yrs, 3 mos, etc.

1771, Mar. 16, Johannes, a son of Henrich Raess, of Indianfield, was buried. He was born 1754, Mar. 26, aged 17 years less 10 das.

1771, Mar. 18, Georg Wagner was buried. He was born 1702, Feb. 2, aged 69 yrs, 1 month, 16 das.

1771, May 8, Cornelius, son of Ernst Harr, of Indianfield, was buried. He was born 1749, Feb. 1, aged 21 yrs, 3 mos, 16 das.

1772, Apr. 5, Eva ---, of Old Goshenhoppen, buried. Born in the year 1699, date unknown, aged about 73 years.

1772, Jun. 13, Henrich Mieker, of Old Goshenhoppen, was buried. He was born 1715, date unknown, aged about 57 years.

1772, May 23, a son of Peter Maener, was buried. Born 1772, Feb. 17, aged 13 weeks and 3 das.

1772, Jul. 12, Johann Cantz was buried. Born 1718, (date unknown, aged about 53 years.

1771 Jul 12, a dau. of Wilhelm Demflin was buried. Born 1771, Aug. 15, aged 10 mos, 3 weeks, 5 das.

1772, Jul. 16, Johann Petrus, son of Johann Leh, was buried. Born 1771, Nov. 14, aged 8 months less a few das.

1772, Jun. 28, a child, named Jacobus was buried. Born 1771, Mar. 10, aged 1 year, 3 mos, 2 weeks and 1 day.

1772, Aug. 25, a child of Johann Mabri was buried. Born 1769, Nov 13, aged 3 yrs, 9 mos, 9 das.

1772, Sept. 28, Johann Mieker was buried. Born 1753, date unknown, aged 20 yrs, etc.

1772, Oct. 14, Heinrich, a son of Henrich Hohl, was buried. Born 1759, May 6, aged 13 years and perhaps 5 months.

1773, Feb. 1, Catharina Schuler was buried. Born May 4, 1695, aged 77 yrs, 3 months and several das.

1773, Jan. 14, a child of Benjamin Schuler was buried. Born 1772, Nov 25, aged 7 weeks.

1773, Feb. 5, a child of Johannes Hudt was buried. Born 1771, Nov. 29, aged 1 year, 2 mos, 4 das.

1773, Mar. 30, a son of Friedrich Mueller was buried. Born 1767, Mar. 1, aged 6 yrs, 4 weeks.

1773, Aug. 12, a son of Henrich Hemsig was buried. Born 1771, Jan. 30, aged 2 years and a half, 11 das.

1773, Aug. 30, a son of Ludwig Hersch was buried. Born 1773, Jul. 21, aged 5 weeks, 4 das.

1774, Jan. 29, a son of Georg Michael Schwartz was buried. Born 1768, Jun. 8, aged 5 yrs, 7 mos, 2 weeks, 5 das.

177, Jan 31, son of Andreas Werner was buried. Born 1773, Nov. 6, aged 14 mos, 3 weeks, 2 das.

17741 May 21, a woman, named --- was buried. Born 1730, Aug. ---, aged 43 yrs, 9 months.

1775, Jan 1, Samuel Schuler was buried. Born 1717, beginning of Feb., aged 58 years.

1775, Mar. 20, the wife of Johann Faust was buried. Born 1720, Jun. 25, aged about 55 years.

1775, Apr. 3, a son of Simon May was buried. Born 1752, day unknown, aged 23 yrs, 6 months.

1775, May 31, a dau. of Johannes Hud was buried. Born 1765, Sept 26, aged 9 yrs, 9 mos, 2 weeks, 4 das.

1775, Oct. 7, Mr. Roerig was buried. Born 1698, day unknown, aged about 77 yrs.

1775, Dec. 13, The wife of Philip Gerig was buried. Born 1696, day unknown, aged about 79 yrs.

1776 Feb. 24 the old Jacob Hauk was buried. Born 1690, day unknown, aged about 87 yrs.

1776, Apr. 9, the old Mrs. Hud was buried. Born 1707, day unknown, aged about 76 yrs.

1776 Jun. 23 the old Mrs. Mebri was burled. Born 1699, beginning of Nov., aged 76 yrs and 7 months and several weeks.

1776, Nov. 30, a son of Andreas Werner was buried. Born 1774, Feb. 1, aged 2 yrs, 10 mos, 3 weeks, 4 das.

1777, Feb. 21, a dau. of Henrich Hemstich was buried. Born 1776, May 18, aged 9 mos, 1 day.

1777, Mar. 21, Joh. Simon May was buried. Born 1701, beginning of Apr., aged 77 yrs.

1777, Jul. 12, a son of Job. Jacobus Schweissfort was buried. Born 1775, Oct. 5, aged 2 yrs less 3 months.

1777, Aug. 11, Erhart Weis, an elder, was buried. Born 1723, Jan. 6, aged 54 yrs, 7 months and some das.

1777, Sept 4, a son of Jacob Wagner was buried. Born 1777, Feb. 14, aged 6 mos, 3 weeks.

1777, Sept. 6 a chil of Philip Bayer was buried. Born 1777, Jan. 1, aged 8 mos, 9 das.

1777, Sept. 6, a child of Peter Hofstatt was buried. Born 1774, Jun. 25, aged 3 yrs, 2 months and some das.

1777, Sept. 6, a dau. of Henrich Werner was buried. Born 1768, Mar. 25, aged 9 yrs, 5 mos, 3 weeks.

1777, Sept. 20, a child of Peter Maener was buried. Born 1776, Mar. 10, aged 1 yr, 4 mos, 8 das.

1777, Sept. 24, a child of Ludwig Moyer was buried. Born 1776, Jul. 28, aged 1 yr, 2 mos, 3 weeks, 2 das.

1777, Sept 29, a son of Peter Maener was buried. Born 1761 Feb. 10, aged 16 yrs, 7 Mos, 2 weeks, 4 das.

1777, Sept. 21, a dau. of Henrich Hut was buried. Born 1769, May 2, aged 8 yrs, 4 mos, 3 weeks.

1777, Oct. 17, a son of Friedrich Rudi was buried. Born 1775, Apr. 9, aged 2 yrs, 6 mos, 8 das.

1777, Oct. 19, a child of Adam Hildebeutel was buried. Born 1773, May 21, aged 4 yrs, 5 months less 3 das.

1777, Dec. 13, the wife of Martin Lichtel was buried. Born 1750, Jan. 12, aged 27 yrs, 11 months.

1777, Nov. 15, a dau. of the old Mr. Goetz was buried. Born 1722, Oct 28, aged 55 yrs, 2 weeks, 1 day.

1777, Dec. 12, Antoni Lichtel was buried. Born 1702, day unknown, aged 75 years and a half.

1777, Dec. 23, the old Mr. Goetz was buried. Born 1696, day unknown, aged 81 years.

1778, Jan. 27, the wife of Johann Huepner was buried. Born 1727, Dec. 1 aged 50 yrs, 1 month, 3 weeks.

1778 Feb. 24 Catharina Kraeber was buried. Born 1709, day unknown, aged about 68 years.

1778, Jun. 5, a son of Joh. Nais was buried. Born 1778, Apr. 10, aged 7 weeks, 5 das.

1778, Jul. 23, a son of Adam Hollebusch was buried. Born 1774, Jul. 14, aged 4 yrs, 9 das.

1778, Jul. 28, the wife of Christian Hollebusch was buried. Born 1709, day unknown, aged 69 years.

1778, Aug. 3, a son of Conrad Rickard was buried; born 1775, Jan. 25, aged 3 yrs, 7 months.

1778, Aug. 27, Christian Hollebusch was buried. Born 1718, Mar. 1, aged 60 yrs, 6 mos, less 6 das.

1778, Nov. 18, a child of Andreas Ohl was buried. Born 1776, ---, aged 2 yrs, 8 mos, 3 das.

The burials during the ministry of Friedrich Daelliker, pastor of this congregation of Old Goshenhoppen.

1783, Feb. 12, Wilhelm, son of Samuel Schuler and wife Elisabeth; aged 2 weeks and 5 das.

1783, May 3, Johann Adam, son of Peter Minner and Barbara, his wife, aged 7 months less 7 das.

1783, Jul. 13, Anna Maria Magdalena Wenz, wife of the late Philip Wenz; aged 61 yrs, 5 mos, 11 das.

1784, Jan 15, Georg, son of Heinrich Faust and Catharina, his wife; aged 3 weeks, 3 das.

Under the ministry of Frid. William Von der Sloot.
1784 Jul 10, Catarina Weigarit, aged 82 yrs, 5 months.

The burials by Joh. Theob. Faber, in the year 1787.

1787, Feb. 27, Elisabeth Huepner was buried; aged 33 years less 1 month.

1787, Apr. 8, the wife of Peter Hauk was buried; aged 62 years 9 months.

1787, May 12, a negro of George Hertzel was buried; aged 19 years less a quarter.

1787, Nov. 15, a child of Jacob Gerhart was buried; aged 3 yrs, 3 mos, 11 das.

1787, Dec. 4, the young Henrich Bok was buried; aged 21 yrs, 4 mos, 3 das.

1788, Apr. 17, a son of our schoolmaster, Johann Daniel Jung, was buried, named Johann Friedrich; aged 4 yrs, 1 month, 12 das.

1788, Apr. 20, Elisabeth Bittel was buried; aged 85 yrs, 3 mos, 1 day.

1788, Apr. 21, the old Mr. Dickenschied was buried; aged about 90 years.

1788, Apr. 29, the old Mrs. Boyer was buried; aged 78 yrs, 8 mos, 17 das.

1788, Oct 6, a dau. of Johann Salate was buried; aged 3 yrs, 11 months less 3 das.

The burials by John Theo. Faber, Jr. in this congregation.

1792, Jun. 22, a dau. of Henrich Faust was buried; aged 4 mos, 14 das.

1792, A daugther of Johannes Buek was buried; aged 5 yrs, 8 mos, 27 das.

1793, Daniel Hofman, aged 66 years.

1793, Mrs. Gremmel, aged 43 yrs, 8 mos, 2 weeks.
1793, Old Mrs. Moy, aged 90 ys.
1793, John Neise's child, aged 9 yrs, 7 mos, 19 das.
1793, Christian Scheid's wife, aged 54 yrs.
1793, John Scheid's child, age 3 yrs, 6 mos, 3 das.
1793, John Saladay's child, aged 6 yrs, 10 mos, 3 weeks, 3 das.
1793, John Saladay's child, aged 3 yrs, 2 mos, 2 weeks, 2 das.
1793, Jacob Weyand's child, aged 9 yrs, 6 mos, 2 weeks, 2 das.
1793, Balser Reed's child, aged 9 yrs, 8 mos, 3 das.
1793, Ludwig Mayer, aged 69 years.
1793, Ludwig Ache's child, (born 1788, May 23),aged 5 yrs, 4 mos, 3 wks.
1793, Ludwig Ache's child, (born 1790, Feb. 20), aged 3 yrs, 8 mos.
1793, William Anderson's child (born 1788, Feb. 12), aged 5 yrs, 8 mos, 1 week, 1 day.
1793, William Anderson's child (born 1790, Aug 5), aged 3 years 2 mos, ? weeks, 3 das.
1793, John Leets (born 1731, Aug.), aged 64 years.
1793, --- Vaust, a small child, a few das old.
1793, George Hertzel's child, Johannes, born 1794, Feb. 27, aged 1 yr, 11 das.

Marriages
Those persons who were united in marriage the year 1767 by John Th. Faber.
1767, Jan. 20, Bernd, son of Friedr. Goetz of Old Goshenhoppen, married Eva. Elisabethia, dau. of Johannes Mack, of New Goshenhoppen.
1767, May 7, Georg, son of Johannes Mack, of New Goshenhoppen, married Elisabetha, dau. of David Martin, of the Oley Mountains.
1767, Sept. 24, Georg, son of the late Mr. Brenneholtz, of New Goshenhoppen, married Anna Maria, dau. of Samuel Mils, of Heidelberg Twp.
1768, Apr. 14, Georg Henrich, son of the late George Schneider, of Philadelphia, married Elisabetha, dau. of Isaac Somni, of Old Goshenhoppen.
1768, May 30, Henrich, son of Henrich Diets, of Upper Salford, married Catharina, dau. of the late Mr. Gerhart, of Franconia Twp.
1768, Sept. 15, Valentin, son of Valentin Haak, of Lower Salford Twp, married Maria Elisabetha, dau. of Petrus Edinger, of Lower Salford.
1768, Sept. 25, Martinus, son of Anton Lichtel, of Upper Salford, married Catharina, dau. of the late Jacob Weidmann, of Upper Salford.
1769, Mar. 28, Wilhelmus, son of Henrich Frey, of Lower Salford, married Christina, dau. of Mr. Heineman, of Lower Salford (the father is still in Germany).
1769, May 23, Joh. Schmidt, son of the late Wilhelm Schmidt, of Falckner Swamp, married Catharine Nungasser, widow of the late Mr. Nungasser, of Old Goshenhoppen.

1769, Aug. 22, Christoph, son of Jacob Bruckert, of Old Goshenhoppen, married Magdalena, dau. of Georg Kuchler, of Old Goshenhoppen.

1769, Nov. 21, Simon Crineus, widower, of Old Goshenhoppen, married Margaretha Klapper, widow, of Old Goshenhoppen.

1770, Jan. 9, Wendel, son of Wendel Wiand, of New Goshenhoppen, married Catharina, dau. of Erhart Weis, of Old Goshenhoppen.

1770, Jun. 21 Johannes Jung (the father is still in Germany), of New Goshenhoppen, married Susanna Walder, dau. of the late Jacob Walder, of Old Goshenboppen.

1771, Apr. 2, Johannes, son of Friedr. Kern, married Maria Magdalena Rudi, dau. of Dietrich Rudi, of Ridgewell.

1771, Jun. 11, Philippus, son of the Georg Schambach, of Lower Salford, married Margaretha Henrich, dau. of Hendrich Hendrich, of Hatfield Twp.

1771, Oct. 27, Jacob Elinger, widower, of Old Goshenhoppen, married Barbara Schenck, widow of Old Goshenhoppen.

1772, Apr 28, Philip Nais, son of the late Joh. Nais, of Old Goshenhoppen, married Elisabetha Leidig, dau. of Jacob Leidig, of Franconia Twp.

1772, May 12, Adam Hiltebeutel, son of the late Martin Hiltebeutel, of Old Goshenhoppen, married Salome Klein, dau. of Johannes Klein, of Old Goshenhoppen.

1772, May 19, Jacob Gerhart, son of the late Peter Gerhart, of Franconia Twp, married Elisabetha Detter, daugther of Conrad Detter, of Franconia Twp.

1772, Jun. 2, Conrad Gerhart, son of the late Peter Gerhart, of Franconia Twp, married Anna Maria Nais, dau. of Johan Nais, of Falckner Swamp.

1772, Sept 15, Benjamin Schuler, son of Samuel Schuler of Old Goshenhoppen, married Catharina Mincker, dau. of the late Henr. Minker, of Old Goshenhoppen.

1772, Nov 17, Rudolph Segler, son of the late Joh. Segler, of Old Goshenhoppen, married Catharina Wolfart, dau. of Nicolaus Wolfart, of Old Goshenhoppen.

1773, May 27, Joh. Hartenstein, son of Ludwig Hartenstein, of Old Goshenhoppen, married Magdalena Hollebusch, son of the late Peter Hollebusch, of Old Goshenhoppen.

1774, Jan 4, Christian May, son of Friedrich May, of Old Goshenhoppen, married Maria Elis. Krein, dau. of the late Joh. Jacob Kein (?), of Old Goshenhoppen.

1774, Jan 6, Andreas Ries, son of the late Henrich Ries, of Old Goshenhoppen, married Margaretha Somni, dau. of Isaac Somni, of Old Goshenhoppen.

1774, Mar. 1, Joseph Werner, son of Joh. Werner, of Old Goshenhoppen, married Barbara Graf, dau. of Jacob Graf, of Old Goshenhoppen.

1774, Mar. 8, Joh. Roerich, son of Nicolas Roerich, of Old Goshenhoppen, married Regina Kaemmer, dau. of the late Jacob Kaemmer, of Old Goshenhoppen.

1774, Aug 21, Abraham Wolfart, son of Nicolaus Wolfart, of Old Goshenhoppen, married Anna Margr. Panebecker, dau. of Weyand Panebecker, of New Goshenhoppen.

1775, Apr 4, Jacob Weiant, son of Georg Weiant, of Old Goshenhoppen, married Salome Renn, dau. of the late Michael Renn, of Old Goshenhoppen.

1775, Nov 2, Paul Knoepper, son of the late Conrad Knoepper, of Lower Salford, married Margaretha Hollebusch, daugther of Christian Hollebusch, of Old Goshenhoppen.

1775, Oct. 29, Hartman Keil, son of the late Adam Keil, of Franconia Twp, married Catharina Herschberger, dau. of Abraham Herschberger, of Franconia Twp.

1776, Jan. 16, Henrich Ohl, son of Andreas Ohl, of Old Goshenhoppen, married Margaretha Sitzman, dau. of Christian Sitzman, of Lower Milford Twp.

1776, May 7, Jacob Wagner, son of the late Michael Wagner, of old Goshenhoppen, married Barbara Deis, dau. of the late Peter Deis, of Lower Salford.

1776, May 14, Philip Weiss, son of Erhart Weiss, of Old Goshenhoppen, married Anna Marg. Schmid, dau. of the late Henrich Schmid, of New Goshenhoppen,

1776, May 26, Abraham Graf, son of Jacob Graf, of Old Goshenhoppen, married Magd. Wagner, dau. of the late Michael Wagner, of Old Goshenhoppen.

1776, Jul. 2, Jacob Schmidt, son of the late Henrich Schmid, of New Goshenhoppen, married Elisabetha Weis, dau. of Erhart Weis, of New Goshenhoppen.

1776 Jul. 2, Jacob Schuler, of Macungie, married Elisabetha Schneider, dau. of Leonhart Schneider, of Old Goshenhoppen.

1776, Aug. 20, Joh. Hiebner, son of Joh. Hiebner, of Old Goshenhoppen, married Maria Naiman, dau. of Marcus Naiman, of Limerick Twp.

1776, Sept. 3, Adam Henrich, son of Joh. Henrich, of Limerick Twp, married Anna Maria Hollebusch, dau. of the late Peter Hollebusch, of Old Goshenhoppen.

1776, Aug. 28, Abraham Berge, son of the late Joh. Ulrich Berge, of lower Salford, married Salome Gerges, dau. of the late Wilhelm Gerges, of Lower Salford Twp.

1776, Oct. 22, Joh. Nais, son of the late Joh. Nais, of Old Goshenhoppen, married Catharina Hud, dau. of Joh. Hudt, of Old Goshenhoppen.

1776, Oct. 31, Joh. Heinemann, son of the late Henrich Heinemann, of Old Goshenhoppen, married Barbara Nais, dau. of Joh. Nais, of Old Goshenhoppen.

1777, Feb. 11, Joh. Schuler, son of the late Samuel Schuler, of Old Goshenhoppen, married Catharina Eitemueller, dau. of Joh. Eitemueller, of Old Goshenhoppen.

1777, Feb. 4, Jonas Schatz, son of the late Philip Schatz, of Old Goshenhoppen, married Catharina Ried, dau. of Phil. Ried, of Old Goshenhoppen.

1777, May 25, Abraham Nais, son of the late Joh. Nais, of Old Goshenhoppen, married Magdalena Cantes, dau. of the late Mr. Cantes, of Old Goshenhoppen.

1777, Aug. 26, Gerhart Bingeman, son of Fried. Bingeman, of Limerick Twp, married Elis. Kentel, dau. of Joseph Kentel, of Limerick Twp.

1777, Nov. 25, Jacob Weiss, son of the late Erhart Weiss, of Old Goshenhoppen, married Elisabetha Schmidt, dau. of the late Henrich Schmidt, of Old Goshenhoppen.

1778, Mar. 10, Johann Gerhart, son of the late Peter Gerhart, of Franconia Twp, married Magdalena Hertzel, dau. of Georg Hertzel, of Old Goshenhoppen.

1778 Jun. 9, Philip Leydich, son of the Rev. Leydich, of Frederick Twp, married Rosina Bucher, dau. of Dietrich Bucher, of Falckner Swamp.

1779 Apr. 11 Martin Lichtel, son of the late Antoni Lichtel, of Old Goshenhoppen, married Catharina Graf, dau. of Joh. Graf, of Upper Salford.

1779, Jun. 13, David Graf, widower, married Anna Maria Henwin, widow, both of Old Goshenhoppen.

1779, Oct. 5, Felix Leh, son of Joh. Leh, of Old Goshenhoppen, married Margaretha Tresman, dau. of the late Joh. Georg Tresman, of Providence Twp.

List of those persons who were united in marriage by me, Friedrich Dellicker.

1782, Aug. 6, Jacob Seibel, son of the late Conrad Seibel, married Anna Magdalena Zern, dau. of Hans Adam Zern, of Malbruk (?) Twp, Philadelphia County.

1782, Sept. 19, Richard Herrison, son of John Herrison, of Union Twp, Berks County, married Catharina Zug, dau. of Abraham Zug, of Old Goshenhoppen.

1782, Sept. 22, Godfrid Wiseler, son of Jacob Wiseler, and Eva Catharina Weiss, dau. of the late Hans Edward Weiss, both of Frederick Twp.

1783, Feb. 20, Peter Dinges married Maria Haas, both of Malbrouk Twp.

1783, May 20, Johannes Buch, son of the late Jacob Buch, married Catharina Schlotter, daugther of Wilhelm Schlotter, of Upper Salford.

List of the persons who were united in marriage by F. W. v. d. Sloot.

1784, Nov. 25, Jacob Schoet, son of Henrich Schoet, of Whitpain Twp, married Elisabetha Bock, dau. of the late Peter Bock, of Marlebrucht (?) Twp.

1794, Aug. 23, Solomon Grimly, son of Solomon Grimly, of Old Goshenhoppen, married Hannah Druckenmiller, also of Old Goshenhoppen.

Persons who were united in marriage by Joh. Theob. Faber.

1787, Feb. 27, Joh. Gipsen married Nensi [Nancy] Mils, both of Old

Goshenhoppen.

1787, Aug. 14, Valentin Kili, of Montgomery towmhip, married Maria Grimli, of Old Goihenhoppen.

1787, Dec. 2, Philip Schillig, of Skippack Twp, married Salome Grimli, both of Old Goshenhoppen.

1787, Mar. 11, Gabriel Schuler married Catharina Ren, both of Old Goshenhoppen.

1788, Apr. 15, Peter Hollebusch, of Old Goshenhoppen, married Susanna Schell, of Falkner Swamp.

GREAT SWAMP CONGREGATION

Burials

Persons were buried by John Theobald Faber:

1767, Apr. 21, the young Eberhard was buried, who lived in the congregation of Great Swamp.

1767, May 14, a son of Joseph Eberhard was buried, named Benshamer, from the Swamp.

1768, May 24, John Phil. Fackenthal was buried, living in the congregation at Springfield.

1768, Oct. 3, Henry Grob was buried. His aged 57 yrs, of the Swamp congregation.

1768, Nov. 19, Franz Russ was buried. His aged 31 yrs, of the Swamp congregation.

1769, Sept. 6, Ulrich Spinner was buried. His age 52 yrs, 3 mos, 3 das, of the Swamp congregation.

1770 Jun. 22 Valentin Dickenschied was buried. His age 36 yrs, 7 mos, and 3 wks less one day.

1771, Jan. 29, Peter Bleiler's dau. was buried, named Anna Catharine, of the Swamp congregation; aged 10 yrs, 11 mos and some das.

1771, Jun. 22, Christian Willatauer was buried, born 1706, Jan 20. His age: 64 yrs, 5 months.

1771, Nov. 18, Joh. Zoeller was married; born 1728, Nov. 16; his age 43 years 2 das.

1772 Jan. 16 (or 23), Mr. Thowwahrt's little son was buried. His name: George Jacob, his aged 2 yrs, 6 weeks and some das.

1772, Oct. 21, Jacob Kehler's dau. was buried; her name Anna Barbara, was born 1768, Feb. 5; her age 4 yrs, 10 mos, 16 das.

1772, Nov. 3, Michael Eberhart was buried; born 1698, Mar. 4th. His aged 74 years and a half and 9 weeks.

1773, Jan 6, Agnes Kaiser was buried; born 1702, the day is unknown, her age about 72 years.

1773, Apr 2, George Mechlin's dau. was buried; born 1771, Feb. 7. Her age 2 yrs, 2 months and 6 das.

1773, Jun 6, the wife of Mr. Zeiner died; born 1738, Dec. 3. Her age 37 years and some months.

1773 Jul 15, Balzer Stiel's child was buried; born 1772, Nov. 27. Age 1 yr, 8 months and some das.

1774, Apr. 1, Peter Linn's dau. was buried; born 1771, Aug. 23. Her age 2 yrs, 7 mos, 7 das.

1774 Apr. 27, son of Ludwig Nusspickel was buried; aged 2 yrs, 2 das.

1774, May 5, dau. of Ludwig Nusspickel was buried; aged 6 yrs, 3 mos, 1 day.

1774, Jun. 15, dau. of Chrisophel Ott buried; aged 4 mos, 28 das.

1775 Jan. 15, Valentin Huper's dau. was buried. Her age 6 yrs, 5 mos, 10 das.

1775, Feb. 22, Theobald Bauchler's dau. vas buried; aged 11 yrs, 3 weeks, some das.

1775, Jun. 24, Anna Margaretha Weis was buried; born Apr. 7, 1706. Her age 69 yrs, 2 months and 2 weeks.

1775, Sept, 15, Jacob Rauber's dau. was buried; born 1773, Oct. 13. Her age 1 year, 11 mos, 2 das.

1775, Oct. 15, Adam Rauchert's dau. was buried; born 1774, Oct. 9; aged 1 year less 17 das.

1775, Nov. 3, John Neukomer's wife was buried; born Feb. 28, 1735. Her age 40 yrs, 8 months.

1776, Aug. 15, Michael Bischoff's wife was buried; born 1722, Mar. 17, her age 54 yrs, 5 months less 2 das.

1776, Nov. 4, Jacob Wittmer's wife was buried; born 1742, about the middle of Sept. Her age 34 years and about 6 weeks.

1777, May 12, John George Schonsebach was buried; born 1746, day unknown. His age, about 51 years.

1777, Aug. 3, Jacob Rauber's dau. was buried; born 1760, Feb. 6. Her age 17 yrs, 6 months less 5 das.

1777, Jul. 25, two children of Daniel Dubs were buried at the same time, namely a son and a dau. The son was born 1775, Sept 7; the dau. 1774, Jan. 20. The age of the boy was 1 year, 10 months and 2 weeks, the girl 3 yrs, 7 months and 4 das.

1777, Aug. 16, Joseph Eberhart's child was buried; born 1769, Jan. 22; aged 8 yrs, 7 months less 6 das.

1777, Aug. 24, Baltzer Stiehl's dau. was buried; born 1759 on Wednesday; her age 17 yrs, 4 mos, 8 das.

1777, Aug. 27, Mrs. Schansebach was buried; born 1723, May 8th, her age 54 yrs, 4 mos, 3 weeks.

1777, Aug. 26, Jacob Wittmer's dau. was buried; born 1765, Aug. 4. Her age 12 years and about 3 weeks.

1777, Aug 31, John Jacobi's child was buried; born 1776, Aug. 2; aged 1 year and 4 weeks. Soon afterwards another one of his children was buried.

1777, Aug. 30, Michael Eberbart's wife was buried; born 1725, Apr. 15, aged 52 yrs, 4 mos, 2 weeks.

1771, Aug. 30, Joseph Eberhart's child was buried; born aged 5 yrs, and 5 mos less 6 das.

1777 Aug 30, Rudi Huper's son was buried; born 1770, Jan 2; aged 7 yrs, 8 months less one day.

1777, Sept. 7, Peter Weber's dau. was buried; born 1768, Apr 15; aged 9 yrs, 5 months.

1777 Sept 22, Felix Bruner's child was buried; born 1772, Jul 14; aged 5 yrs, 2 mos, 7 das.

1777, Oct. 14, John Lohe's child was buried; born 1770, Jul. 10; aged 7 yrs, 3 mos, 2 das.

1777, Oct. 3, George Mack's dau. was buried; born 1776, Jun. 23, aged 1 year, 3 mos, 1 week, 3 das.

1777, Oct. 5, Henr. Ott's child was buried; born 1777, Apr. 4th; aged one half a year.

1777, Oct. 6, Georg Kern's son was buried; born 1772, Apr. 23; aged 5 yrs, 5 months; 10 das.

1778, Jan. 8, Henry Huper was buried; born 1715 Apr 15th; aged 62 Yrs, 9 momths less 7 das.

1778 Mar. 6, Felix Bruner's dau. was buried; born 1774, Nov 19; aged 3 years 3 months 5 das.

1779, Feb. 9, the old Mrs. Schutz was buried; born 1698, Aug. 20; aged 8o yrs, 5 mos, 3 weeks.

1779, Feb. 10, the old Mrs. Willauer was buried; born 1710, about Nov., aged about 68 yrs, 3 months.

1779, Mar. 29, Rudolph Huper was buried; born 1722, May 1st; aged 56 yrs, 10 mos, 4 weeks.

1779, Apn 16, Nicolaus Biber's dau. was buried; born 1776, Nov, 27; aged 2 yrs, 4 mos, 2 weeks, 4 das.

1779, Jun. 11, Heter (?) Bock's child, named Susanna, was buried; born 1778, Sept. 18th; aged 8 mos, 3 weeks and one day.

Those who died and were buried under the ministry of Fr. Delliker:

1783, Apr. 17, Michael Eberhard, aged 51 yrs, 2 weeks.

1783, Apr. 18, Anna Maria Scholl, widow of the late Peter Scholl. Her age 65 yrs, 1 month, second weeks.

1783, Apr. 27, Verena Rudolph, widow of the late Heinrich Rudolph; her age 64 yrs, 10 months.

1783, May 4, Margreth Holzhauser, wife of Caspar Holzhauser, aged 79 years.

1783, Oct. 24, Anna Huber, widow of the late Heinrich Huber, aged 67 years.

Buried by Frederick William Von der Sloot.

1784, Sept. 6, Ulrich Rieser, born 1709, Apr 8, aged 75 yrs, 4 mos, 20 das.

1785, Feb. 25, Daniel Hitz was buried, aged 85 yrs, 7 months.

Sept. 7, Valentin Kaiser, aged 76 yrs, 11 months.

1785, Mar. 26, Anna Maria Bleiler was buried, aged 82 yrs, 10 months.

1785, Apr. 3, John Mombauer's child, John David.

Those persons who were buried by me, John Theobald Faber.

1786, Aug. 17, a dau. of Daniel Dubs was buried, named Catharine, aged 2 yrs, 8 mos, 10 das.

1786, Nov. 20, Peter Eberhart, a deacon, was buried, aged 42 years and a half year.

1786, Dec. 1, Peter Eberhart's wife was buried, aged 40 yrs, 4 mos, 9 das.

1787, Jan. 6, dau. of Henry Huper, named Anna, was buried, aged 11 mos, 1 day.

1787, Apr. 5, the old Mrs. Hitz was buried; aged 76 year, 2 weeks, 1 day.

1787, Oct. 11, the old Mr. Reiswig was buried; aged 77 yrs, 5 mos, 18 das.

1788, Feb. 28, Felix Bruner's dau., Magdalene, was buried; aged 8 mos, 2 das.

1788, Apr. 8, Anna Maria Sax was buried; aged 35 yrs, 2 mos, 3 weeks and one day.

1788, May 31, Anna Rosina Bergheimer was buried; aged 37 years.

Sept. 28, John Georg Muller's child was buried; aged 7 months.

1788, Oct. 22, David Spinner's dau. named Maria, was buried, aged 3 yrs, 2 mos, 2 das.

N. Pomp, pastor.

1790,Apr 4, Anna Margaretlia Reisswig, a widow, 77 years old.

Those persons who were buried by John Theobald Faber [Jr.]

1790, John Swenk, a child, 3 yrs, 7 mos, das.

1792, --- Breuchler, a child.

1793, Jacob Huber's child, 7 yrs, 2 weeks, 6 das.

1793, Jacob Mory, 66 yrs, 4 mos less 2 das.

1793, Henr. Huber's child. -

1794, Jonathan Klein, born Dec. 24, 1794, aged 1 yr, 2 weeks, 6 das.

1794, Anna Barbara, his wife, born Apr. 4, 1732, aged 62 yrs, 10 mos, 6 das.

1794, Anna Maria Hillegas, born 1746, Oct. 25; aged 48 yrs, 5 Mos, 3 das.

MARRIAGE RECORD

Those persons who were joined in marriage by me, John Theobald Faber.

1767, Mar. 5, Georg Sem, son of Georg Sem, of Lower Milford, and Elisabeth Reiswig, dau. of John Reiswig, of Upper Milford, were married.

1768, Mar. 8, David Mehin, son of Adam Mehin, of Great Swamp, and

Elisabetha Redelmeyer, dau. of the late Martin Redelmeyer, of New Goshenhoppen.

1768, Apr. 4, Peter Linn, son of the late Peter Linn, of Upper Saucon, and Catharina Cock, dau. of the late John Cock, of Upper Saucon.

1768, May 26, Peter Schuller, son of Adam Schuller, of Upper Milford, and Maria Catharina Riser, dau. of Ulrich Riser, of Upper Milford.

1768, Nov. 17, Friedr. Dill, son of the late Simon Dill, of Pikeland Twp, Bucks County, and Susanna Spinner, dau. of Ulrich Spinner, of Great Swamp.

1768, Dec 4, Jacob Mack, son of Wilhelm Mack, of Rockbill Twp, Bucks County, and Catharine Drumbauer, dau. of Andreas Drumbauer, of Franconia Twp, Phila. County.

1769, Jan. 3, Joh. Nicolaus Diets, son of Adam Diets, of Upper Saucon, and Catharine Bischoff, dau. of Michael Bischoff, of Swamp.

1770, Aug. 26, Joh. Nicolaus Sanfels, son of the late Carl Sanfels, of Lower Milford, and Anna Elis. Ott, dau. of Her. Ott, of Upper Milford.

1771, May 14, Henr. Ott, widower, of Great Swamp, and Margretha Ziegenfuss, widow, of Tohickon.

1771, Nov. 17, Joh. Olinger, son of the late Carl Olinger, of Great Swamp, and Anna Maria Ott, dau. of Henr. Ott, of Great Swamp.

1771, Nov. 26, Joh. Petrus Reiswig, son of Joh. Reiswig, of Great Swamp, and Maria Eva Engelman, dau. of Andreas Engelmann, of Great Swamp.

1772, May 5, Joh. Hermer, son of Joh. Georg Hermer, of Springfield, and Susanna Reiswich, dau. of John Reiswig, of Upper Milford.

1772, Nov. 22, Joh. Hauser, son of Jacob Hauser, of Macungie Twp, and Anna Maria Barb. Wolf, dau. of Wm. Wolf, of Macungie Twp.

1772, Nov. 30, Christoffel Ott, son of Henr. Ott, of Great Swamp, and Attli Hupper, dau. of Rudi Hupper, at Great Swamp.

1773, Jan. 17, Joh. Jacobi, son of the late Peter Jacobi, of Hekok (?) Twp, and Anna Eberhart, dau. of the late Michael Eberhart, of Great Swamp.

1774, Aug. 16, Philip Hederig, son of Peter Hederig, of Richland Twp, and Cath. Scheib, dau. of Martin Scheib of Hekok Twp.

1775, Nov. 14, Georg Adam Dorr, son of the late Georg Dorr, of Old Gosbenboppen, and Christina Heger, dau. of Philip Heger, of Great Swamp.

1775, Nov. 28, Henr. Weis, widower, of Great Swamp, and Margreta Burger, widow, of Great Swamp.

1776, Feb. 13, Philip Mombauer, son of Nicolas Mombauer, of Great Swamp, and Barbara Spinner, dau. of the late Ulrich Spinner, of Great Swamp.

1776, Aug. 11, Joseph Hornecker, son of the late Ulrich Hornecker, of Upper Saucon, and Hanna Weber, dau. of Henr. Weber, of Upper Saucon.

1777, Febr, 4, Henr. Weber, son of Henr. Weber, of Upper Saucon, and Margareta Hornecker, dau. of Ulrich Hornecker, of Rockhill Twp.

1778, Feb. 8, Michael Ott, son of Henr. Ott, of Great Swamp, and Hanna Braun, dau. of Daniel Braun, of Upper Saucon.

1778, Apr. 21, Jacob Huper, son of Rudolph Huper, of Great Swamp, and Anim Maria Heres, widow of the late Mr. Heres, of Lower Milford.

1778, Jun. 4, Jacob Klemer and Elisabetha Andres, both of Lower Milford.

1778, Sept. 15, Jacob Wittmer and Smanna Mack dau. of John Mack, of New Goshenhoppen.

177S, Sept. 29, Joh. Becker, of Upper Milford, and Elisabetha Berger, of Upper Milford.

1779, Apr. 11, Daniel Klein, son of Michael Klein, of Great Swamp, and Magdalena Bauchler, dau. of Theabald Brauchler of Great Swamp.

1779, May 23, Michael Rudolph, son of Henr. Rudolph, and Margareta Ott, dau. of Henr. Ott, both of Upper Milford.

Great Swamp Marriages

1779, Aug. 9, Georg Michael Trumbauer, son of Andres Trumbauer, and Cath. Bock, dau. of Peter Bock, of Lower Milford Twp.

List of persons married by Friedrich Delliker.

1782, Apr. 23, Georg Doerr, son of Hannes Doerr, of this congregation, and Sophia Steder, dau. of the late Henrich Stetler, of New Goshenhoppen.

1782, Oct. 29, Peter Kufer, son of Johan Kufer, of Tinicum Twp, and Cath. Elisab. Engelmann, dau. of Andres Engelman, of Upper Milford.

1782, Nov. 26, David Spinner, son of the late Urich Spinner, and Catharine Herlacher, dau. of Georg Herlacher, of Lower Milford.

1783, Apr. 1, Heinrich Mumbauer, son of Niclas Mumbauer, and Catharina Didlo, dau. of Abraham Didlo, both of Lower Milford, Bucks County.

Persons married by Friedrich Wilh. Von der Sloot.

1784, Jun. 20th, Caspar Mumfeld, son of Henrich Mumfeld, and Catharina Schanzenbach, dau. of George Schanzenbach.

1784, Aug. 10, Jacob Tracksel, son of Peter Tracksel, and Margaretha Eberhart, dau. of Joseph Eberhard.

1784, Dec. 2, Philip Eberhard, son of the late Michael Eberhard, of Upper Milford Twp, and Margaretlia Hillegas, oldest dau. of Johannes Hillegas, of Upper Milford Twp.

1785, Aug. 23, Georg Ditlo, son of Abraham Ditlo, and Maria Magdalena Meier, oldest dau. of Wendel Meier.

1785,Sept. 6, Peter Weber, son of Peter Weber and Maria Reichenbach.

Persons who were married by John Theob. Faber:

1786, Nov. 21, Henr. Grob, of Lower Milford Twp, and Margareta Schutz, of -- - Twp.

1787, May 15, John George Ott, of Upper Milford, and Catharina Bishof, of Lower Milford.

1787, Apr. 13, Philip Bitting and Elis. Derrschiam, both of Great Swamp.

These persons were married by John Faber, Jr., in the year 1792.

1792, --- Brauchler and --- Mack.

1793, Nov. 28, Christian Heger and Caty Long, of Great Swamp.

INDIAN CREEK (INDIAN FIELD) REFORMED

Marriages by John Theobald Faber, 1782-1786.

Aug 13, 1782 Jacob Edelmann of Rockhill Twp. and Anna Gloria Benner of Hilltown Twp.

Sept 19, 1782 George Trumbore of Franconia Twp. and Susanna Cassel of Domensen (Towamencin) Twp.

Oct 10, 1782 George Mayer of Upper Salford Twp. and Catharine Geiger of Heidelberg Twp.

Sept 7, 1782 Morris Fell of Bucks County and Tetsi Thomas of Philadelphia County.

Sept 15, 1782 George Sheib of Hatfield Twp. and Catharine Kern of Hilltown Twp.

Jan 7, 1783 John Jacob Lang and Sarah Gomer of Hilltown Twp.

Mar 20, 1783 Isaac Dill and Anna Benner of Franconia Twp.

Apr 29, 1783 John Reis and Elisabeth Schwenk, both of RockhillTwp.

May 27, 1783 Philip Mumbauer and Magdalena Leidi of Hilltown Twp.

Oct 7, 1783 Jacob Conwor and Elisabeth Riedt both of Hatfield Twp.

Oct 28, 1783 Henry Hertzel and Susanna Dickeshshut of Rockhill and Salford Twp.

Dec 9, 1783 John Ernst Herr and Charlotte Rautebush of Rockhill Twp.

Apr 15, 1784 Ludwig Weil and Anna Nesch of Rockhill Twp.

Apr 17, 1784 Henry Seltzer and Laetitia Thomas of Hatfield Twp.

Mar 29, 1785 Jacob Schmit of Upper Salford and Margaret Waller of same Twp.

Apr 7, 1785 Henry Huber of Great Swamp and Maria Scholl.

Apr 14, 1785 Andrew Trumboor of Rockhill and Margaret Hunsberger of same Twp.

Apr 21, 1785 Martin Sheib and widow ---.

Apr 21, 1785 Peter Conver of Hatfield and Elisabeth Bruner of Franconia.

May 12, 1785 --- Huber and ---- Schol.

May 12, 1785 --- Hertzel and --- Huber.

---, 1785 Phil. Solber of Hatfield and Margaret Rautebush of Rockhill Twp.

Mar 21, 1786 Nicholas Frantz of Hilltown and Christina Kramer of same.

Mar 28, 1786 Jacob Kop of Hilltown and Catharine Henge of Franconia Twp.

Marriages by John Michael Kern, 1788.
Feb 17, 1788 Henry Cyriacus Muller and Maria Charlotte Wambold.

Marriages by John William Ingold, 1788-1789.
Oct 28, 1788 John Jacob Rees and Anna Maria Scheib.
Mar 31, 1789 William Schmidt and Catharine Weidknecht.
May 10, 1789 Joseph Hoffart and Maria Hauskupper.
May 26, 1789 John George Grub and Magdalena Rees.
Sep 22, 1789 Philip Scholl and Elisabeth Hahngen.
Oct 8, 1789 Amos Meiner and Elisabeth Beringer.
Jan 28, 1790 Paul Frantz and Maria Dames (Thomas.)
Mar 4, 1790 Johannes Reit and Susanna Kramer.
Apr 15, 1790 George Beringer and Magdalena Mesemer.

Marriages by Nicholas Pomp, 1791-1797
Jan 11, 1791 Joseph Narrengang and Anna Rosenberger.
Apr 5, 1791 William Weil and Barbara Weymer.
Apr 21, 1791 John Frantz and Catharine Seller.
Oct 11, 1791 Samuel Jones and Hannah Clayton.
Nov 29, 1791 Jacob Wambold and Elisabeth Marck.
Mar 22, 1792 Henry Dotterer and Nancy Davies.
Apr 9, 1792 Benjamin Braun and Margaret Keyser.
Apr 12, 1792 Henry Hertzel and Susanna Allum.
May 1, 1792 George Bolig and Christina Schwartzlander.
June 19, 1792 Abraham Scheib and Anna Maria Hamscher.
Aug 20, 1792 Martin Conrad and Elisabeth Reifschneider.
Aug 30, 1792 George Hange and Maria Geliste.
Sep 4, 1792 Ludwig Sommer and Catharine Emmerich.
Sep 18, 1792 Abraham Scholl and Magdalena Ments.
Apr 11, 1793 Philip Hertzel and Elisabeth Gerhard.
Apr 18, 1793 John Gross and Christina Vollmer.
May 14, 1793 Henry Kop and Elisabeth Seller.
May 23, 1793 Jacob Rodlein and Margaret Reid.
May 28, 1793 Henry Antes and Susanna Hahn.
Sep 3, 1793 Christian Hunschberger and Hannah Seller.
Oct 3, 1793 Benjamin Harkin and Sarah Frantz.
Mar 18, 1794 Jacob Ratzel and Hannah Fowler.
Apr 3, 1794 George Raudenbusch and Elisabeth Gerhard.
May 13, 1794 Abraham Kolb and Barbara Seller.
May 11, 1794 Henry Fried and Catharine Ruhl.
Jun 12, 1794 Paul Kromer and Susanna Rothlein.
Nov 13, 1794 Abraham Seller and Catharine Kolb.

Dec 30, 1794 Samuel Mayer and Elisabeth Scholl.
Feb 19, 1795 Michael Nees and Elisabeth Hertzel.
Feb 24, 1795 John Schieb and Catharine Heller.
Apr 21, 1795 Henry Mayer and Elisabeth Wenz.
Jun 9, 1795 Jacob Ruckstuhl and Maria Barbara Nees.
Jul 21, 1795 Henry Rosenberger and Maria Holzhauser.
Nov 19, 1795 Isaac Kop and Sarah Miller.
Jan 14, 1796 Henry Kremer and Gothy (I) Conrad.
Mar 6, 1796 Abraham Gerhard and Margaret Kern.
Mar 15, 1796 Adam Reimer and Elisabeth Scheib.
Aug 12, 1796 George Herzel and Catharine Kron.
Oct 18, 1796 John Adam Gresman and Catharine Hertzel.
Nov 7, 1796 Peter Hederich and Christina Kuntzer.
Nov 22, 1796 Theobald Nees and Anna Weickel.
Nov 30, 1796 John Leister and Elisabeth Wenz.
Apr 4, 1797 Philip Brunner and Catharine Kern.
Apr 4, 1797 Frederick Jordan and Catharine Hertzel.
Apr 6, 1797 John Segler and Elisabeth Scholl.
May 29, 1797 John Mayer and Rebekah Kob.

Burials by Rev. John Theobald Faber, 1782-1786
Dec 2, 1782 Philip Schambach's child, age 10 mos, 8 day.
Jan 6, 1783 Jost Follmer's child, age 5 mos.
Jan 7, 1783 John Seller, age 51 yrs, 3 mos.
Jan 15, 1783 Child of Seller's son-in-law, age 4 yrs, 8 mos.
Mar 25, 1783 Philip Henry Seller, age 53 yrs.
May 20, 1783 Old Mrs. Weytemayer, age 83 yrs, some mos, some wks.
Jun 17, 1783 Schellenberger's child, age 4 mos, 4 wks.
Jul 18, 1783 Conrad Leydi's child, age 4 yrs, 4 mos, 13 days.
Aug 14, 1783 Wife of Paul Franz, age 49 yrs, 10 mos.
Aug 15, 1783 A woman at Skippack, age 85 yrs.
Aug 16, 1783 ---- Gerhart, age 66 yrs.
Aug 26, 1783 Wife of Mr. Schambach, age 60 yrs, 5 mos, some wks.
Oct 3, 1783 Christian Dedere, age 40 yrs, 7 mos. 11 days.
Nov 18, 1783 Jacob Wentz, age 36 yrs, 4 mos, less 4 days.
Feb 25, 1784 Old Mrs. Hertzel, age 65 yrs, several mos.
Jun 23, 1784 Old Mr. Hertzel, age 67 yrs, 5 mos, 10 days.
Jul 14, 1784 John Shellenberger's child, age 2 yrs, 1 mos, 3 days.
Oct 10, 1784 Old Mrs. Gresman, age 80 yrs.
Oct 17, 1784 Conrad Leidi's child, age 9 mos, 1 day.
Feb 25, 1785 Servant of Mr. Pilger, age 12 yrs.
Feb 27, 1785 Old Mr. Leidy, age 56 yrs, 2 mos.
Jul 6, 1785 Carl Schellenberger's child, age 10 mos.

Aus 15, 1785 Conrad Hilligas' child of New Gosh, 4 yrs, 3 mos, 6 days.
Sep 19, 1785 Jacob Mayer, age 33 yrs, 1 mo, 3 weeks.

Burials During the Ministry of John Michael Kern, 1787-1788
Dec 2, 1787 Catharine Gerhard, age 5 yrs, 10 mos, 12 days.
Dec 7, 1787 Henrich Rees, age 68 yrs.
Dec 22, 1787 Magdalena Mayer, age 6 yrs, 6 mos, 20 days.
Jan 26, 1788 John Jost Frederich, age 88 yrs.
Feb --, 1788 Lydia Seller age 2 yrs, 2 mos, 14 days.

Burials During the Ministry of John William Ingold, 1788.
Jul 28, 1788 Jacob Schellenberger's son, age 1 yr, 4 mos, 3 wk, 3 days.
Oct 1, 1788 Elisabeth Scholl, single, age 18 yrs, 2 wks, 4 days.
Oct 26, 1788 John Scholl age 16 yrs, 4 mos, 9 days.
Dec 18, 1788 Susanna Scholl age 18 yrs, 8 mos, 13 days.
Jan 10, 1789 Nicholas Franz's child, age 5 mos, 3 wks, 5 days.
Mar 29, 1789 Mrs. Catharine Barbara Ingold, wife of minister, aged 40 yrs, 6
    mos, 3 wk, 4 days.
Apr 12, 1789 John Gerhard's two children, one aged 5-6 hrs, the other lived only
    two hours.
May 11, 1790 Catharine Hahnge, age 83 yrs, 6 mos.

Burials by Nicholas Pomp of the Indian Creek Congregation
Maria Catharine, dau of Jacob Klein, d. August 24,1790; buried Aug 26, 1790;
    aged 20 yrs, 2 mos. 11 days.
May 14, 1791 Joseph, son of Philip Rieth.
Sep 3, 1791 John, son of Philip Schellenberger.
Sep 3, 1791 John Henry, son of Henry Scheib, age 8 yrs.
Jan 18, 1792 Catharine Elisabeth, widow of the late Isaac Hunsberger, d. Jan 16;
    buried Jan 18; aged 75 yrs, 9 mos, 1 days.
Feb 8, 1792 Enosh, son of Samuel Seller, 1 yr.
Jul 26, 1792 Magdalena, dau of Jacob Leidy, drowned in millrace, buried Jul
    26; age 2 yrs, 6 mos, 27 days.
Aug 2, 1792 Catharine, dau of Henry Hertzel, age 3 yrs, 7 mos, 2 days.
Sep 8, 1792 Ernst Herr, member of Lutheran congregation.
Dec 18, 1792 Elisabeth, dau of H. Dreisbach.
Aug 16, 1793 William Seibel, son of Henry Seibel, age 6 yrs, 7 mos, 7 days.
Aug 24, 1793 George Scheib, died of dropsy, aged 69 yrs, 7 mos, 6 days.
Sep 5, 1793 Anna Scholl, wife of Tobias Scholl, d. after long illness, aged 51
    yrs, 2 mos, 6 days.
Sep 26, 1793 Samuel Brod, of dysentery, aged 67 yrs, 7 mos, 2 days.
Oct 28, 1793 Michael Scholl's son, d. of dysentery, age 15 yrs, 7 mos, 22 days.
Nov 8, 1793 William Weil's child, d. of dysentery, age 1 yrs, 7 mos, 26 days.

---, 1793 Catharine Mayer, d. of dysentery, a widow, age 67 yrs.

Jan 31, 1794 Jacob, son of Jacob Schellenberger, d. of dysentery, age 3 yrs.

Aug 26, 1794 Catharine Kramer, wife of Henry Kramer, d. Aug 24, buried Aug 26; aged 34 yrs, 8 mos, 9 days.

Aug 3, 1794 Elisabeth Kope, wife of Henry Kope, d. of dysentery, together with her small child, buried with her, Aug 3. She was 24 yrs, 3 mos, 11 days.

Aug 16, 1794 Benjamin, a boy raised by Jacob Klein, d. of consumption, aged 17 yrs, 4 mos.

Aug 19, 1794 Jacob Leidy, d. of fever, aged 75 yrs, less 5 days. He left behind 8 children and 66 grandchildren and 8 great-grandchildren.

Mar 31, 1795 John Schellenberger, d. of fever, aged 82 yrs, 8 mo, 26 days. He left behind 10 children, 64 grandchildren and 17 great-grandchildren.

---, 1795 John Henry Resch, aged 17 yrs, 5 mos, d. of consumption.

Feb 1, 1796 Paul Franz, d. of apoplexy, aged 61 yrs, 7 mos.

Nov 25, 1796 Peter Gerhard, d. probably of apoplexy, aged 44 yrs, less 5 days.

FAULKNER SWAMP REFORMED

Marriages by the Rev. John Philip Leydich, 1748-1775.

Nov 9, 1748 Jacob Liebegut and Christine Brand.

Nov 17, 1748 John Conrad Lorsbach and Susanna Herb.

Jan 17, 1749 Gottfried Langenbein and Anna Margaret Schmied.

Jan 23, 1749 Peter Liebegut and Christine Mohn.

Feb 14, 1749 John George Voegle and Philippina Crebill.

Mar 28, 1749 Adam Boehmer and Anna Margaret Seiwell.

Jul 18, 1749 Jacob Krem and Friderica Catharine Tups.

Dec 12, 1749 John Grob and Anna Ella Christman.

Jan 9, 1750 Peter Dietz and Catharine Frohnbach.

Aug 7, 1750 Philip Faas and Margaret Barbara Mombauer.

Aug 7, 1750 John Eberle and Catharine Stempel.

Aug 21, 1750 John Jacob Reinhard and Anna Margaret Holb.

Sep 4, 1750 John Christian Hahn, schoolmaster and precentor here at the present time and Anna Maria-Freyer.

Oct 31, 1751 John Philip Lauterbach and Gertrude Engel.

Oct 31, 1751 John Henry Schneider and Catharine Renar.

Feb 13, 1752 Warner Pieters and Catharine van der Sleys.

Feb 13, 1752 Melchior Huebner and Barbara Fischer.

Apr 21, 1752 Sylvester Otho and Maria Catharine Born.

Nov 28, 1752 John Peter Reimer and Rachel Ziber.

Jul --, 1753 John Julius Coerper and Catharine Reimer.

Nov 20, 1753 Henry Happel and Catharine Mueller.

Dec 18, 1753 Sebastian Schales and Maria Christine Graf.

Dec.25, 1753 John George Happel and Maria Elizabeth Lantes.

Feb 25, 1755 John Michael Lautenschlaeger and Anna Eliz. Saeler.

Feb 25, 1755 Jacob Bleiler and Agnes Engel.

Persons who were married by the Rev. Nicholas Pomp, 1765-1783.

Mar 27, 1769 Daniel Beker, son of Joseph, and Anna Hab.

Apr 2, 1769 Peter Eschenfelder, son of Philip Jacob and Eliz. Rieser.

Mar 17, 1772 John Sieber and Elizabeth Merkel.

Mar 17, 1772 Gottfried Seeler and Veronica Schmid.

Mar 17, 1772 John Jahn and Maria Betz.

Apr 7, 1772 John Schmid and Elizabeth Hellwich.

Apr 23, 1772, N. Pump, V.D.M. and Elizabeth Dotter.

May 19, 1772 Philip Aker and Elizabeth Fidele.

Jun 4, 1772 Nicholas Reil and Margaret Schuhler.

Jun 9, 1772 John Neuman and Elizabeth Merkel.

Aug 11, 1772 Peter Busch and Mary Costert.

Aug 11, 1772 Bastian Wagener and Margaret Schneider.

Dec 3, 1772 William Rittenhause and Margaret Welker.

Dec 6, 1772 Peter Schmid and Anna Maria Goetzelman.

Dec 22, 1772 John Dotterer and Anna Maria Schmid.

May 9, 1773 John Peter Diener, son of Henry Diener and Margaret Mayer.

May 11, 1773 John Carl of Bercks Twp., Chester Co. and Cath. Wagener.

Nov 23, 1773 John Hippel and Anna Maria Jaeger.

Dec 19, 1773 Christopher Clauss and Catharine Haeng.

Jan 25, 1774 Lorentz Hippel and Margaret Stein.

Apr 4, 1774 John Goetz and N.N.--- (N.N. - Nomen nescio)

Oct 18, 1774 Daniel Meins and Sarah Huber.

Nov 1, 1774 Jacob Bernhard and Anna Dotter.

Oct 25, 1774 Jost Freyer and Barbara Dotter.

Oct 25, 1774 Frederick Loesch and Barbara Derr.

Mar 14, 1775 Henry Laubach and Anna Maria Defrehn.

Mar 21, 1775 Nicholas Miller and Maria Schmid, dau of John Schmid.

Apr 30, 1775 Philip Seeler and Elizabeth Carl, both of Brickland Twp., Chester County.

May 30, 1775 John Huwen (Haven?) and Anna Maria Kyly of Limrick Twp.

May 30, 1775 Henry Schneider and Susanna Mathew, both of New Hanover Twp., Philadelphia County.

Jun 5, 1775 John Mose and Magdalene Koenig, both of Brickland Twp.

Aug 17, 1775 Frederick Antes and Catharine Schuler.

Nov 7, 1775 Moses Kehl and Catharine Spiess.

Dec 6, 1775 Christian Bauer and Catharine Seibert.

Jan 7, 1776 Andrew Schneider and Magdalene Schneider.

Feb 20, 1776 Adam Miller and Elizabeth Brendel.

Mar 26, 1776 Elias Werner and Catharine Schlaider.
Apr 2, 1776 John Engel and Anna Margaret Georg.
May 7, 1776 Peter Schnack and Catharine Fren.
May 12, 1776 Peter Jung and Catharine Schneider.
Feb 25, 1777 Peter Loewenberg and Justina Scherrard.
Apr 1, 1777 John Steger and Elizabeth Steger.
Apr 8, 1777 Jacob Steger and Catharine Steger.
May 14, 1777 Peter Seibert and Anna Maria Ruthrauff.
May 18, 1777 George Scheffe and Anna Margaret Weinerich.
Aug 24, 1777 --- Bingeman and Elizabeth Kendel.
Mar 3, 1778 Andrew Maccason and Elizabeth Clears.
May 12, 1778 Joseph Serben and Elizabeth Frehn.
May 12, 1778 Conrad Grob and Amelia Grob.
Apr 14, 1778 Nicholas Niebel and Catharine Miller.
Oct 22, 1778 John Schultz and Elizabeth Geyer.
Jan 13, 1779 Valentine Bayer and N. Geist.
Feb 9, 1779 Nicholas Gilbert and Mary Neiss.
Mar 18, 1779 John Clayfield and Catharine Eichelberger, widow.
Apr 6, 1779 Peter Specht and Margaret Neuman.
May 18, 1779 Peter Fink and Catharine Jung.
Jun 22, 1779 John Specht and Catharine Neuman.
Apr 25, 1779 John Schneider's son of Beickland and Koenig's dau.
Jul 11, 1779 John Conrad Dewitz and Eva Dehlinger.
Aug 10, 1779 Nicholas Mack and Magdalene Hellwich.
Aug 17, 1779 George Dengeler and Anna Maria Spiess.
Aug 17, 1779 Jacob Kuhly and Catharine Sassamenhausen.
Sep 12, 1779 Adam Stein and Catharine Hippel.
Oct 24, 1779 Henry Maurer and Magdalene Vollmar.
Nov 11, 1779 Joseph Butterweck and Margaret Strieker.
Nov 16, 1779 John Jost and Benigna Dotter.
Nov 23, 1779 Francis Picany and Maria Brand.
Dec 14, 1779 John Nagel and Christine Bruner.
Feb 17, 1780 Michael Kolb and Magdalene Leidig.
Apr 24, 1780 George Drees and Catharine Schlonecker.
Apr 24, 1780 Abraham Herb and Sibylla Vuchs.
May 16, 1780 Andrew Biedel and Barbara Neuman.
May 23, 1780 Philip Fillman and Elizabeth Scherer.
May 30, 1780 John Maurer and Catharine Hillegass.
May 30, 1780 Michael Huber and Elizabeth Hillegass.
Nov 7, 1780 Jacob Berninger and Salome Jost.
Jun 6, 1780 Jacob Schneider and Magdalene Gerhard.1
Nov 14, 1780 Conrad Mayer and Maria Hartranft.
Nov 14, 1780 Michael Schwartz and Maria Frey.

Dec 5, 1780 John Schneider and Susanna Stein.

Jan 2, 1781 John Reiffschneider and Dorothea Beck.

Mar 13, 1781 George Jodde and Anna Maria Neuman.

Apr 17, 1781 Henry Gratzer and Elizabeth Bernhard.

May 2, 1781 John Jackson and Elizabeth Berninger.

May 3, 1781 Henry Knauss and Elizabeth Ried.

May 7, 1781 Jacob Mayer and Sarah Mayer.

May 15, 1781 Jacob Gehry and Elizabeth Lauer.

Jun 19, 1781 Henry Hippel and Hannah Schneider.

Jul 3, 1781 Henry Maurer and Philippina Dotter.

Nov 20, 1781 Conrad Neuman and Catharine Bender.

Dec 4, 1781 Henry Reiffschneider and Sophia Beck.

Jan 15, 1782 Henry Pfalzgraff and Anna Maria Huber.

Jan 29, 1782 Michael Esterlein and Elizabeth Faust.

Mar 19, 1782 John Huber and Anna Erbach.

1782 --- David Evans's mulatto, James, and Jacob Krauss's mulatto, of
    Longswamp.

Apr 2, 1782 George Herbst and Elizabeth Wiebel.

May 9, 1782 Jacob Buchwalter and Magdalene Acker.

Apr 16, 1782 Jacob Arndt and Elizabeth Neiss.

Apr 18, 1782 John Jaeger and Magdalene Knerr.

Nov 5, 1782 Samuel Hirsch and Susanna Andre.

Dec 25, 1782 Michael Decker and Elizabeth Fertig.

Jan 18, 1783 Matthew Liebegut and Catharine Schuster.

Feb 18, 1783 Frederick Conrad and Catharine Schneider.

Mar 16, 1783 George Freyer and Maria Schneider.

Mar 25, 1783 Matthew Regener and Elizabeth Huber.

Mar 27, 1783 William Becker and Maria Reiffschneider.

Apr 10, 1783 Jacob Schwenck and Elizabeth Reimer.

Apr 22, 1783 Jacob Schmid of Towamensing Twp, Philadelphia County and
    Maria Scherer.

Apr 22, 1783 Peter Roshon and Maria Wolfanger.

May 8, 1783 Jacob Steger and Elizabeth Schoenholtz.

May 20, 1783 Philip Bernhard and Elizabeth Antes.

May 27, 1783 Conrad Schmid and Margaret Spiess.

Jun 24, 1783 Adam Andreas and Catharine Ache.

Aug 19, 1783 Jacob Engel and Elizabeth Bucher.

Marriages by Frederick Dellicker

Apr 13, 1784 Henry, son of Peter Roshong(2) of Frederick Twp. and Catharine,
    widow of Michael Trumbauer of Marlborough Twp.

Apr 20, 1784 Henry, son of Adam Boshard and Gertrude, dau of Andrew Jung,
    both of Goshenhoppen.

Apr 20, 1784 John, son of Jacob Dengeler and Magdalene, dau of Andrew Schmid, both of this congregation.

May 9, 1784 George, son of the late John Moor of Marlborough Twp., and Barbara, dau of Frederick Langbein of Limerick Twp., Philadelphia County.

May 25, 1784 Christopher, son of the late Henry Scheffy of Frederick Twp., and Catharine, dau of Philip Roshong of Limerick Twp.

Jun 29, 1784 Rev. Frederick William van der Schlott, preacher at Goshenhoppen and Anna Margaret Ried, dau of Jacob Ried of Hatfield Twp.2

Oct 7, 1784 John, son of the late Isaac Meyer of Tulpehocken and Catharine, dau of Philip Hahn of this congregation.3

Oct 16, 1784 Jacob, son of Henry Freyer and Susanna, dau of Sebastian Eichelberger, both of this congregation.

Nov 9, 1784 Adam, son of Philip Luckhart and Anna Barbara, widow of Jacob Erni, both of this congregation.

Nov 16, 1784 Philip, son of the late George Meklein and Margaret Barbara, dau of Philip Jacob Schmid, both of this congregation.

Nov 23, 1784 John George Gaukler and Dorothea, dau of Gottlieb Zink, both Lutherans of Old Goshenhoppen. 1

Dec 14, 1784 John, son of Henry Schneider and Susanna, dau of John Schmid, both of this congregation.

Dec 30, 1784 Henry, son of the late Ludwig Hartenstein and Magdalene, dau of Michael Renn, both of Old Goshenhoppen.

Jan 30, 1785 Henry, son of the late Henry Grote and Elizabeth, dau of Christian Wood of New Hanover Twp.

Apr 12, 1785 Henry, son of the late George Goetz, and Maria Catharine, dau of Casper Bucher.

May 19, 1785 George, son of George Neiss, and Elizabeth, dau of Jacob Christman of Frederick Twp.

Apr 14, 1785 Henry Neuman, son of Henry Neuman and Magdalene, dau of John Kohn.

Aug 28, 1785 Martin Zieler, widower, and Catharine, dau of Carl Kichlein of Frederick Twp.

Aug 10, 1785 Jacob, son of the late Jacob Dengeler and Catharine, dau of Leonard Walder of this congregation.

Sept 20, 1785 Ludwig, son of Ludwig Bender and Rosina, dau of Ludwig Schik of this congregation.

Oct 9, 1785 John, son of Henry Huber and Magdalene, dau of the late Adam Sorg.

Oct 13, 1785 Jacob, son of John Schellenberger of Hatfield Twp, and Christine, dau of John Jost.

Oct 25, 1785 Jacob, son of the late Andrew Jorger and Catharine Schmidt, dau of John Schmid, of this congregation.

Dec 10, 1785 Henry son of Henry Freyer and Anna Maria, dau of Moses
    Bender.

Jan 29, 1786 Peter, son of John Schmid of Limerick and Elizabeth, dau of Isaac
    Felix of Reading.

Feb 7, 1786 Daniel, son of John Jost of this congregation and Barbara, dau of
    Conrad Hillegass of New Goshenhoppen.

Feb 25, 1786 Peter, son of the late Jeremiah Osterlein, and Magdalene, dau of
    Conrad Doderer.

Apr 4, 1786 Jacob, son of Michael Stoffelet and Eva, dau of Jacob Mayer.

Apr 4, 1786 George, son of the late Simon Graff, and Christine, dau of Philip
    Jahn.

Apr 11, 1786 Peter, son of Casper Erb and Christine, dau of Wendel Renninger.

May 9, 1786 Christian, son of late Conrad Specht and Barbara, dau of the late
    Martin Sinzendorfer.

May 23, 1786 Conrad, son of the late George Voegely and Catharine, dau of
    the late Matthew Fux.

May 30, 1786 Jacob, son of the late John Grob and Elizabeth, dau of Adam
    Kalb.

Oct 12, 1786 Frederick Delliker, V.D.M. and Maria Magdalena
    Schuvena(Juvenal), widow of Northern Liberties, near Philadelphia.

Nov 21, 1786 Henry, son of John Schellenberger of Hatfield Twp. and Barbara,
    dau of John Schmid of Frederick Twp.

Dec 5, 1786 Henry, son of Henry Kihly and Hannah, dau of John Kember of
    Skippack Twp.

Jan 30, 1787 Conrad, son of the late Jacob Dieterich and Elizabeth, dau of the
    late Philip Susholtz.

Mar 6, 1787 John, son of the late John George Fierer and Margaret, widow of
    Peter Gorchy.

Apr 12, 1787 Daniel, son of Matthias Doderer and Barbara, dau of Adam
    Muthard of Berks County.

May 22, 1787 Casper Erb, widower, and Catharine Reinheim, widow of George
    Reinheim, Lutherans.

Jul 24, 1787 John, son of the late Philip Steipers and Elizabeth, dau of the late
    Valentine Hahs of Limerick Twp.

Aug 11, 1787 Philip, son of Henry Freyer and Elizabeth, dau of the late
    Christian Reinheim.

Sept 18, 1787 Jacob, son of Nicholas Dering and Catharine, dau of John Henry
    Ekelman.

Oct 9, 1787 Abraham, son of Henry Bleuler of Great Swamp, and Margaret, dau
    of Ludwig Bender.

Oct 30, 1787 Philip, son of Michael Brand, and Catharine, dau of the late Henry
    Schaeffy.

Dec 25, 1787 Frederick, son of Michael Schwartz and Maria, dau of Frederick

Lord.

Jan 1, 1788 Jacob, son of Conrad Reiffschneider, and Catharine, dau of Henry Devertshauser.

Feb 26, 1788 John, son of Zacharias Neiss and Hannah, dau of the late David Reinert.

Mar 11, 1788 Henry, son of Jacob Stetler and Sarah, dau of the late Valentine Haas.

Mar 13, 1788 Jacob, son of the late Christian Weyerman, and Elizabeth, dau of Carl Haven.

Apr 1, 1788 Daniel, son of the late Daniel Benner, and Anna Maria, dau of John Schoener.

Apr 22, 1788 John, son of the late John Zoller and Anna Maria, dau of John Erny.

Apr 22, 1788 George, son of David Haag, and Anna, dau of Conrad Weyerman.

Apr 22, 1788 Abraham, son of the late Joseph Zimmerman of Sussex County of Jersey and Nancy, dau of Geo. Neiss.

Jun 5, 1788 John Jacob, son of Philip Roschong and Anna Barbara, dau of John Creider.

Nov 20, 1788 Abraham, son of Hans Adam Zaern and Magdalene, dau of Jacob Kehl.

Dec 14, 1788 William, son of Frederick Stillwagen and Elizabeth, dau of Joseph Kolb of New Goshenhoppen.

Dec 16, 1788 George, son of the late George Dieterich Bucher and Christine, dau of the late John Schneider.

Dec 30, 1788 Jacob, son of John Frey and Catharine, dau of Sebastian Reiffschneider.

Mar 3, 1789 Frederick, son of Hans Adam Zarn, and Anna Margaret, dau of Abraham Tris.

Mar 10, 1789 Daniel Koch and Magdalene, dau of the late Fred. Betz.

Mar 10,1789 George, son of Peter Gugger and Christine, dau of Anthony Spies.

Mar 17,1789 John Pitterman, widower and Susanna, dau of Michael Brand.

Mar 31,1789 Jacob, son of John Roscher, and Hannah, dau of the late Frederick Weiss.

Apr 7,1789 John, son of the late Jacob Detweiler, and Magdalene, dau of Peter Gugger of New Goshenhoppen.

Apr 14,1789 Frederick, son of George Hubener and Christine, dau of Peter Roschong.

Apr 28,1789 George Freyer, widower, and Maria, dau of the late Philip Doderer.

May 17,1789 Adam, son of John Jost, and Susanna, dau of Conrad Hillegass of New Goshenhoppen.

May 17,1789 John, son of William Geyer and Anna Maria, dau of the late Hans Adam Hillegass of New Goshenhoppen.

Jun 25,1789 John, son of Anthony van der Schleiss and Elizabeth, dau of the late Herman Neuman of Providence.

Jul 6,1789 George, son of the late Matthias Krieg of Oley, and Catharine, dau of Gottfried Langbein.

Oct 22,1789 John Nicholas, son of Peter Faust and Elizabeth, dau of the late Nicholas Walbert of Frederick Twp. 1

Oct 22,1789 John, son of Christian Sheid and Magdalene, dau of the late Peter Bock of Old Goshenhoppen.2

Nov 30,1789 Bernhard, son of Michael Bar of Oley, and Margaret, dau of Gottfried Langbein.

Jan 26, 1790 George, son of the late Michael Huber, and Elizabeth, dau of Ludwig Bender.

Jan 26, 1790 Samuel Bertoly, widower, and Elizabeth Frey.3

Feb 2, 1790 Jacob, son of Frederick Rudy and Catharine, dau of Christian Scheid of Old Goshenhoppen.

Feb 5, 1790 Nicholas Pfuhl, widower, and Elizabeth, dau of Michael Brand.

Mar 2, 1790 Francis, son of Christian Zoller, and Catharine, dau of Jacob Wolfinger.

Mar 25, 1790 Samuel, son of Peter Vedder of Reading Twp. and Maria, dau of the late George Dieter Bucher.

May 18, 1790 Isaac, son of William Deising, and Sarah, dau of Jacob Frey.

May 18, 1790 George, son of Gottfried Langbein and Eva, dau of Peter Fischer.

Aug 17, 1790 John, son of the late John Berger and Christine, dau of Peter Faust of Ridgeland Twp.

Sept 14, 1790 Christian, son of Conrad Bikhard and Anna, dau of George Schlotter of Old Goshenhoppen.

Oct 2, 1790 Abraham, son of Henry Huber and Margaret, dau of the late Dewald Grub.

Oct 26, 1790 John Baedman and Hannah, dau of Michael Brand.

Dec 14, 1790 Conrad, widower, son of Peter Minner and Elizabeth, dau of the late Peter Schmid.

Dec 14, 1790 Jacob, son of John Nicholas Bauer and Anna, dau of Peter Fried.

Jan 31, 1791 John, son of John Lee, and Hannah, dau of Nicholas Henry of Frederick Twp.

Mar 2, 1791 Christian, son of Henry Freyer, and Christine, dau of Jacob Fillman.

Mar 17, 1791 John, son of the late John Schneider, innkeeper, and Catharine, dau of the late Jacob Dengeler.

Mar 17, 1791 John Viery, widower, and Barbara, dau of Joseph Speidel.

Apr 12, 1791 Conrad, son of the late Sebastian Bucher, and Anna Maria, dau of Henry Engel.

Apr 14, 1791 John, son of John Greder and Christine, dau of the late Herman Neuman.

May 10, 1791 Conrad, son of John Kihler and Elizabeth, dau of the late Robin Edward.

Jun 2, 1791 Elias Watts and Elizabeth Hornback.

Jun 6, 1791 Doctor Joseph Rass and Maly Maria McClintik.

Aug 21, 1791 John, son of the late Valentine Buff and Christine, dau of the late Matthias Scheuffley. 1

Aug 23, 1791 Samuel, son of the late Leischer David and Margaret, dau of the late John Nicholas Bauer.

Aug 23, 1791 John, son of Adam Livegood and Elizabeth, dau of William Reifschneider.

Sept 1, 1791 John, son of Frederick Cuntz, and Elizabeth, dau of Conrad Beyer.

Sept 18, 1791 Henry, the son of John Cohl and Barbara, dau of the late Sebastian Eichelberger.

Sept 27, 1791 John, son of Casper Baret, and Margaret, dau of Henry Sell of Upper Hanover Twp.

Nov 3, 1791 Matthias, son of George Deker, and Maria, dau of Casper Bernhard.

Dec 11, 1791 Jacob, son of the late George Oberdorff and Maria, dau of John Lee.

Dec 20, 1791 Thomas, son of the late George Bohlich, and Elizabeth, dau of Jacob Kehl.

Jan 3, 1792 Henry, son of Jacob Craus and Sophia, dau of Christian Zoller.

Jan 24, 1792 John, son of Thomas Wilson and Elizabeth, dau of Joseph Speidel.

Feb 7, 1792 Peter, son of Adam Livegood, and Catharine, dau of Daniel Lintzenbugler.

Feb 21, 1792 William, son of Michael Schmid Elizabeth, dau of Daniel Merz.

Mar 13, 1792 John, son of Stephen Crumrein and Elizabeth, dau of Peter Martin.

May 12, 1792 John Michael, son of Michael Mueller of Northern Liberties, and Catharine, dau of the late George Mechlein.

Jun 19, 1792 Abraham Grob, widower and Margaret, dau of Christian Zoller.

Jun 24, 1792 Peter, son of the late Peter Bock, and Esther Beringer, dau of the late Joseph Beringer of Old Goshenhoppen.

Jun 28, 1792 Lawyer Edmund Key from Maryland and Ruth Anna Potts.

Jul 3, 1792 Peter Reifschneider, widower, and Barbara, dau of the late Nicholas Lachmund.

Oct 2, 1792 Philip, son of Jacob Livegood and Elizabeth, dau of the late Joseph Mebbery.

Oct 30, 1792 George, son of George Bechtel and Hannah, dau of John Schweinhart.

Nov 5, 1792 John, son of John Schlichter and Magdalene, dau of Jacob Frey.

Nov 6, 1792 John, son of the late Samuel Sens and Catharine, dau of John Schoener.

Nov 20, 1792 John Brooks and Mary Keppner.

Dec 18, 1792 Abraham, son of Bernhard Doderer and Elizabeth, dau of Sebastian Reifschneider.

Apr 2, 1793 John Neuman, widower and Elizabeth Schilchy, widow.

Jun 23, 1793 Christopher Scheffy, widower and Catharine, dau of the late Joseph Mebbery.

Jul 18, 1793 Henry Seyler, widower, and Susanna, dau of Peter Gugger.

Jul 25, 1793 John Jost, widower and Maria, dau of Valentine Seipel.

Aug 13, 1793 Christian, son of the late John Betto, and Barbara, dau of Ludwig Schik.

Sept 17, 1793 Michael, son of John Wien and Anna Maria, dau of --- Geyer.

Sept 24, 1793 Jacob, son of John Kihly and Maria, dau of Philip Beyer.

Sept 29, 1793 John, son of Leonard Beyer and Barbara, dau of Michael Zigler.

Sept 29, 1793 John, son of Peter Moser and Hannah, dau of David Weidner.

Oct 29, 1793 David Bruch, widower, and Anna Kihler, widow.

Nov 4, 1793 Charles Jolly and Sophia Mebbery. 1

Nov 26, 1793 John, son of Henry Geyer and Margaret, dau of Conrad Jeger.

Dec 24, 1793 Andrew, son of Andrew Schmid and Maria, dau of George Gresch.

Dec 26, 1793 John, son of Michael Leidner and Catharine, dau of Casimir Misemer.

Jan 2, 1794 Doctor William Arch Cozem and Charlotte Maus.

Feb 27, 1794 Philip, son of Bernhard Freyer and Elizabeth, dau of Henry Schneider.

Mar 2, 1794 George Ovenshane and Mary Taylor.

Mar 25, 1794 John, son of the late Jacob Livegood and Christine, dau of John Beker.

Apr 13, 1794 Nicholas Lachmund and Catharine Thomas.

Apr 15, 1794 Samuel, son of Michael Ziegler and Christine, dau of Henry Schneider of Marlborough Twp.

May 6, 1794 John, son of Ludwig Bender and Catharine, dau of Michael Albrecht.

May 25, 1794 John Spengler, widower and Elizabeth, dau of Andrew Schmid.

Aug 3, 1794 Henry, son of Andrew Schmid and Christine, dau of the late George Dieter Bucher.

Sept 11, 1794 Levi Coulston and Sarah Evans.

Oct 12, 1794 John, son of Wendel Reninger and Anna Catharine, dau of Adam Kalb.

Oct 19, 1794 Henry, son of Philip Roschong and Anna Maria, dau of William Major.

Oct 28, 1794 George, son of Henry Keiser and Eva, dau of Joseph Speidel.

Nov 6, 1794 John, son of Herman Achy, and Barbara, dau of Andrew Jung.

Nov 18, 1794 Benjamin, son of George Brand and Elizabeth, dau of the late Abraham Meyer.

Nov 27, 1794 Conrad, son of Conrad Reifschneider, and Elizabeth, dau of John Wien.

Dec 25, 1794 Peter, son of John Fritz and Susanna, dau of Andrew Schoener.

Apr 2, 1795 Abraham, son of Abraham Sell and Barbara, dau of Peter Guker of New Goshenhoppen.

Apr 26, 1795 Abraham, son of the late Peter Edinger and Elizabeth, dau of Martin Lichty of Old Goshenhoppen.

May 5, 1795 George, son of John Schmid and Catharine dau of Valentine Scheelkof. 1

May 25, 1795 Henry Schueg and Elizabeth Jung.

Jun 21, 1795 John, son of Ludwig Schik and Maria, dau of Bernhart Gilbert.

Aug 23, 1795 William, son of William Axt and Anna, dau of Jacob Wolfinger.

Sept 17, 1795 John, son of Peter Roshing and Magdalene, dau of John Johnsen (Jans).

Oct 15, 1795 The Rev. William Hendel, minister in Tulpehocken, etc. and Margaret, dau of Philip Hahn.

Oct 25, 1795 Michael, son of Michael Ziegler and Maria, dau of Henry Sasseman.

Oct 6, 1795 John, son of William Major and Elizabeth, dau of Michael Neuzehnholtzer.

Nov 3, 1795 Matthias, son of the late Valentine Shilich and Catharine, dau of John Eschenfelder.

Nov 19, 1795 Jacob, son of Michael Schmid and Maria, dau of the late Matthias Rittenhauser.

Dec 1, 1795 Jacob, son of William Lik, and Catharine, dau of Conrad Jeger.

Feb 9, 1796 John, son of Herman Reifschneider and Catharine, dau of Andrew Schoener.

Feb 13, 1796 William Meberry And Anna Hakley.

Feb 23, 1796 William, son of the late George Beyer and Catharine, dau of Henry Groll.

Mar 3, 1796 John Jolly and Rebecca Mebbery.

Mar 22, 1796 John, son of Henry Hohlenbusch and Sarah, dau of Frederick Kuntz.

Mar 26, 1796 Valentine, son of Peter Steltz and Magdalene, dau of Michael Kuntz or Cuntz.

Mar 26, 1796 George Pfeihl and Elizabeth Obryen (O'Brien).

Apr 5, 1796 Peter, son of the late John Schweitzford and Maria, dau of Conrad Bikhard.

Apr 5, 1796 Michael, son of the former Mark Kihler and Elizabeth, dau of Michael Ziegler.

Mar 12, 1796 Henry, son of Adam Hohlenbusch and Maria, dau of John

Hildenbeutel.

May 1, 1796 Jacob Roschong, widower, and Anna Major.

May 1, 1796 Andrew Tacy and Becky Williams.

Aug 10, 1796 John, son of Frederick Kehr and Maria, dau of Thomas Kemel of Pottstown.

Aug 14, 1796 Carl Geyer, widower and Margaret Specht, widow.

Aug 21, 1796 John, son of Peter Sebold and Catharine, dau of the later Nicholas Lachmund.

Sept 11, 1796 Benjamin, son of John Stetler and Hannah, dau of John Kepler of Trappe.

Nov 29, 1796 John, son of the late Sebastian Bucher and Elizabeth, dau of Andrew Schoener.

Dec 8, 1796 Henry, son of the late John Lee and Catharine, dau of Philip Mud.

Mar 5, 1797 John, son of George Bechtel and Maria, dau of John Misemer of Pottstown

Mar 7, 1797 Abraham Schunk and Patty Thomas.

Mar 14, 1797 Samuel Potts and Maty (Martha) Jus.

Apr 17, 1797 Edward, son of the late Isaac Connel, and Susanna, dau of Henry Keyser.

Apr 20, 1797 John, son of Peter Steltz and Catharine, dau of John Schnell.

Jun 4, 1797 Thomas, son of John Brok and Elizabeth, dau of John Misemer.

Aug 31, 1797 Henry, son of John Kihly and Catharine, dau of Conrad Beyer.

Oct 17, 1797 Daniel, son of Valentine Kratz and Elizabeth, dau of Matthias Geist of Old Goshenhoppen.

Nov 3, 1797 Philip, son of Philip Gabel and Catharine, dau of Henry Schneider of Upper Salford.

Dec 31, 1797 Benjamin, son of Jacob Reiff and Anna, dau of the late Michael Groll.

Jan 28, 1798 Philip, son of the late Martin Kreis and Catharine, dau of David Bruch.

Feb 14, 1798 Henry, son of Henry Ekelman and Elizabeth, dau of Philip Roschong.

Mar 13, 1798 John, son of the late John Willauer and Catharine of the late Jacob Livegood.

Mar 20, 1798 Frederick, son of Frederick Delliker, pastor of this place, and Catharine, dau of the late John Geo. Beitman.

May 6, 1798 Conrad, son of John Cohl and Hannah, dau of the late John Werly.

May 8, 1798 Joseph, son of the late Lorenz Schmid and Maria, dau of Peter Acker.

Jun 7, 1798 Rasmus Lever and Maria Freyer.

Jul 10, 1798 Jacob, son of John Jost and Hannah, dau of Philip Schwarzlender.

Jul 25, 1798 Henry, son of John Jost and Margaret, dau of the late John Rikert.

Aug 19, 1798 Jacob son of the late Michael Groll and Sarah, dau of Philip

Beyer.
Aug 19, 1798 Isaac, son of the late Frederick Beker and Elizabeth, dau of
Christian Ziegler.
Sept 16, 1798 John, son of James Thomas and Maria Catharine, dau of
Frederick Delliker, pastor of this place.
Oct 1, 1798 George, son of John Heist, and Susanna, dau of Rein Kihler.
Oct 1, 1798 Nathaniel Bolton and Susanna Updegraf.
Nov 18, 1798 Joseph Jost and Elizabeth Kepler.
Nov 29, 1798 Conrad Bikhard and Elizabeth Schweisforth.
Dec 4, 1798 Mahlon Long and Pahly (Polly) Benjamin.
Dec 6, 1798 George Dieterich and Catharine Kehr.
Nov 9, 1798 Nathan Bolton and Susanna Upthegraf.

Marriages by Frederick Herman
May 26, 1799 Frederick Weiss and Barbara Kurtz.
Aug 4, 1799 James M'Clintuk and Martha, dau of Thomas Bull, Esq. of Chester
County.
Sept 3, 1799 Christian Steltz and Catharine, dau of John Schmitt.
Oct 15, 1799 David Lubold, of Berks County, and Hannah Gehrling of Chester
County.
Dec 24, 1799 Jacob Carl and Elizabeth Hippel, both of Chester Co.
Dec 30, 1799 Jacob Fisher and Elizabeth Weidner.
Dec 31, 1799 George Missimer and Elizabeth Thomas.
Dec 31, 1799 Frederick March and Susanna Kiehler.

Burials by the Rev. John Philip Deydich, 1748-1752.
Dec 26, 1748 died; Dec 27, buried; Christine, dau of Jacob Bayer age 1 yr, 8
mos.
Jan 6, 1749 died; Jan 8 buried; Eva Elizabeth, dau of Valentine Kiel, age about
4 yrs.
Feb 9, 1749 died; Feb 11, buried, Joseph Freyer, age 65 yrs.
Feb 25, 1749 died; Feb 26 buried; Jacob Mayer, alias Walldoerffer; age about
59 yrs.
Feb 28, 1749 died; Mar 2; buried; Christina, wife of Henry Dieringer, age 45
yrs.
Mar 16, 1749 died; Mar 18 buried; Jenicke, dau of the late John Neiss, age in
her eighth year.
Apr 5, 1749 died; Apr 7 buried; Matthew Speck, age 68 yrs.
In this year 1750, none given properly to my care died.
--- 1751, died ---- buried; Jacob, son of Mr. John Miller, age in his 2nd year.
Jan 15, 1752 died about 12 p.m. the wife of Casper Singer, age 45 yrs.
Sept 17, 1755 died; Sept 18 buried; Mr. John Miller, at the time a deacon, age
54 yrs.

Nov 22, 1751 in the evening, died; Nov 24 buried; Elizabeth, dau of Mr. John
Eshbach, age 2 yrs, 7 mos.

Burials of the Rev Nicholas Pomp, 1772-1783

Feb 3, 1772 died; Feb 5 buried; Catharine, dau of J. Uhlerich, age 9 yrs,10
mos,5 days.

Feb 5, 1772 died; buried Feb 7; Margaret Barbara, wife of Jacob Hauch, age 86
yrs (in the Zieber-Schwenck Cemetery).

Mar 25, 1772 died; Mar 27 buried; Jacob, son of John Schneider, age 15 yrs, 11
mos, 10 days.

Jan 6, 1773 died; buried Jan 8; Margaret, wife of Matthias Reichert.

Jan 30, 1773 died; buried Feb 1; a child of Mr. Ekelman.

Feb 25, 1773 buried; Elizabeth, dau of Henry Freyer.

Mar 5, 1773 buried; Peter., son of Henry Freyer.

Apr 6, 1773 buried; Christine, little dau of Mr. Hamsher.

Apr 10, 1773 buried; Henry, little son of Mr. Hamsher.

Jun 2, 1773 buried; Philippina, little dau of John Plet.

---, 1773 Conrad Schmid's little son.

---, 1773 Jacob Frack's child.

Jan 19, 1774 died; buried Jan 21; Maria, nee Betz.

Feb 6, 1775 died; buried Feb 8; Barbara Antes, wife of Frederick Antes.

Mar 13, 1775 died; buried Mar.15; Henry Schleicher.

May 21, 1775 buried; Elizabeth, dau of Philip Jahn age 14 days, died of
smallpox.

Jun 1, 1775 buried; Maria Christina and Jacob, children of Andrew Schmid,
died of smallpox. Ages respectively 7 yrs, 7 mos, and 3 yrs, 4 mos, 25 days.

Jun 21, 1775 buried; Margaret, dau of John Gerling.

Mar 19, 1777 died; buried Mar 21; M. Sibylla Neuzenhoeltzer.

Feb 26, 1777 died; buried Mar 1; Eva Catherine, dau of Valentine Kehly, age
13 yrs.

Feb 28, 1777 died; buried Mar 2; Conrad Specht, age 54 yrs, 5 mos.

Mar 15, 1777 died; Mar 17 buried; John Zoller, Age 73 yrs, 8 mos.

Mar 3, 1777 died; Mar 5 buried; Bastian Eichelberger, age 56 yrs, 18 days.

Mar 15, 1777 died; Mar 17 Buried; Sibylla Euster, Widow, age 56 yrs, 15 days.

Mar 25, 1777 Died; Mar 23 buried; John Reifschneider, son of William
Reifschneider, age 28.

Mar 27, 1777 died; buried Mar 29; Hannah, wife of Balthasar Maurer.

Apr 10, 1777 buried; David Bruch's child.

May 4, 1777 Buried Jacob Bauman's wife.

May 22, 1777 Buried; Apollonia Kuntz.

Jul ---, 1777 Buried Joachim Gottschalk's wife.

Aug ---, 1777 Buried Conrad Richtsein's dau.

Aug ---, 1777 Buried Christian Steltz.

Aug ---, 1777 Buried George Pfalzgraff's child.
Jul ---, 1777 Buried the late John Zoller's child.
Sep ---, 1777 Buried Christian Zoller's child.
Nov ---, 1777 Buried Peter Meffert.
Dec ---, 1777 Buried Jacob Bingeman.
Dec ---, 1777 Buried George Neiss's child.
Dec ---, 1777 Buried Catharine Reegner.
Jan 1, 1778 Buried Christian Neuman.
Jan 10, 1778 Buried Christian Weber.
Jan 13, 1778 Buried Henry Geyer's wife.
Jan 16, 1778 Buried Bastian Bucher.
Jan 24, 1778 Buried John Hippel.
Feb 2, 1778 Buried Herman Neuman.
Feb 8, 1778 Buried Sophia Bucher.
--- , 1778 Buried child of the late Peter Meffert.
Mar 2, 1778 Buried Christopher Neuman.
Mar 2, 1778 Buried Mauren (Mason) Derk's child.
Mar 26, 1778 Buried Conrad Grobt's wife, (b. 1714. Buried in Zieber-
    Schwenck Cemetery.)
---, 1778 Buried N. Ludwig Stark.
---, 1778 Buried a single Person from Philadelphia.
---, 1778 Buried George Dieder Bucher's little girl.
---, 1778 Buried Michael Ludwich's child.
---, 1778 Buried May 21st, George Dieder Bucher's daughter, who was shot
    accidentally.
Jun 20, 1778 Buried Nichoas Schuhriemen, who met death through a fall.
Jun 21, 1778 Buried Adam Esch.
Jul 20, 1778 Buried James Schriber, a man from the poor house.
Aug 15, 1778 Buried Thomas, son of Casper Schneider.
---, 1778 Buried Conrad Scherer's little son.
---, 1778 Buried Peter Miller's little dau.
Sept 18, 1778 Buried Peter Seeler's little son.
---, 1778 Buried John Hoffman' little dau.
---, 1778 Buried Conrad Scheer's little dau.
---, 1778 Peter Miller's wife.
---, 1778 Buried John Hoffman's little son.
---, 1778 Buried John Mayer's wife.
---, 1778 Buried Catharine Engel.
---, 1778 Buried Catharine Knauss.
Feb 13, 1780 Buried John Pauss.
Feb 2, 1780 Buried Henry Deringer, age 87 years.
Mar 19, 1780 Buried Anna Martha Neuman, age 66 yrs.
Mar 29, 1780 Buried Henry Landau's child.

May 11, 1780 Buried Henry Stetler, age 48 yrs. (b. 1732, buried in Leydy's Cemetery.)

Aug 30, 1780 Buried Herman Sassamanshausen,

Sept 13, 1780 Buried Martin Bitting's Widow.

Oct 15 Buried William, son of Conrad Reifschneider.

Nov 28 Buried Casper Kriessemer's son.

Nov 30 buried John Derr's daughter.

Jan 21, 1781 Buried Anna Maria, Wife of Michael Dotterer.

Jan 31, 1781 Buried John Plett's little daughter.

Mar 4, 1781 Buried Widow Scheffe.

Mar 5, 1781 Buried Thomas Goerger

Mar 6, 1781 Buried John Loch's child.

---, 1781 Buried Abraham Faust.

Jun 2, 1781 Buried Jacob Neuman.

Jun 6, 1781 Buried Conrad Rauch.

Jun 11, 1781 Buried John Dudiere's daughter.

Aug 26, 1781 Buried Henry Jung Age 93 yrs, New Goshenhoppen Ch.

Nov 6, 1781 Buried, two sons of Conrad Jager, one 8 Yrs.old, buried Nov 2; the other 10 Yrs. buried Nov.6.

Dec 31, 1781, died; buried Jan 2,1782, Jacob Barrall.

Jan 11, 1782 Buried Maria Margaret Fisher.

Mar 23, 1782 Died; Mar 25 Buried; Peter du Freher.

Apr 14, 1782 Buried Philip Baltener, a Lutheran.

Jul 15, 1782 Buried Michael Deny.

Dec 9, 1782 Buried Thomas Schneider.

Dec 19, 1782 Buried Joseph Freyer's child.

Jan 22, 1783 Buried Eva Berninger.

Feb 13, 1783 Buried Margaret, Wife of William Reifschneider.

Feb 19, 1783 Buried Mathias Eyerman's child.

Mar 18, 1783 Adam Imbody's child.

Mar 27, 1783 Buried John Peter, son of Peter Sebold.

Mar 30, 1783 Buried Adam Asher, M. Goshon's teamster.

Mar 16, 1783 Buried Henry Neuman's child.

Apr 30, 1783 Buried Anna Maria, dau of George Dengler, age 2 yrs, 10 mos.

May 9, 1783 Buried Jacob Gashong's dau.

Deaths and Burials in My Ministry, Fredrick Dellinger, 1784-1799.

May 9, 1784 A most pathetic beginning of this year was made by my own wife, Maria Barbara, with a child under her heart. She was born Jan 8 1746; died May 7, 1784, in the morning between 12 and 1 o'clock, age 38 yrs, 4 mos less 1 day. Her burial services were conducted by the Rev. Mr. Von der Schloot, Pastor of Goshenhoppen, who delivered a most touching discourse, from the Words of Paul, Philip. I:23.

Jul 1, 1784 Henry Roschong, age 53 yrs, 8 mos, less 8 days.

Aug 3, 1784 Maria, dau of John M'Calister and wife, Christine, age 6 yrs, 3 mos, and a number of days.

Sept 3, 1784 Christine Margaret, wife of Philip Reier, age 27 yrs, 11 mos, 7 days.

Sept 4, 1784 Henry Koch, age 64 yrs, 2 mos less 4 days.

Sept 7, 1784 John George Voegeli, age 58 yrs, 7 mos, 12 days.

Sept 17, 1784 Valentine Killy, age 67 yrs, 11 mos, 5 days.

Sept 29, 1784 John Meyer, age 78 yrs, 8 mos.

Oct 1, 1784 Jacob Bernhard, age 72 yrs.

Oct 9, 1784 Gertrude, wife of Peter Steltz, age 36 yrs, 7 mos.

Dec 17, 1784 Frederick, son of Conrad Richtstein, age 24 yrs.

Dec 20, 1784 Philippina, wife of Martin Zieler, age 31 yrs,3 mos, less 8 days.

Dec 21, 1784 Jacob, son of Michael Decker, and wife, Elizabeth, age 1 yr, 4 mos, 2 wks.

Feb 14, 1785 Anna Maria, wife of John Neiss, age 83 yrs, 8 mos, 14 days.

Feb 22, 1785 Anna Elizabeth, wife of Daniel Neier of New Goshenhoppen, age 51 yrs, 10 mos, and a number of days.

Feb 25, 1785 Anna Maria, Wife of George Adam Hellebard, age 84 yrs. A Lutheran.

Mar 8, 1785 Catharine Margaret, wife of Casper Erb, age 53 yrs, 5 mos, 3 wks, 2 das. A Lutheran.

Apr 21, 1785 Henry Schenkel, age 67 yrs, less 1 mo, 7 days.

May 3, 1785 Catharine, dau of Jacob Witz, and wife, Maria of Pottstown, age 10 yrs, 5 days.

May 3, 1785 Rebecca, dau of Same Parents; age 4 yrs, less 1 day.

May 28, 1785 Anna Elizabeth, dau of Peter Bernhard and wife, Anna Maria, age 6 wks, 1 day.

Jun 4, 1785 Ann Maria, wife of Henry Schmid, age 83 yrs; buried (in Leidy's Cemetery.) These old people have lived in marriage with each other 60 years, and he also is 83 years; though several months younger than his wife. This is a circumstance not often met with.

Jul 6, 1785 Jacob Dengler, age 54 yrs, 2 mos, less 2 days.

Jul 29 Marcus, son of John Richard, Esq. and wife, Sophia, both Lutherans, age 7 mos, 3 wks.

Sept 9, 1785 John, son of John Nagel, and wife, Christina, age 1 yr, 5 mos, 1 day.

Sept 12, 1785 Peter, son of the same parents, age 3 yrs, 5 mos, less 2 days.

Oct 14, 1785 John Meklein, age 79 yrs, 7 mos, less 3 days. A Lutheran.

Oct 25, 1785 Elizabeth, dau of Joseph Brendlinger and Anna Rosina, Lutherans, age 7 yrs, 4 mos, less 3 days.

Nov 29, 1785 Erhard Schick, age 85 yrs, 1 mo, less 5 days. A Lutheran.

Dec 26, 1785 John, son of John Goezelman and wife, age 27 yrs, 8 mos, 1 da.

Apr 3, 1786 George Michael Frederick, age 82 yrs, 3 mos, 2 days; a Lutheran.

Apr 7 Michael Doderer, age 87 yrs, 11 mos and a number of days.

May 24, 1785 Thomas Schoen, age 87 yrs, less 1 mo.

Aug 16, 1785 George Andrew Schweinhardt, age 61 yrs, less 3 mos. A Lutheran.

Dec 2, 1785 Anna Helena, widow of Jacob Gilbert, age 80 yrs, A Lutheran..

Jan 5, 1727 Christina, dau of Casper Bucher, and his wife, Catherine, age 13 yrs, 9 mos, 16 days.

Jan 6, 1787 Eva Catharine, wife of Carl Weiss, age 58 yrs,8 mos.

Jan 8, 1787 Jacob, age 7 mos, 7 days, son of Philip Jost and his wife, Rosina.

Jan 11, 1787 Andrew Reifschneider, age 83 yrs.

Feb 12, 1787 Catharine, wife of Abraham Bopp, age 39 yrs, 1 mo.

Mar 12, 87 Daniel Hingerer, age 87 yrs, A Lutheran.

Mar 14, 1787 Elizabeth Kihly, age 65 yrs, widow of Valentine Kihly.

Apr 3, 1787 Catherine Rubert, age 77 yrs, widow of Valentine Rubert. A Lutheran.

May 1, 1787 Jacob Stoffellet, age 22 yrs.

May 18, 1787 Henry, age 7 wks, 3 days, son of John Betz and wife, Elizabeth.

Jun 17, 1787 Susanna Bender, age 46 yrs, 7 mos, 3 wks, 5 days, widow of Elias Bender.

Jul 7, 1787 Maria Elizabeth Wortman, a Lutheran, age 85 yrs, 9 mos, widow of Adam Wortman. She is survived by 8 children, 85 grandchildren, 71 great-grandchildren.

Jul 23, 1787 John, son of Peter Martin and wife, Catharine, age 6 yrs, 5 mos, less 2 days.

Jul 27, 1787 John Conrad, son of John Geiger, age 21 yrs, 5 mos, 3 days. He was without understanding and speech from his birth. A Lutheran.

Jul 31, 1787 Jacob, son of John Klein and wife, Magdalene, age 2 yrs, 3 mos, 2 wks. Lutherans.

Aug 6, 1787 Catharine, dau of John Romich, and wife, Anna Maria, age 13 yrs, 3 mos, 3 wks, 3 days. Lutherans.

Sept 1, 1787 Andrew Kihn, age 25 yrs, 5 mos, less 10 days.

Sept 11, 1787 Sibylla Balter, widow of Philip Balter, age 73 yrs. A Lutheran.

Sept 13, 1787 John George Schleier, age 66 yrs, 7 mos, less 10 days. He broke his neck, while hauling hay.

Dec 20, 1787 Anna Maria, wife of George Freyer, age 27 yrs, 7 mos, 21 days.

Dec 25, 1787 David Jag, age 74 yrs, 5 mos, 4 days. A Lutheran.

Dec 30, 1787 Elizabeth, dau of George Erb and wife, Catharine, age 1 yr, 9 mo, 23 days. Lutherans.

Jan 18, 1788 Maria Margaret, wife of Conrad Miner, age 17 yrs, 8 mos, 5 days.

Mar 7, 1788 Henry, son of Michael Neunzehnhoelzer, and wife, Elizabeth, age 18 yrs, 5 mos, 10 days. No religion. The father is to blame.

Mar 15, 1788 Peter, son of Jacob Kehl and wife, Barbara, age 6 yrs, 9 mos, less

6 days.

Mar 20, 1788 John, son of Martin Zieler and Margaret, age 1 yr, 8 mos.

Apr 15, 1788 Frederick Weiss, age 51 yrs, 5 mos, buried in Leidy' s Cemetery.

Apr 18, 1788 Magdalene, dau of Adem Krebs and his wife, Catharine, age 9 yrs, 1 mo, 4 ½ days. Lutheran.

Apr 22, 1788 Jacob Stichter, age 27 yrs, 3 mos, 2 days. A Lutheran.

May 3, 1788 Helena, Widow of George Beck, age 73 yrs, 1 mo. Lutheran.

---, 1788 Veronica, dau of Conrad Neuman and wife, Catharine, age 2 yrs, 6 mos, 10 days.

May 10, 1788 Maria Margaret, wife of William Sterk, age 72 yrs, A Lutheran of Hill Church.

May 15, 1788 Catharine, dau of George Herbst, and his wife, Barbara, age 10 yrs, 7 mos, 24 days. Lutherans.

May 17, 1788 Elizabeth, dau of Frederick Delliker, Pastor and his wife, Maria Magdalene, 8 mos, 17 days.

Jun 4, 1788 Dieterich Martin, age 79 Years.

Jun 5, 1788 Henry Neumann, age 27 yrs, 1 mo, 10 days.

Jun 29, 1788 Elizabeth, wife of John Pitterman, age 20 yrs, 4 mos, 8 days.

Aug 9, 1788 Elizabeth, widow of David Jag, age 73 yrs, Lutheran.

Aug 14, 1788 George Diterich Bucher, age 52 yrs, 6 mos, less 6 days.

Aug 21, 1788 Anna Barbara Joerger, age 75 yrs, 9 mos, widow of Martin Joerger. She was drowned in Swamp Creek. A Lutheran.

Aug 30, 1788 John Adam Neuman, son of George Neuman and his wife, Catharine, age 17 yrs, 7 mos, 5 days.

Nov 20, 1788 Margaret, dau of Christian Specht and wife, Barbara, age 1 yr, 9 mos, 18 days.

Dec 6, 1788 Maria Catharine, widow of Peter Seeler, age 77 yrs,

Feb 7, 1789 Margaret, widow of Christian Steltz, age 83 yrs, 1 mo.

Feb 8, 1789 Anna Catharine, wife of Eberhard Lachmann, age 73 yrs, a Lutheran.

May 25, 1789 John Philip Mueller, age 73 yrs,4 mos, 7 days. Lutheran.

Jun 2, 1789 Mary Magdalene, wife of Nicholas Pfuhl, age 32 yrs, 10 mos, A Lutheran.

Jun 9, 1789 Peter, son of Peter Specht and wife, Margaret, age 3 yrs, 3 mos, 13 days. The child fell from a wagon and was injured by one of the wheels. He died soon after this.

Jun 28, 1789 Hannah, dau of Christian Specht and wife, Barbara, age 10 mos, 26 days.

Jul 14, 1789 David, son of Conrad Diffenbacher and wife, Catharine, age 4 wks, less 3 days.

Jul 22, 1789 Hannah, dau of Christian Stetler and wife, Catharine, age 20 yrs, 6 mos, 2 wks. A Lutheran buried in Leidy's Cemetery.

Aug 4, 1789 Jacob, son of Jacob Dering and wife, Catharine, age 1 yr, 1 mo.

Aug 7, 1789 John, son of the above Jacob Dering, age 1 yr, 1 mo. 1 day.

Sept 1, 1789 Anna Maria, dau of John Vogely and wife, Anna Maria, age 2 mos, 7 days. Lutherans.

Sept 10, 1789 Anthony, son of George Dengler and wife, Anna Maria, age 3 yrs, 3 mos, 3 wks, 5 days.

Sept 11, 1789 Jacob Patton, Colonel, age 62 yrs.

Sept 12, 1789 Conrad Jeger, age 32 yrs, 9 mos, less 6 days. Lutheran.

Oct 15, 1789 Christina Bernhard, widow of Jacob Bernhard, age 75 yrs, 2 mos, 3 wks, less 3 days

Nov 8, 1789 George Neiss age 64 yrs, 8 mos.

Nov 13, 1789 Catharine, wife of Christopher Scheffi, age 29 yrs., 5 mos.

Jan 5, 1790 Anna Maria, widow of Frederick Erny, age 81 yrs.

Jan 26, 1790 Sarah, dau of John Pitterman and his late wife, Elizabeth, age 2 yrs, 5 mos, 6 days.

Feb 10, 1790 Jacob Neumann, age 62 yrs, 8 mos, 24 days.

Mar 19, 1790 Margaret, wife of John Viery, age 29 yrs.

Mar 19, 1790 John, son of John Viery and his deceased wife, Margaret, age 11 mos. Mother and child rest side by side, in one grave and remain united in death.

Apr 22, 1790 Hannah, widow of Conrad Jeger, age 37 yrs, 11 mos.

May 28, 1790 Andrew, son of Frederick Nebe and wife, Catharine, age 4 mos, 4 days.

Oct 19, 1790 Joseph Meberry, age 15 yrs and several months.

Jan 28, 1791 Wiliam, son of William Geyer and his wife, Anna Maria, of New Goshenhoppen, age 22 yrs, 2 mos.

Feb 3, 1791 Anna Maria, dau of Francis Zoller and his wife, Catharine, age 3 mos, 2 wks. 1 day.

Apr 9, 1791 John Philip, son of Jacob Brand and his wife, Maria, age 3 mos, 2 wks.

Apr 23, 1791 George Diterich, son of George Bucher and his wife, Christine, age 5 wks, 5 days.

May 1, 1791 John Michael Krebs, age 47 yrs, 3 mos, 5 days. A Lutheran.

Jun 22, 1791 Sarah, wife of Abraham Grob, age 38 yrs, 7 mos, 6 days.

Jun 23, 1791 John George, son of Jacob Schneider and his wife, Magdalene, age 1 mo, 1 wk, 5 days..

Aug 23, 1791 Esther, son of Bernard Freyer and his wife, Anna Maria, age 1 yr, 8 days.

Aug 30, 1791 John Casper Bernhard, age 73 yrs, 3 mos, 3 wks, 4 days.

Oct 3, 1791 Anna Maria, dau of John Klein and wife, Magdalene, age 4 yrs. 6 mos, 5 days.

Jan 5, 1792 Thomas Lord, age 37 yrs, 2 mos, 3 wks.

Feb 10, 1792 Anna Catharine, wife of Peter Reifschneider, age 40 yrs, 7 mos, 2 wks.

Feb 29, 1792 Benjamin, son of John Copplin and his wife, Susanna, age 4 mos, 3 wks.

Mar 1, 1792 Anna Maria, widow of Matthew Fuchs, age 55 yrs, 3 mos, 2 wks.

Mar 9, 1792 Jacob, son of Abraham Huber and wife, age 3 mos, 2 wks, 5 days.

May 28, 1792 Margaret, wife of John Neuman, age 40 yrs.

Aug 27, 1792 John, son of Henry Bernhard and wife, Sophia, age 3 yrs, 1 wk.

Oct --, 1792 Anna Maria, dau of Conrad Neuman,and wife, Catharine, age 1 yr, 1 mo, 5 days.

Oct --, 1792 Anna, dau of Henry Neuman and wife, Maria, age 10 mos, 6 Davs.

Nov 1, 1792 Helena, widow of Frederick Heim, age 74 yrs, 7 mos.

Nov 8, 1792 Jacob, son of Jacob Roschong and wife, Barbara, age 2 yrs, 3 mos, 3 wks.

Dec --, 1792 John Kehl, age 72 yrs.

Dec 29, 1792 Jacob, son of George Dengler and wife, Anna Maria, age 10 mos.

Jan 3, 1793 Peter Faust, age 67 yrs, 8 mos, 7 days.

Feb --, 1793 Elizabeth, wife of Henry Seyler, age 29 yrs, 24 days.

Mar. 7, 1793 Anna Maria, wife of Sebastian Reifschneider, age 54 yrs, several mos.

Mar 2, 1793 Catharine, dau of Francis Pigoney, and wife, Maria, age 12 yrs, 3 mos, 9 days.

Mar 8, 1793 Jacob, son of John Eschendelder, and wife, Sarah of Trappe, age 6 yrs, 3 mos, 15 days.

Apr 4, 1793 Henry Schmid, age 90 yrs, 4 mos buried in Leidy's Cemetery. N.B. He was struck dead by his own roof in a windstorm.

May 4, 1793 Barbara, widow of Hartman Haas of Trappe, age 64 yrs,

Jun 3, 1793 John Motzer, age 77 yrs, 5 mos, 3 wks, 5 days.

Aug 25, 1793 Anna Margaret, widow of John Swaner, age 80 yrs, less 3 wks.

Sept 16, 1793 Jacob Dering, age 30 yrs, 9 mos.

Nov 4, 1793 Jacob, son of Henry Craus and his wife, Sophia, age 1 yr, 3 mos.

Nov 5, 1793 Jacob, son of Francis Zoller and his wife, Catharine, age 1 yr, 8 mos.

Nov 8, 1793 John, son of George Sperry, and his wife, Elizabeth, age 15 yrs, 10 mos, 6 days.

Jan 6, 1794 Joseph, son of Ludwig Worman and his wife, Hannah, age 9 mos, less 1 day.

Jan 19, 1794 Catharine Margaret Sophia, wife of John Christian Breyman, age 44 yrs, 6 mos, less 2 days. A Lutheran.

Jan 20, 1794 Conrad Seeler, age 59 yrs.

Feb 2, 1794 Jacob Pitterman of Trappe, age 39 yrs, 1 mo. 2 wks.

Mar 30, 1794 Jacob Brand, age 60 yrs, 7 mos.

Apr 22, 1794 Susanna, dau of John Dengler and wife, Magdalene, age 10 mos, less 4 days.

Apr 29, 1794 Elizabeth, dau of Thomas Bolich, and his wife, Elizabeth, age 2 yrs, less 3 days.

Jun 24, 1794 Elizabeth, dau of Peter Sebold, and his wife, Magdalene, age 11 yrs, less 6 wks.

Jul 29, 1794 Salome, dau of Jacob Pitterman, and his wife, Susanna, age 7 yr, 7 mos, 3 wks, 4 days.

Aug 13, 1794 Michael Brand, age 70 yrs, 2 mos.

Aug 22, 1794 Catharine Schleicher, unmarried, age 48 yrs.

Oct 27, 1794 Elizabeth, dau of Jacob Kihly and his wife, Maria, age 10 mos.

Nov 2, 1794 Anna Maria, dau of John Viery and his wife, Barbara, age 2 yrs, 9 mos, 2 wks.

Nov 4, 1794 John, son of Jacob Hebenheimer, and his wife, Elizabeth, age 6 yrs, 8 mos, 3 days.

Nov 4, 1794 David, son of Jacob Hebenheimer, and wife, Elizabeth, age 4 yrs, 7 mos, 1 day.

N.B. In 8 days, the above parents lost 3 children from dysentery. The two recorded above were buried on the same day.

Dec 11, 1794 Samuel, son of Nicholas Pfuhl, and his wife, Elizabeth, age 4 yrs, 1 mo. 3 wks. 3 days.

Jan 13, 1795 Maria, widow of Nicholas Schneider, age 67 yrs, from Trappe.

Feb 18, 1794 George Adam Egolf, age 71 yrs.

N.B. The household sons and daughters, are Lutheran, after the will of the mother.

Mar. 17, 1794 Elizabeth, wife of Jacob Filman, age 31 yrs, 6 mos, 2 wks. 2 days.

Apr 9, 1794 Jacob Damm, age 54 yrs,

May 9, 1794 John, son of Henry Grob and his wife, Barbara, age 7 yrs, 2 mos, 3 wks, 3 days, buried in Leidy Cemetery.

May 10, 1794 Adam, son Henry Bosshard and Catharine, age 2 wks, 3 days.

Jun 17, 1794 Jacob, son of John Neuman and wife, Elizabeth, age 1 yr, 6 mos, 2 days.

Jul 28, 1794 Joachim Nagel, age 89 yrs, 5 mos 5 days.

N.B. He lived in marriage with his wife, Catharine 63 yrs. She survives him.

Aug 5, 1794 George Keyser, age 82 yrs,

Aug 7, 1794 Peter Specht, age 40 yrs, 6 mos.

Aug 18, 1794 Jacob,son of Conrad Jeger and wife, Deborah, age 2 yrs, 10 mos.

Aug 20, 1794 Valentine, son of Jacob Filman and his wife, Elizabeth, age 5 yrs, 2 mos, 15 days.

Aug 29, 1794 Jacob, son of Jacob Reifschneider and his wife, Catharine, age 6 yrs, 6 mos, 2 wks.

Aug 31, 1794 Catharine,, dau of Jacob Reifschneider and his wife, Catharine., age 4 yrs, 3 wks. 3 days.

Sept 2, 1794 Elizabeth, dau of Felix Christman and his wife, Margaret, age 9 yrs, 4 mos.

Sept 11, 1794 Catharine, dau of George Keiler, and his wife, Elizabeth, age 7 yrs, 7 mos, 3 wks.

Sept 19, 1795 Jacob, son of John Baer and his wife, Elizabeth, age 1 yr, 1 mo, 1 wk, 5 days.

NB. The last seven children died of dysentery.

Sept 26, 1795 Sophia, dau of Jacob Craus and wife, Christine, age 21 yrs, 10 mos,

Sept 27, 1795 Anna Maria, dau of Peter Jorger and his wife, M. Barbara, age 16 yrs, 9 mos.

Oct 1, 1795 Henry, son of Jacob Kehl and his wife, Barbara., age 9 yrs, less 3 mos,

Oct 14, 1795 Sophia, dau of Philip Leydich and his wife, Rosina, age 15 yrs, 9 mos, less 4 days, buried in Leidy Cemetery.

Oct 10, 1795 Michael Bauer of Trappe, age 85 yrs.

Oct 16, 1795 Conrad, son of John Geyer and his wife, Margaret, age 3 wks.

Oct 23, 1795 Veronica, dau of Anthony Spies and his wife, Margaret, age 18 yrs, 6 mos, less 8 days.

Oct 26, 1795 Philip Livegood of Pottstown, age 44 yrs, 3 days.

Dec 2, 1795 Christine, dau of Jost Freyer and wife, Barbara, age 18 yrs, 9 mos.

Dec 9, 1795 Hannah, dau of John Reichert, Esq. and wife, Sophia, age 9 wks. 4 days. Lutherans.

Dec 24 Margaret Schleicher, age 86 yrs.

Feb 4,1796 Salome, dau of Peter Reifschneider and wife, Barbara, age 1 yr, 4 mos,

Feb 13,1796 Maria, dau of George Orthlieb and wife, Veronica, age 5 yrs, 4 mos, 2 wks.

Feb 17,1796 Michael, son of Henry Raudenbusch and wife, Catharine of Trappe, age 1 yr. 3 mos, 10 days.

Mar 12,1796 Michael Spatz, age 76 yrs, a Lutheran.

Mar 30,1796 Barbara, widow of late Conrad Specht, age 62 yrs, less 11 days.

Apr 5, 1796 Jost Suess, age 24 yrs, 2 mos, Pottsgrove.

Apr 29, 1796 Elizabeth, widow of Lorentz Reimert, age 85 yrs.

May 7,1796 Henry Geiger, age 82 yrs, 4 mos.

Jun 6,1796 Maria Catharine, dau of Jost Suess, deceased and his wife, Maria Suess, age 4 mos; 9 days.

Jun 20,1796 Elizabeth, dau of John Amman and wife, Elizabeth, age 1 yr, 3 mos, 4 days.

Jun 20,1796 George, son of Jacob Pitterman and his wife, Susanna of Trappe, age 3 yrs.

Jun 22,1796 John, son of Isaac Weber, and wife, Margaret of Trappe, age 4 yrs.

Sept 26,1796 Elizabeth, wife of Daniel Pfeil, age 65 yrs.

Oct 3,1796 Maria, dau of Benjamin Misemer, and wife, Elizabeth, of Pottstown, age 5 yrs, 3 mos, 2 days.

N.B.She fell into a kettle of soft soap.

Nov 14,1796 Elizabeth, wife of John Betz, age 50 yrs, 9 mos,1 wk.

Nov 20,1796 Anna Christine, wife of George Stetler, age 80 yrs, 11 mos.

Nov 20,1796 Daniel, son of John Betz, and wife, Elizabeth, age 19 yrs, 10 mos.

Nov 29,1796 Samuel, son of Philip Freyer, and wife, Elizabeth, age 10 mos, 7 days.

Dec 17,1796 John Schmid, age 87 yrs, 10 mos.

N.B.He was blind for 5 yrs, He lived 64 yrs, in wedlock with his wife; she also is 87 yrs.

Jan 5, 1797 Michael Craus, age 55 yrs, buried in Leidy's Cemetery.

Jan 7, 1797 John Schneider, age 32 yrs, 4 mos, 10 days.

Feb 14, 1797 John George Schedel, age 76 yrs, 5 mos from Pottsgrove.

Feb 16, 1797 Maria Catharine Henrich, age 83 yrs from Pottsgrove.

Feb 20, 1797 John George Maser, age 31 yrs, 4 mos from Pottsgrove.

Mar 13, 1797 John, son of Conrad Minner and wife, Elizabeth, from Pottsgrove.

Mar 14, 1797 John Deheve, age 43 yrs, 2 mos,

Apr 9, 1797 Margaret Jolly, an illegitimate girl, bound out to John Neis, age 9 yrs, 2 mos.

Jun 11, 1797 John George, son of George Bucher and wife, Christine, 3 wks, 1 day.

Jul 4, 1797 Jacob Seibert, son of Jacob Seibert and wife, Philippina, age 19 yrs.

Jul 10, 1797 Henry Neuman almost 80 yrs, of age.

Aug 18, 1797 John, son of George Langbein and wife, Eva, age 4 yrs, 2 mos.

Aug 20, 1797 John, son of Adam Schloneker and wife, Sarah, age 2 yrs, less 1 day.

Aug 21, 1797 Magdalene, wife of Conrad Doderer, age 82 yrs, 3 mos.

N.B. This couple lived together 65 yrs, 7 mos.

Aug 26, 1797 Anna, dau of Samuel Schmid and wife, Susanna, age 1 yr, 2 mos, 2 days.

Sept 15, 1797 Henry, son of Philip Wits, and wife, Barbara, age 4 yrs, 9 days.

N.B. He was killed by boards carelessly laid.

Dec --, 1797 Elizabeth, wife of Abraham Doderer, age 32 yrs, 1 mo, 2 days.

Dec 29, 1797 George Kien, age 72 yrs.

--- 18, 1798 Jacob Wits, Esq. age 48 yrs, 10 mos, 6 days.

Mar 22, 1798 Conrad Grob, age 83 yrs, 1 mo, 8 days.

Apr 10, 1798 Tobias, son of Philip Jost, and wife, Rosina, age 6 yrs, 6 mos, 19 days.

May 21, 1798 Samuel, son of Jacob Berlinger, and his wife, Salome, age 16 yrs.

Sept 27, 1798 Margaret, widow of Zacharias Neiss, age 60 yrs, 3 mos.

Dec --, 1798 Veronica, wife of Philip Jost, age 73 yrs, 11 mos.

Jan 15, 1799 The very Reverend Frederick Delliker, who had server his congregation as preacher for almost 15 years,w as buried. He died on the 13th of this month, age 60 yrs, 10 mos, 17 days.

Records of the Deaths and Burials by the Rev. Federick Herman, 1799-1800

May 26, 1799 John Specht, age 19 yrs, 7 mos.

Jul 26, 1799 John Steltz, son of Peter Steltz, age 24yrs, 11mos.

Aug 25, 1799 John Nagel's dau, age 3 yrs.

Sept 4, 1799 Abraham Maurer's son, age 1 yr, 3 mos.

--- --, 1799 Juliana Reifschneider, age 95 yrs, 8 mos.

--- --, 1799 John Reifschneider's child, age 5 yrs, 7 mo, 8 days.

Oct 7, 1799 William Witz, a child, no age.

--- --, 1799 T.Wagner's child, no age.

Oct 18, 1799 Michael Berninger, no age.

Oct 18, 1799 John Jung's child, no age.

--- --, 1799 Henry Keyer, age 55 yrs, 2 mo, 24 days.

--- --, 1799 Reifschneider's child, no age.

Dec 2, 1799 Frederick Brandt, 34 yrs, 1 mo, 18 days.

Dec 13, 1799 Jacob Keely's son, 1 yr.

Dec 22, 1799 Jacob Keely's dau, 2 yrs.

Dec 30, 1799 Daniel Koch, age 50 yrs.

Jan 9, 1800 John Maenner's child, age 1 yr.

Jan 11, 1800 Mr. Fischer's mother, age 82.

Jan 12, 1800 J. Kiehler's son, age 17.

Jan 28, 1800 Mr. John Richard's negro man, age 30 yrs.

Feb 1, 1800 Gabriel Eisenberger, age 31 yrs.

Feb 6, 1800 Thomas Liendner's child, age 3 yrs.

Feb 11, 1800 Nicholas Kresch's child, no age.

Feb 13, 1800 Susanna Hahlman, age 21 yrs.

Mar 3, 1800 John Herb, age 52 yrs.

Mar 18, 1800 Jacob Engel's child, no age.

Mar 19, 1800 John Engel's child, no age.

Jun 26, 1800 Conrad Specht, age 18 yrs, 8 mo, 11 days.

Jul 10, 1800 Jacob Livegood's widow, no age.

Jul 15, 1800 N. Backer's grandchild, no age, from Pottsgrove.

Aug 15, 1800 Michael Straub, age 23 yr, 3 mo, 8 days.

Aug 14, 1800 Joseph Brendlinger, age 10 yrs, 2 mo,s 21 days.

Sep 25, 1800 Ludwig Bender's child, no age.

Oct 2, 1800 John Schmitt of Pottsgrove, no age.

Nov 4, 1800 Ludwig Worman's child, no age.

Nov 16, 1800 Salome Ludy, age 57 yrs.

Nov 17, 1800 Conrad Gerber's child, from Pottsgrove, no age.

--- --, 1800 John Brandt, age 32 yrs, 10 mo, 20 days.

Dec --, 1800 John Herger's widow, age 81 yrs, 7 mos, 20 days, buried in Leidy's
   Cemetery.   .

-A-

ABERNATHY, Jane, 63
ABERNETHY, Jane, 63
ACHE, Catharine, 146; Jacob, 124;
    Ludwig, 129; Maricha, 124
ACHUFF, Hannah, 63, 78; Jacob, 63,
    78; Thomas, 63
ACHY, Herman, 152; John, 152
ACKER, Anna Maria, 90; Anthon,
    90; Johan Jurg, 93; Magdalene,
    146; Maria, 154; Peter, 154;
    Susanna, 93
ACKERS, ---, 87
ACKLY, Elizabeth, 63, 70; Thomas,
    51
ADAM, John, 104; Maria
    Magdalena, 104
ADAMS, Abigail, 87; Benjamin, 23;
    Catharine, 86; Elizabeth, 63, 80;
    James, 63, 68; Jane, 55, 63, 75;
    Jedediah, 55; Jediah, 23; John,
    63, 80; Margaret, 63; Margret,
    80; Rachel, 63, 68; Sarah, 63, 64;
    William, 63, 64
ADDIS, Elizabeth, 62; John, 62
AKER, Philip, 144
AKIN, Andrew, 63, 65; Susannah,
    63, 65
ALBERSON, Benjamin, 21; Sarah,
    21
ALBERTSON, Benjamin, 22, 48, 58;
    Jacob, 48; Susanna, 58; Thomas,
    22
ALBRECHT, Adam, 93; Catharine,
    152; Eva Barbara, 93; Michael,
    152
ALLEMANNIN, Elisabeth, 91
ALLEN, Elizabeth, 60; Sarah, 60
ALLISON, James, 93
ALLUM, Susanna, 140
ALLWEIN, N., 109

ALSENTZ, Johann Georg, 124;
    Johannes, 124
ALSOP, Mary, 30; Ruhamah John,
    30; Scrivener, 30
ALTHAUSIN, Anna Maria, 91
AMBLER, Ann, 45; Edward, 24;
    John, 49; Joseph, 45, 46, 47, 48,
    49; Mary, 48; Sarah, 46
AMBLERSON, Edward, 42; Joseph,
    42
AMBORN, Christoph, 82;
    Christopher, 101; Susanna, 82
AMMAN, Elizabeth, 165; John, 165
ANDERS, Maria, 109
ANDERSON, Hanna, 92; Sarah, 63,
    71; William, 92, 129
ANDRE, Susanna, 146
ANDREAS, Adam, 146
ANDRES, Elisabetha, 138
ANGEL, Anna Maria, 84; Philip, 84
ANTES, Barbara, 156; Elizabeth,
    146; Frederick, 144, 156; Henry,
    140
APPELE, George, 82; Maria Juliana,
    82
ARBUCKLE, James, 5
AREND, Abraham, 104; Catharina,
    104
ARENDSEN, Anna Barbara, 90;
    Peter, 90
ARMITAGE, Barbara, 63, 78;
    Elizabeth, 63, 81; Enoch, 63, 78;
    Jacob, 60; Rebecca, 60
ARMSTRONG, Caleb, 63, 78;
    Elizabeth, 63, 68; Jane, 63;
    Joseph, 63, 68; Mary, 63, 78;
    Thomas, 63
ARNDT, Jacob, 146
ARWYN, Rebecca, 31, 32; William,
    31, 32, 33
ASCHENFELDERN, Maria

DARRAH, Archibald, 66, 78; Sarah,
66, 78
DARROUGH, Ann, 66, 73; Derick,
66; Derrick, 73
DARY, Jane, 67
DATISMANN, Magdalena, 120
DATISMON, Jacob, 120
DAVENPORT, Winifred, 33
DAVID, Hugh, 35; James, 59, 60;
Leischer, 151; Margaret, 60;
Meredith, 45; Rees, 32, 38;
Samuel, 151
DAVIDS, Ann, 32, 33; Benjamin, 32,
33; Margaret, 32; Sarah, 33
DAVIDSIN, Maria, 83
DAVIDSON, Hannah, 68; Hester, 66,
68; Robert, 66, 68
DAVIES, Abraham, 35; Ann, 66;
Anne, 34; Catharine, 92; David,
43; Elizabeth, 42; Gwen, 31;
Henry, 66, 68; John, 34, 41;
Margaretha, 98; Mary, 34, 39,
40, 66, 76; Meredith, 31, 41;
Nancy, 140; Nathan, 34; Patty,
66, 68; Rachel, 35; Rebecca, 66,
69; Richard, 31, 32; Robert, 35;
William, 40, 66
DAVIS, Ann, 72; Anna, 87; David, 5,
8, 53, 59; Edmund, 66, 68;
Elisha, 96; Elizabeth, 5, 66, 79;
Hannah, 14, 64, 67, 79; Isaac, 91;
Jane, 67; John, 32, 33, 67, 77, 87;
Margaret, 32; Margareta, 89;
Mary, 9, 66, 68, 84; Meredith,
42, 43; Nathaniel, 64, 67; Peter,
2; Samuel, 44; Sarah, 43, 96;
Simon, 89; Sophia, 91; Thomas,
14; William, 6, 72
DAVY, Jane, 75
DAWES, Abraham, 31, 39, 45;
Abram, 31; Francis, 39; John, 31,
34; Mary, 31, 34, 39; Rachel, 45;
Samuel, 31

DAWS, Abraham, 40, 41, 42, 43, 44;
Edith, 44; Elisabeth, 42; Isaac,
42; Lydia, 40; Mary, 40; Tacy,
43
DAY, Susan, 41; William, 41
DE BLEMA, Le Miatta, 109
DE HAVEN, Abraham, 102; Mary,
102; Sara, 105
DE WRANGEL, Provost, 96
DEAL, Hannah, 67; Joseph, 67;
Mary, 65, 67; Samuel, 21; Sarah,
67
DEAN, Hannah, 66; Joseph, 66;
Mary, 95; Samuel, 54; Sarah, 77;
William, 95
DEAVES, Abraham, 22; Martha, 22
DECKER, Elizabeth, 159; Jacob,
159; Michael, 146, 159
DECORSEY, Hannah, 67, 71;
William, 67, 71
DECORSY, Hannah, 70
DEDERE, Christian, 141
DEELBICH, Dunwik, 67; Isaac, 67
DEELBICK, Hoortsey, 67; Issac, 67
DEFREHN, Anna Maria, 144
DEGEN, Catharina, 94; Henrich, 94
DEHEVE, John, 166
DEHLINGER, Eva, 145
DEIS, Barbara, 131; Peter, 131
DEISING, Isaac, 150; William, 150
DEKER, George, 151; Matthias, 151
DELGIN, Anna Sevela, 60
DELLICKER, Frederick, 146
DELLIKER, Elizabeth, 161; Fr., 135;
Frederick, 154, 155, 161;
Frederick V.D.M., 148;
Friedrich, 116, 121, 138; Maria,
155; Maria Magdalene, 148, 161;
Reverend Frederick, 167
DELLINGER, Maria Barbara, 158;
Minister Frederick, 158
DELWORTH, Isaac, 60; Sarah, 60
DEMFLIN, Wilhelm, 125

Other Heritage Books by Charlotte Meldrum:

Abstracts of Bucks County, Pennsylvania Land Records, 1684-1723

Early Church Records of Burlington County, New Jersey
Volumes 1-3

Early Church Records of Chester County, Pennsylvania, Volume 2
Charlotte Meldrum and Martha Reamy

Early Church Records of Gloucester County, New Jersey

Early Church Records of Salem County, New Jersey

Early Records of Cumberland County, New Jersey

Johnston County, North Carolina Marriages, 1764-1867

Marriages and Deaths of Montgomery County, Pennsylvania, 1685-1800

6910114R0